# eCommerce in the Cloud
## *Bringing Elasticity to eCommerce*

*Kelly Goetsch*

Beijing · Boston · Farnham · Sebastopol · Tokyo

**eCommerce in the Cloud**

By Kelly Goetsch

Printed in the United States of America.

Published by O'Reilly Media, Inc., 1005 Gravenstein Highway North, Sebastopol, CA 95472.

O'Reilly books may be purchased for educational, business, or sales promotional use. Online editions are also available for most titles (*http://safaribooksonline.com*). For more information, contact our corporate/institutional sales department: 800-998-9938 or corporate@oreilly.com.

**Editor:** Ann Spencer
**Production Editor:** Melanie Yarbrough
**Copyeditor:** Kiel Van Horn
**Proofreader:** Sharon Wilkey

**Indexer:** Ellen Troutman-Zaig
**Interior Designer:** David Futato
**Cover Designer:** Karen Montgomery
**Illustrator:** Rebecca Demarest

April, 2014:       First Edition

**Revision History for the First Edition**
2014-04-18:   First release
2016-06-24:   Second release

See *http://oreilly.com/catalog/errata.csp?isbn=9781491946633* for release details.

978-1-491-94663-3

[LSI]

# Table of Contents

Preface. . . . . . . . . . . . . . . . . . . . . . . . . . . . . . . . . . . . . . . . . . . . . . . . . . . . . . . . . . . . . . . . . . ix

Introduction. . . . . . . . . . . . . . . . . . . . . . . . . . . . . . . . . . . . . . . . . . . . . . . . . . . . . . . . . . . xv

## Part I. The Changing eCommerce Landscape

### 1. The Global Rise of eCommerce. . . . . . . . . . . . . . . . . . . . . . . . . . . . . . . . . . . . . . . . . . 3
Increasing Use of Technology     4
    Internet Connectivity     4
    Internet-Enabled Devices     5
Inherent Advantages of eCommerce     5
    Price Advantage     5
    Convenience     7
    Large Product Assortment     7
Technological Advances     8
    Closer Tie-in with the Physical World     8
    Increasing Maturity of eCommerce Offerings     10
Changing Face of Retail     19
    Omnichannel Retailing     22
    Business Impact of Omnichannel     25
    Technical Impact of Omnichannel     26
Summary     29

### 2. How Is Enterprise eCommerce Deployed Today?. . . . . . . . . . . . . . . . . . . . . . . . . . . . 31
Current Deployment Architecture     32
    DNS     33
    Intra Data Center Load Balancing     34
    Web Servers     35
    eCommerce Applications     39
    Application Servers     41
    Databases     41

        Hosting                                                            44
    Limitations of Current Deployment Architecture                         46
        Static Provisioning                                                46
        Scaling for Peaks                                                  47
        Outages Due to Rapid Scaling                                       49
    Summary                                                                51

# Part II.    The Rise of Cloud Computing

**3. What Is Cloud Computing?** . . . . . . . . . . . . . . . . . . . . . . . . . . . . . . . . . . . . . . . . **55**
    Generally Accepted Definition                                          55
        Elastic                                                            57
        On Demand                                                          58
        Metered                                                            59
    Service Models                                                         61
        Software-as-a-Service                                              63
        Platform-as-a-Service                                              64
        Infrastructure-as-a-Service                                        65
    Deployment Models                                                      66
        Public Cloud                                                       67
        Hybrid Cloud                                                       68
        Private Cloud                                                      68
    Hardware Used in Clouds                                                69
        Hardware Sizing                                                    70
    Complementary Cloud Vendor Offerings                                   72
    Challenges with Public Clouds                                          73
        Availability                                                       73
        Performance                                                        75
        Oversubscription                                                   77
        Cost                                                               78
    Summary                                                                80

**4. Auto-Scaling in the Cloud** . . . . . . . . . . . . . . . . . . . . . . . . . . . . . . . . . . . . . . . . **81**
    What Is Auto-Scaling?                                                  81
    What Needs to Be Provisioned                                          82
        What Can't Be Provisioned                                         84
    When to Provision                                                     85
        Proactive Provisioning                                           85
        Reactive Provisioning                                            87
    Auto-Scaling Solutions                                               87
        Requirements for a Solution                                      88

Building an Auto-scaling Solution                                      92
Building versus Buying an Auto-Scaling Solution                        94
Summary                                                               94

**5. Installing Software on Newly Provisioned Hardware........................ 95**
What Is a Deployment Unit?                                             95
Approaches to Building Deployment Units                               97
Building from Snapshots                                                97
Building from Archives                                                 99
Building from Source                                                  100
Monitoring the Health of a Deployment Unit                           102
Lifecycle Management                                                 107
Summary                                                              108

**6. Virtualization in the Cloud............................................ 109**
What Is Virtualization?                                              110
Full Virtualization                                                 110
Paravirtualization (Operating System–Assisted Virtualization)       112
Operating System Virtualization                                     113
Summary of Virtualization Approaches                                115
Improving the Performance of Software Executed on a Hypervisor       116
Summary                                                             119

**7. Content Delivery Networks............................................ 121**
What Is a CDN?                                                       123
Are CDNs Clouds?                                                     124
Serving Static Content                                               125
Serving Dynamic Content                                             128
Caching Entire Pages                                                 129
Pre-fetching Static Content                                         132
Security                                                             133
Additional CDN Offerings                                            135
Frontend Optimization                                               135
DNS/GSLB                                                             136
Throttling                                                           138
Summary                                                             139

**Part III.   To the Cloud!**

**8. Architecture Principles for the Cloud.................................. 143**
Why Is eCommerce Unique?                                             143

Revenue Generation                                                      143
Visibility                                                              144
Traffic Spikiness                                                       144
Security                                                                144
Statefulness                                                            144
What Is Scalability?                                                    146
Throughput                                                              146
Scaling Up                                                              147
Scaling Out                                                             148
Rules for Scaling                                                       149
Technical Rules                                                         150
Nontechnical Rules                                                      160

9. Security for the Cloud. . . . . . . . . . . . . . . . . . . . . . . . . . . . . . . . . . . . . . . . . . . . . . . . . . . . .  163
General Security Principles                                             165
Adopting an Information Security Management System                      166
PCI DSS                                                                 167
ISO 27001                                                               169
FedRAMP                                                                 171
Security Best Practices                                                 172
Defense in Depth                                                        172
Information Classification                                              173
Isolation                                                               174
Identification, Authentication, and Authorization                       175
Audit Logging                                                           177
Security Principles for eCommerce                                       177
Security Principles for the Cloud                                       179
Reducing Attack Vectors                                                 180
Protecting Data in Motion                                               183
Protecting Data at Rest                                                 185
Summary                                                                 187

10. Deploying Across Multiple Data Centers (Multimaster). . . . . . . . . . . . . . . . . . . . . . .  189
The Central Problem of Operating from Multiple Data Centers             191
Architecture Principles                                                 192
Principles Governing Distributed Computing                              193
Selecting a Data Center                                                 197
Initializing Each Data Center                                           198
Removing Singletons                                                     198
Never Replicate Configuration                                           199
Assigning Customers to Data Centers                                     200
DNS                                                                     200

    Global Server Load Balancing    203
  Approaches to Operating from Multiple Data Centers    207
    Active/Passive    207
    Active/Active Application Tiers, Active/Passive Database Tiers    209
    Active/Active Application Tiers, Mostly Active/Active Database Tiers    210
    Full Active/Active    212
    Stateless Frontends, Stateful Backends    213
  Review of Approaches    214
  Summary    215

**11. Hybrid Cloud.** . . . . . . . . . . . . . . . . . . . . . . . . . . . . . . . . . . . . . . . . . **217**
  Hybrid Cloud as a By-product of Architecture for Omnichannel    219
  Connecting to the Cloud    224
    Public Internet    224
    VPN    225
    Direct Connections    225
  Approaches to Hybrid Cloud    226
    Caching Entire Pages    226
    Overlaying HTML on Cached Pages    228
    Using Content Delivery Networks to Insert HTML    230
    Overlaying HTML on the Server Side    232
    Fully Decoupled Frontends and Backends    233
    Everything but the Database in the Cloud    235
  Summary    236

**12. Exclusively Using a Public Cloud.** . . . . . . . . . . . . . . . . . . . . . . . . . . . . . . . **239**
  Why Full Cloud?    239
    Business Reasons    239
    Technical Reasons    240
  Why Not Full Cloud?    241
  Path to the Cloud    243
  Architecture for Full Cloud    246
    Review of Key Principles    246
    Architecture for Omnichannel    248
    Larger Trends Influencing eCommerce Architecture    249
  How to Select a Cloud Vendor    249
  Summary    251

**Index.** . . . . . . . . . . . . . . . . . . . . . . . . . . . . . . . . . . . . . . . . . . . . . . . . . . **253**

# Preface

Among all enterprise workloads, ecommerce is unique because of the extreme variability in traffic. The chart in Figure P-1 shows the number of page views per second over the course of the month of November for a leading US retailer.[1]

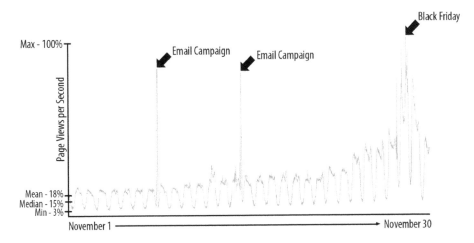

*Figure P-1. November page views for a leading US retailer*

The amount of hardware required varies substantially over the course of a month, day, or even hour, yet provisioning a production environment to 500% of annual peak for the *entire year* is common. A large US retailer recently sold $250 million online over a seven-day period, yet their CPU utilization, which is their bottleneck, never topped 15%.

---

1 Data courtesy of Akamai Technologies, 2013.

Having spent my career deploying large ($1 billion+/year in annual revenue) ecommerce platforms and later building the technology under these platforms, I am always struck by the fear-driven inefficiencies and fashion-driven dogmatism that permeates every aspect of our trade. Aside from being wasteful, the real problem is distraction from your core business. We are at a juncture in history where a fundamental change is required. We can do better than the status quo.

Cloud computing, having matured over the past decade, is now to the point where it can finally be used for large-scale ecommerce. Cloud offers the promise to scale up and down dynamically to match your real-time needs. You pay for only what you need and you can use as much as you want. The cloud vendor deals with all of the work that goes into building infrastructure, platforms, or services, allowing you to focus on your core business. "It just makes so much sense," is what most people say about the combination of ecommerce and cloud, yet "Are you crazy?" is what most people say when you actually propose its use.

In this book, I'll show you how cloud computing, particularly public Infrastructure-as-a-Service, is *evolutionary* from a technology standpoint and *revolutionary* from a business standpoint. Using what you already know, I'll show you how you can quickly and incrementally adopt cloud computing for any ecommerce platforms, whether packaged or custom and new or legacy. Cloud computing is firmly on the "right" side of history, and I hope you'll join me in exploring how it can be applied to the most challenging of use cases: ecommerce.

 Software-as-a-Service ecommerce offerings are not in the scope of this book.

# Intended Audience

This book is for architects and aspiring architects who wish to learn more about cloud computing and how the top ecommerce vendors can leverage the cloud. While the first chapter focuses on the current state of ecommerce, the remainder of the book focuses on the architecture required to use the cloud for ecommerce. The principles contained within are also easily applied to other transactional web applications. If you can deploy a large-scale ecommerce platform in a cloud, you can deploy anything.

# Contents of This Book

This book is organized into three parts.

In Part I, we'll look at the current trends in ecommerce in Chapter 1 and the prevailing deployment architecture in Chapter 2.

In Part II, we'll focus on cloud computing and its various incarnations. We'll start out in Chapter 3 by discussing what cloud actually is, followed by how to auto-scale in Chapter 4, and how to automatically install and configure your software on the newly provisioned hardware in Chapter 5. Virtualization will be discussed in Chapter 6 and Content Delivery Networks in Chapter 7.

In Part III, we'll discuss how to use cloud computing for ecommerce. We'll start by discussing key architecture principles in Chapter 8, followed by security in Chapter 9, and then how to deploy to multiple geographically distant data centers in Chapter 10. In Chapter 11, we'll discuss how to use a hybrid cloud. Chapter 12 discusses how to serve an entire platform from the cloud.

## Conventions Used in This Book

The following typographical conventions are used in this book:

*Italic*
: Indicates new terms, URLs, email addresses, filenames, and file extensions.

`Constant width`
: Used for program listings, as well as within paragraphs to refer to program elements such as variable or function names, databases, data types, environment variables, statements, and keywords.

**`Constant width bold`**
: Shows commands or other text that should be typed literally by the user.

*`Constant width italic`*
: Shows text that should be replaced with user-supplied values or by values determined by context.

 This element signifies a tip or suggestion.

 This element signifies a general note.

This element indicates a warning or caution.

# Safari® Books Online

 *Safari Books Online* is an on-demand digital library that delivers expert content in both book and video form from the world's leading authors in technology and business.

Technology professionals, software developers, web designers, and business and creative professionals use Safari Books Online as their primary resource for research, problem solving, learning, and certification training.

Safari Books Online offers a range of plans and pricing for enterprise, government, education, and individuals.

Members have access to thousands of books, training videos, and prepublication manuscripts in one fully searchable database from publishers like O'Reilly Media, Prentice Hall Professional, Addison-Wesley Professional, Microsoft Press, Sams, Que, Peachpit Press, Focal Press, Cisco Press, John Wiley & Sons, Syngress, Morgan Kaufmann, IBM Redbooks, Packt, Adobe Press, FT Press, Apress, Manning, New Riders, McGraw-Hill, Jones & Bartlett, Course Technology, and hundreds more. For more information about Safari Books Online, please visit us online.

# How to Contact Us

Please address comments and questions concerning this book to the publisher:

O'Reilly Media, Inc.
1005 Gravenstein Highway North
Sebastopol, CA 95472
800-998-9938 (in the United States or Canada)
707-829-0515 (international or local)
707-829-0104 (fax)

We have a web page for this book, where we list errata, examples, and any additional information. You can access this page at *http://oreil.ly/ecommerce_in_the_cloud*.

To comment or ask technical questions about this book, send email to *bookquestions@oreilly.com*.

For more information about our books, courses, conferences, and news, see our website at *http://www.oreilly.com*.

Find us on Facebook: *http://www.facebook.com/oreilly*

Follow us on Twitter: *http://www.twitter.com/oreillymedia*

Watch us on YouTube: *http://www.youtube.com/oreillymedia*

## Acknowledgments

This book is the direct result of people who have invested in me—from my family to the hundreds of people who have helped me in some way throughout my career. I am perpetually humbled by people's capacity for selfless acts of kindness.

Specifically, I'd like to thank my uncle, David Kroening, for introducing me to technology at an early age; my early mentor, Guy Morazain, for introducing me to ecommerce and launching my career; and Mohamad Afshar, for encouraging me to write this book and for mentoring me on the business side of technology.

I'd also like to thank my reviewers Mark Scarton, Devon Hillard, Vaskin Kissoyan, Scott Van Ummersen, Andy Powers, Leo Dolan, Jags Krishnamurthy, and Glen Borkowski for keeping me honest and for providing insights that have shaped this book.

Finally, I'd like to thank my amazing wife, Melissa. It's only with her support that I was able to write this book and am able to focus on my career. She's the best.

# Introduction

We are in the midst of an ecommerce-driven revolution in retail. Prior to the mid-1990s, ecommerce didn't exist. Today, business-to-consumer (B2C) ecommerce is a $1 trillion per year business worldwide,[1] directly accounting for 7.3% of total global retail sales.[2] Over 1.7 trillion[3] of retail sales in the US are now influenced by ecommerce. Emerging markets like Brazil, Russia, India, and China offer nearly limitless growth potential.

 For the purposes of this book, *ecommerce* is defined as any commercial transaction facilitated between two parties using the Internet. This book will be most useful to those running $100 million/year businesses selling physical goods and services over the Internet to end consumers, though the principles will be applicable to all forms of ecommerce.

## eCommerce Deployment Architecture: Frozen in Time

In addition to becoming increasingly important to business, ecommerce is a fairly unique use case within information technology (IT). It's perhaps the most visible platform a retailer has, either influencing or directly contributing around half of revenue.[4] Failures lead to front-page news, disclosures in earnings calls, reduction in stock price, and firings. Most applications are just not that important—if payroll is processed five hours late, nobody cares. All customer touchpoints are increasingly

---

1 "Global Retail E-Commerce Keeps On Clicking," *http://bit.ly/1BGipZ5* (2015).

2 "Global e-commerce sales set to grow 25% in 2015," *http://bit.ly/1Dc5vT7* (2015)

3 Lobaugh, Simpson, Ohri, et al. "Navigating the New Digital Divide," Deloitte Digital (2015), *http://bit.ly/1PbPKfr*.

4 *http://bit.ly/1fwVX2r*

likely to be facilitated by ecommerce, as point-of-sale systems are being replaced with tablets that connect to a single ecommerce platform. An outage now is the equivalent of barring customers from entering all physical stores.

Because of increasing competition and the maturity of offerings, customers are increasingly fickle about performance. They expect response times to be instant. Akamai recently found that half of consumers *expect* a web page to load in less than two seconds, with the 30% expecting a page to load in less than one second[5] Amazon.com saw a 1% increase in revenue for every 100 milliseconds of response-time improvement.[6] In today's world, milliseconds matter.

Availability and performance are becoming increasingly difficult to offer as traffic has become more prone to rapid spikes due to an increasing reliance on promotions and marketing-driven events. We'll discuss this more later, but it's not uncommon to see spikes in traffic that are one or two orders of magnitude above steady state. Social media–based marketing can lead to campaigns going viral. From an IT administrator's standpoint, the traffic can come so quickly that it looks like a distributed denial-of-service attack, when in reality it's likely to be a few million kids hitting refresh on their pages in anticipation of the release of the latest hot basketball shoe.

While ecommerce has been maturing over the past two decades, the prevailing deployment architecture looks largely as it did in the beginning—mostly static environments fronted by web servers deployed out of a single data center. Many simply guess at what their peaks will be and then multiply that number by five for safety. Hardware is statically deployed and idle for most of the year. It's been done this way for four reasons:

- IT administrators fear losing their jobs because of outages. It's simply less risky to throw hardware at problems.

- For a while, ecommerce deployments were small enough that the hardware cost was negligible.

- There hasn't been a good alternative to the static approach—cloud in its present form didn't exist until very recently, and it's matured only recently.

- The old models of hosting had more accountability. If there was an outage, you could always escalate to your vendor.

---

5 "Performance Matters, 9 Consumer Insights," *https://content.akamai.com/PG2920-Performance-Matters.html* (FYI, someone uploaded the actual report to *http://www.joecolantonio.com/downloads/Perf2015trends.pdf*) (2015)

6 Greg Linden, "Make Data Useful," Amazon.com and Findory, *http://bit.ly/1k7ypZw* (PowerPoint file download).

The current approach to ecommerce deployment architecture is not scalable. The rise in traffic has ballooned environments from dozens to hundreds or even thousands of servers. Given today's extremely competitive business climate, it's not feasible to have hundreds or thousands of servers sit idle for all but a few hours out of the year. It's also increasingly difficult to predict traffic. Most important, and central to this book, is that cloud computing has matured to the point where it can be used for ecommerce.

## What Is Cloud?

*Cloud* is one of those ineffable terms that has been redefined to encompass everything, yet means nothing. For the purposes of this book, the cloud is best characterized by three adjectives: elastic, on demand, and metered. Let's look at each in greater detail:

*Elastic*
> To be considered cloud, you must be able to increase or decrease a given resource either automatically or on demand by using self-service user interfaces or APIs. A resource can include anything you have in your data center today—from commoditized hardware running Linux (Infrastructure-as-a-Service), to application servers (Platform-as-a-Service), up to applications (Software-as-a-Service). The "what" doesn't matter all that much; it's the fact that you can provision new resources.

*On Demand*
> Seeing as *elastic* is the first word used to describe the cloud, you must be able to provision a resource precisely when you need it and release it when you don't.

*Metered*
> You should pay only for what you use. This has enormous implications, as the costs directly reflect usage and can therefore be substantially lower.

When the term *cloud* is used in this book, it generally refers to public Infrastructure-as-a-Service. We'll spend Chapter 3 describing cloud in more detail.

## Why Is the Cloud a Fit for eCommerce?

Cloud is a natural fit for ecommerce because you can provision and pay for resources when you need them instead of building enormous static environments scaled for peaks. The goal is to provision automatically, which we'll discuss in Chapter 4. Without the cloud, environments are statically built and scaled for peak load. It doesn't make sense when you can use a cloud. The problem of underutilization is even worse for preproduction environments, many of which are built to some scale of production yet sit even more idle than production. Most deployments have approximately the following environments:

- Two production environments (each capable of handling 500% of the peak production traffic)
- Three staging environments (each being 50% of production)
- Three QA environments (each being 25% of production)
- Three or more development environments (each being 10% of production)

The staging environments are likely to be used for some form of automated testing about once a week or so. QA environments are likely to be used by a handful of QA testers. But that's it. If you look at the average CPU usage of all these preproduction environments, it's likely to be less than 1% for any given week, yet these environments consume the equivalent of multiple production environments' worth of hardware. The situation is slightly better with production but not much.

In addition to being wasteful, building out and maintaining these environments is likely not your core competency as an organization and is likely distracting you from what you do best—whether that's selling the latest iPhone or selling diapers. Let the few major cloud vendors hire the right talent to build infrastructure. Cloud computing makes so much sense for ecommerce that its proper use can provide you with serious competitive differentiation while lowering costs. Let's explore how ecommerce and retail are changing.

# PART I

# The Changing eCommerce Landscape

# CHAPTER 1

# The Global Rise of eCommerce

The growth of ecommerce around the world is unstoppable, with double- or even triple-digit growth seen annually since its emergence in the mid-1990s. This growth has enormous technical implications for both application and deployment architecture, with all indications that this growth is likely to continue for the coming decades. According to a 2013 report by Morgan Stanley, global ecommerce as a percentage of total retail sales is expected to grow by 43%, between 2012 and 2016.[1]

The reasons for this growth are as follows:

- Increasing use of technology
    - Internet use
    - Internet-enabled devices
- Inherent advantages of ecommerce
    - Price advantage
    - Convenience
    - Large product assortment
- Technological advances
    - Closer tie-in with the physical world
    - Increasing maturity of ecommerce offerings

Let's explore each of these further.

---

[1] eCommerce Disruption: A Global Theme Transforming Retail, 6 January 2013.

# Increasing Use of Technology

## Internet Connectivity

Ubiquitous internet connectivity has been a direct driver of ecommerce growth, as the Internet is a prerequisite to the "e" in "ecommerce." In developed countries, 77% of individuals use the Internet, whereas in developing countries, that figure is a lower 31%.[2]

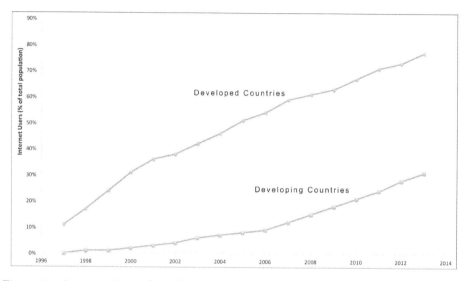

*Figure 1-1. Internet Users of Developed and Developing Countries (% of total poulation), 1997-2013*

Internet users heavily skew young. In the US, 97% of 18–29 year olds are Internet users, but that figure drops to 57% for those aged 65 and older. Over time, Internet use will increase to nearly 100% across all age groups.

 Forty percent of men aged 18–34 in the US agree with this statement: "Ideally, I would buy everything online."[3]

---

2 *http://bit.ly/1gELPFo, http://bit.ly/QYg8Cq.*

3 eMarketer, "Millennial Men Keep Their Digital Lives Humming," (23 September 2013), *http://bit.ly/OqrRYw.*

---

As ISPs mature, the reliability and bandwidth of their offerings has increased, while the cost has dropped. At the same time, there are an increasing number of devices that can be used to access the Internet.

## Internet-Enabled Devices

Internet-enabled devices of all types now make it easier to shop wherever and whenever. It wasn't too long ago that the only way to get online was through a stationary computer connected to the Internet over a dial-up modem. Today, the primary means of Internet access around the world is through mobile devices. They're everywhere and always connected. An incredible 84% of UK citizens won't leave home without their cellphones.[4] Tablets have gone from being nonexistent to almost a billion in circulation projected by 2017. In North America, 60% of Internet users are expected to own a tablet by 2017.[5] These devices are ubiquitous and each one of them is capable of facilitating ecommerce, with many ecommerce vendors offering custom applications specifically built for each device.

Even when customers visit a physical retail store, they often research products and check prices online while in the store. A recent survey found that 77% of all American customers have done this, while those in the millennial generation do this 85% of the time.[6] Customers want information about the products they're buying and they want to make sure they're paying a fair price.

Today's customers, especially younger ones, want to be able to make purchases on their own terms. They want full control over when, where, and how they shop.

# Inherent Advantages of eCommerce

## Price Advantage

Many customers believe that pricing is better online. For example, an Accenture survey showed that 52% of customers in the US and UK believed that prices online were cheaper than in store.[7] For the most part, this is true. Lower overhead, lower taxes, and disintermediation have all played roles in driving down prices online.

---

4 Alamo, "Phone Home!" (March 2009), *http://bit.ly/MrUC5Q*.

5 Natasha Lomas, "Forrester: Tablet Installed Base Past 905M By 2017, Up From 327M In 2013," TechCrunch (6 August 2013), *http://techcrunch.com/2013/08/06/forrester-tablets/*.

6 Pymnts.com, "Online Versus In-Store Shopping Trends: What Drives Consumer Choice," (18 December 2012), *http://bit.ly/1k7ytsc*.

7 Accenture Interactive, "Today's Shopper Preferences: Channels, Social Media, Privacy and the Personalized Experience," (November 2012), *http://bit.ly/MrUBPf*.

Online-only vendors have much less overhead, and ecommerce around the world is led by *pure play* vendors—online-only vendors whose business model is to not operate out of physical stores. For example, Macy's, a retailer with a physical and online presence, is investing $400 million in the renovation of its flagship store in New York.[8] With even the largest ecommerce implementations costing less than $100 million, the return on investment is much higher than $400 million spent on one physical store. The fixed costs are so high in traditional retail that some retail chains are seen by investors as real estate investment firms first and retailers second. The lower overhead of pure play ecommerce vendors often translates to lower prices.

Taxes are another downward driver on prices. Taxes on goods purchased in a physical retail store in most developed markets can exceed 20%.[9] The regulations that apply to physical retailers often don't apply to ecommerce vendors, especially those across borders. Many jurisdictions charge taxes only when the retailer physically has a presence in that jurisdiction. For cross-border shipping, especially of expensive electronics and luxury goods, this is often not the case. The cost savings can be substantial.

Disintermediation continues to play a big role in pushing down prices, as manufacturers set up direct-to-consumer ecommerce platforms and sell on marketplace-like exchanges. Prior to ecommerce, manufacturers had to sell to wholesalers who then sold to retailers. Now it's fairly easy, at least technically, to set up a direct-to-consumer business and keep those margins.

Online prices are not always lower, though. An advantage ecommerce offers is the ability to price discriminate based on anything—from previous purchasing history, to geographic location, to demographic information like gender and income. For example, an Australian retailer was recently found to be imposing a 6.8% surcharge on all Internet Explorer 7 users.[10] Prices can be set however and whenever the vendor pleases. Outside of not causing public relations headaches or running afoul of local laws, there are no rules or restrictions online. In physical stores, it's a logistical nightmare to change prices, and it's often impossible to charge people different prices for the same goods. Coupons and targeted promotions can help, but the sticker prices are exceedingly hard to change.

---

8 *The Economist*, "Retailers and the Internet: Clicks and Bricks," (25 February 2012), *http://econ.st/1k7yrRe*.

9 Ernst and Young, "Worldwide VAT, GST, and Sales Tax Guide," (May 2013), *http://bit.ly/MrUAe3*.

10 Steven Vaughan-Nichols, "Australian Retailer Charges Customers IE 7 *Tax*," (14 June 2012), *http://zd.net/1k7ys7K*.

# Convenience

The costs to customers of shopping in a traditional retail store can be substantial. Quantifiable costs include the following:

- Time away from home or work
- Transportation costs, including fuel for your car or public transportation costs
- Often higher costs due to an inability to comparison shop

Unquantifiable costs include listening to your toddler scream for candy at checkout, among others.

The costs of online shopping are virtually nothing. It takes seconds to purchase a product from a vendor that you've done business with in the past and it can even be done from the convenience of a smartphone. Even when shopping with new retailers, it takes no longer than a few minutes to find and buy the product you're looking for. Return-friendly policies make it easy to return products that may not fit properly, like shoes or clothing. And the maturity of ecommerce, as we'll discuss shortly, makes it easy to quickly find exactly what you're looking for.

# Large Product Assortment

Most physical retail stores are small—between 3,000–10,000 square feet, usually selling a few hundred products in one category of merchandise. For example, it would be very difficult to find this book and car parts in the same physical store. Even larger-format hypermarkets, which can be as large as 260,000 square feet,[11] sell only a few thousand products. Their assortment tends to be wide but not very deep. It's hard to sell a wide range of products in physical stores because retailers have to procure and take physical possession of products, get the products to each physical store, continually stock the shelves, and so on. This is all very capital and labor-intensive, resulting in low margins.

Large ecommerce vendors sometimes don't even take physical possession of the goods they sell, using arrangements such as *drop shipping*, whereby the manufacturer or wholesaler ships directly to the end customer. Many ecommerce vendors are using marketplaces where the sellers are clearly identified as being a third party, usually the manufacturer or a small wholesaler. Both drop shipping and marketplaces have eliminated a lot of inventory, risk, capital, and labor associated with carrying that inventory.

---

11 Associated Press, "260,000-square-foot Wal-Mart in Upstate NY," (20 March 2008), *http://nbcnews.to/MrUCCR*.

To further add to the benefits of ecommerce, products can be shipped from a few centrally located warehouses, with the vendors having to worry about keeping only a few warehouses stocked, as opposed to thousands of physical stores. Amazon.com ships its products out of over 80 physical warehouses around the world, with many over one million square feet.[12] It can still be profitable for an ecommerce vendor to sell 100 units of a given product, whereas it would never be profitable for a physical retailer. This has revolutionized entire industries, like book selling and auto parts distribution, as people want to buy niche products that aren't economically feasible to stock in physical retail stores.

# Technological Advances

## Closer Tie-in with the Physical World

Because of its nature, ecommerce has some distinct advantages and disadvantages over traditional retail. We discussed many of the advantages earlier, including price, convenience, and assortment. The main disadvantages, also discussed earlier, include the inability to see and/or try on goods, and shipping. This is where ecommerce vendors with physical stores can have an edge over pure play ecommerce vendors. They can leverage their physical stores to bridge the gap between the virtual and physical worlds.

Let's start with the inability to see and try on goods. Many retail stores, whether belonging to the ecommerce vendor where the purchase is ultimately made or not, have become virtual showrooms. *Showrooming* refers to the trend of customers viewing and trying on the products in physical stores but then buying online. Traditional retailers without a strong ecommerce offering abhor this behavior and have even hidden barcodes in a feeble attempt to stop it. Retailers with a strong ecommerce offering have even begun to encourage the practice by offering free in-store WiFi, advertising wider assortments that are available online, encouraging customers to view product reviews online, and offering detailed content that's featured only online. The thought behind this is that it's better to cannibalize revenue from your physical stores with your ecommerce offering as opposed to someone else's ecommerce offering. Having a strong physical and ecommerce presence is what's required to succeed in today's increasingly digital world.

Many ecommerce vendors with physical stores now offer in-store pickup and in-store return of goods purchased online. A few offer fulfillment from physical stores, meaning any item from any physical store can be picked off the shelves and delivered to customers. This makes all of the inventory from a retailer's entire network avail-

---

12  Neal Karlinsky and Brandon Baur, "From Click to Delivery: Inside Amazon's Cyber Monday Strategy," ABC News (26 November 2012), *http://abcn.ws/1k7ysEQ*.

able to anybody in the world. Certain types of ecommerce vendors, like grocers, have always featured in-store fulfillment as well as delivery from the local store. In the UK, this is a $10 billion/year business, with physical retail stores both fulfilling and shipping (via delivery vans) the goods to individuals.[13] Other categories of goods that have traditionally been fulfilled from local retail stores include large electronics, furniture, and other items that are too big to ship or require custom installation.

To compensate for the advantage that retailers with physical stores have, leading-edge online-only ecommerce vendors are experimenting with same-day delivery and offering customers the ability to pick up goods from *drop boxes*, which are simply automated kiosks containing your goods that you unlock with a code. Often these drop boxes are scattered throughout metropolitan areas in places like convenience stores. This makes it faster for customers to receive and return goods while lowering shipping costs.

### Customer-friendly policies

By its nature, ecommerce is at a distinct disadvantage over traditional retailers because of the physical distance between the products and the customers. In a purely physical retail world, this isn't an issue. You pay for the products at a point-of-sale terminal and walk out the door with your products in hand. Specific problems with ecommerce and shipping include the following:

- Cost of outbound shipping (sending goods from vendor to customer)
- Cost of inbound shipping (sending returned goods from customer back to vendor)
- Time it takes to receive goods
- Delays and taxes incurred at border crossings
- Cost/time to return

These problems are made worse by the fact that customers want to physically see and try on goods. There's a reason that many physical retail stores, especially those selling higher-end noncommoditized merchandise, sometimes spend hundreds of thousands of dollars for lighting and changing rooms in their stores. Customers often want to see and try on those categories of goods including clothing, shoes, leather goods, jewelry, watches, and so on. You can't do that with ecommerce, so the return rates tend to be higher. Return rates can be as high as 20%–30% for apparel.[14]

---

13 Reuters, "Online Grocery Sales to Double in Key European Markets by 2016—IGD," (23 October 2013), *http://reut.rs/MrUCTm*.

14 Mark Brohan, "Reducing the Rate of Returns," Internet Retailer (29 May 2013), *http://bit.ly/1k7ytIW*.

To compensate for these deficiencies, many vendors offer these incentives:

- Free inbound and outbound shipping to at least some customers—often those who are the most loyal or those who need to be enticed to complete a purchase
- Reduced-price expedited shipping, sometimes offered as part of an annual membership
- Free same-day delivery, especially in smaller countries or large metro areas
- In-store pickup and returns for vendors with physical stores
- Depot-based pickup, where you can have your goods delivered to a secure locker in a local convenience store or gas station

Customer-friendly policies such as free shipping and free returns are cutting into margins less as shipping costs are being reduced. The clear trend of the past decade has been away from giant monolithic fulfillment centers to smaller, more regional centers that are closer to customers. A package is going to cost less to ship and will show up faster if it has to travel 500 miles instead of 2,000. These policies hurt margins in the short run but ultimately lead to satisfied customers who buy more in the long run.

## Increasing Maturity of eCommerce Offerings

We've come a long way since the beginning of modern ecommerce in the mid-1990s. Back in the early days of the Internet, ecommerce suffered from a dearth of Internet-enabled devices, slow connection speeds, little or no web browser standardization, and little public awareness. The year 1994 was the turning point, when people in the US began to buy personal computers for the first time and hook them up to the Internet. Netscape, the original web browser for the masses, began in early 1994 and supported Security Sockets Layer (SSL) later that year. Dial-up Internet, while slow, was better than the nothingness that preceded it. Money follows eyeballs, as the old adage goes, and ecommerce began to grow in tandem and then much faster than Internet use. As people began to use ecommerce, established retailers and entrepreneurs of all stripes began to invest. For example, Amazon.com was founded in 1994, and eBay was founded in 1995. This cycle of investment and growth has been repeated in countries all around the world, beginning when Internet access is available to the masses.

The investments in ecommerce have led to both incremental improvements and major innovations, including:

- Better functionality through new tools and features that make it easier to shop
- A more personalized shopping experience
- Use of social media to both directly transact and influence sales

- Rich interfaces offered across multiple device types
- Transfer of control from IT to business
- Improvements in underlying technology that improved performance and availability
- Customer-friendly policies, like free shipping and no-hassle returns
- Closer tie-in with the physical world—from in-store returns to kiosks in public places

While innovation is always good, it has come at the cost of complexity. It's not uncommon for a large ecommerce platform to have over a million lines of actual source code. You need to integrate or build solutions for management, monitoring, ratings and reviews, product recommendations, load balancing, static content serving, load testing, and more. You need dozens of products or services, each having its own lifecycle and service-level agreements. It's a lot of work. But it's precisely these technologies and newfound ways of using them that have led to the widespread and rapid adoption of ecommerce around the world.

Let's explore each of these further.

### Better functionality

Over the years, ecommerce has evolved from a collection of more or less static HTML pages to a rich shopping experience, complete with tools and features to help you find and purchase the goods or services you may or may not even know you want. Shopping online is now so enjoyable that many prefer to do it under the influence of alcohol when they're in a good mood.[15] Not many intoxicated customers feel inclined to walk into a physical retail store in the middle of the night.

The better ecommerce vendors offer advanced tools to help you find exactly the product you're looking for. For example, *Netshoes.com.br* is the largest online apparel retailer in the world. *Netshoes.com.br* has no physical stores and specializes in selling shoes online. To better compete against physical retail stores, *Netshoes.com.br* invested in technology to perform 3D scans of shoes. When you create your profile, you can enter in the model number and size of the shoes that fit you best. When browsing for new shoes, you can compare the fit of your old shoes versus new shoes and see how the fit actually differs, as shown in Figure 1-2.

---

15 Stephanie Clifford, "Online Merchants Home In on Imbibing Consumers," *New York Times* (27 December 2011), *http://nyti.ms/MrUDXc*.

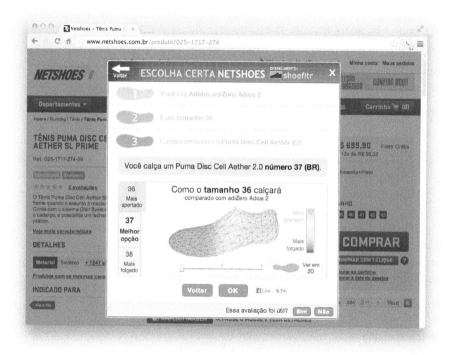

*Figure 1-2. Netshoes.com.br's shoe-fitting tool*

Innovations like this highlight the advantage that ecommerce offers. In a physical retail store, you'd have to try on many pairs of shoes until you found the ones that fit you perfectly. Each physical store is unlikely to have as many shoes to choose from.

Another benefit of ecommerce is the ability to customize products and see accurate visualizations of customizations. Customized products sell for a premium and keep customers more engaged. NFLShop.com, for example, does this with custom jerseys.

Enhanced photography, including 360° videos, make it easier to see products. Innovations in static image serving and devices capable of connecting to the Internet have made it easier than ever to deliver and render high-resolution images.

Enhanced search has made it trivial to search, browse, and refine your results to pinpoint exactly what you're looking for. Modern ecommerce preceded Google's founding by four years. For the first few years of ecommerce, search didn't exist or wasn't accurate. For the most part, you had to manually browse through categories of products until you found what you were looking for. In the 2000s, ecommerce search began to take off, though it didn't really mature until the mid-2000s. For many years, search results were fairly inaccurate, as they simply did keyword matching against each SKU's metadata. The goal of retail has always been to get the right products in front of the right customer at the right time. Accurate search enables that.

Modern search is very mature, offering accurate search with the ability to refine by price, manufacturer, and other product-specific metadata. For example, a search for "usb flash drive" across any popular ecommerce website will offer customers the ability to refine by the capacity and USB specification. The ability to quickly refine results has been a substantial driver of conversions.

Maturing ecommerce search functionality has also helped ecommerce vendors by allowing business users to boost results, bury results, redirect to a special page for a given term, and so on. This maturation of technology has allowed today's business users to help customers find exactly what they're looking for while maximizing revenue and margins.

Category-specific tools and guides have also made shopping easier for novices. For example, buying memory has never been easier because of a proliferation of memory finder tools, as depicted in Figure 1-3.

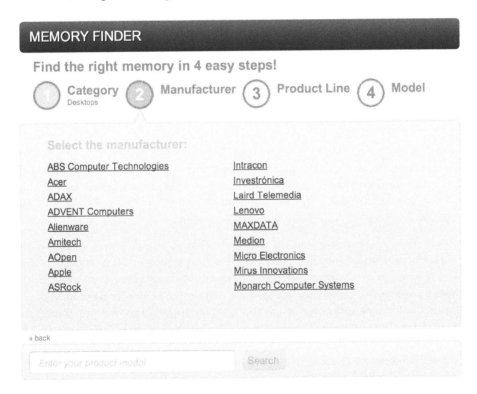

*Figure 1-3. Memory finder tool*

Empowered by these tools, novices can get what they need without having to chat or call a customer service representative. Customer enablement is a key driver of ecommerce's success, and these tools exemplify that trend.

Over the years, ecommerce has moved from being more transactional to more solution-oriented. Many customers now want bundles of products that work better together. For example, viewing the product detail page of a TV now commonly triggers cross-sells, as shown in Figure 1-4.

*Figure 1-4. Example of a cross-sell*

These cross-sells are often high-margin goods for vendors, and they help the customer by completing the solution.

## Personalized shopping

Personalization has proven to be a powerful driver of both customer satisfaction and higher revenue. Broadly, *personalization* is the ability to customize a shopping experience to individual customers or groups of customers based on an attribute or behavior. Effective personalization drives sales in the way that an attentive sales staff does, except you don't have to pay commission to algorithms.

*Attribute-based personalization* often uses demographic information captured during registration, and sometimes browsing behavior. For example, as an apparel retailer, you may want to show your Wisconsin customers winter gloves and your Florida customers swimsuits in January. Customers in Wisconsin simply have little use for swimsuits in January and may not advance past the home page when presented with such irrelevant information. Or imagine a man being presented with the latest lipstick. Chances are, these recommendations are going to be entirely ignored or even perceived as offensive. Outside of a few stores in the world, sales people in traditional retail stores would be fired if they presented a man with lipstick as they walked in the door.

*Behavior-based personalization* is triggered by specific events—often the viewing of specific products. For example, based on my browsing history, this ecommerce website has determined that I would be interested in the following, shown in Figure 1-5.

*Figure 1-5. Example of behavior-based personalization*

Behavior-based personalization is often preferred to attribute-based personalization because it's based on what customers actually do as opposed to stereotypes about what they should do. For example, someone located in Wisconsin could be buying a swimsuit for an upcoming trip to Florida. Displaying related swimsuits because a customer has already viewed five others in the same session is perfectly normal.

From an ecommerce vendor's standpoint, personalization serves simply to increase sales. Going back to *Netshoes.com.br*, one of their specialties is selling team apparel for soccer teams in Latin America. Soccer, as with many other sports and activities, can be a very serious matter to many fans.[16]

> "Corinthians is like a nation, a religion…people are borrowing money from banks, from relatives to come here. They are quitting their jobs, selling their bikes, their cars, even their fridges. It's true."
>
> —A Corinthian's fan (Sao Paulo's hometown club) on the legions of fans that followed the team to Japan for an important match

Now imagine this fan creating an account on *Netshoes.com.br*, identifying as a Corinthians fan during registration, and then seeing apparel from their archrival, Pameiras, on the home page. It would be an insult and it would show that Netshoes.com doesn't understand him. It's highly unlikely that a Corinthians fan will ever buy a Pameiras–branded item. In fact, being presented with a Pameiras item is likely to prevent the sale of a Corinthians item to this fan. Presenting customers with a personalized shop-

---

16 James Montague, "Corinthians: Craziest fans in the world?" CNN (14 December 2012), *http://cnn.it/1k7yvAr.*

ping experience has proven to be a substantial driver of sales for many ecommerce vendors.

Imagine the advantages this has over traditional retail, where there's virtually no personalization whatsoever. A sales associate on a store floor is likely to know nothing about any given customer, whereas the Web has purchase history, browsing history, and a complete demographic profile of each shopper available to build a personalized ecommerce shopping experience.

Personalization can also be used to price discriminate. For example, men between the ages of 30–45 who make greater than $150,000/year have a very inelastic demand for the latest technology gadget and always could be shown the list price. Women aged 60+ are likely to have very elastic demand for the latest gadget and may be more willing to make a purchase with a 30% off discount or free shipping. Price discrimination is a part of our everyday lives, from the price of airfare to how much you pay for your bathroom renovation. Traditional retailers would do it more if they could. It's shockingly easy to do it with ecommerce.

## Social media

Social media, virtually nonexistent a few years ago, has come to be a substantial influencer and even driver of ecommerce sales. Today it's estimated that 74% of customers have a commercial interaction with social media prior to an ecommerce purchase.[17] Customers interact with social media to learn about products, search for discounts, and then tell others about their experience shopping and consuming the product. The reach of social media today is extensive, with the average Facebook user having 245 friends[18] and Twitter delivering more than 200 billion tweets per day.[19] It's ubiquitous and becoming an increasing part of our daily lives.

Customers are increasingly taking to social media to research purchases and then tell their friends about their shopping experiences—whether good or bad. Before social media, an upset customer was likely to tell a few close friends about their experience. Now, it's easy to tell hundreds or even thousands of people in the few seconds it takes to compose a Tweet or update your Facebook status.

Purchases are increasingly no longer made in isolation. Influences come far and wide, especially from social media.

---

17  Cooper Smith, "Pinterest Is Powering A Huge Amount of Social Commerce, and Twitter Isn't Too Shabby Either," *Business Insider*, (4 September 2013), *http://read.bi/MrUDXp*.

18  Hayley Tsukayama, "Your Facebook Friends Have More Friends Than You," *Washington Post* (3 February 2012), *http://bit.ly/1k7yufM*.

19  Twitter, Inc., "Amendment No. 1 to Form S-1 Registration Statement" (15 October 2013), *http://1.usa.gov/MrUGlZ*.

---

### Rich interfaces across multiple devices

In the early days of ecommerce, ecommerce applications were fairly static. You went to *http://www.website.com* from a web browser and received a single static HTML page as your response, formatted for an 800×600 pixel display. It was probably built exclusively for Internet Explorer.

Today, most ecommerce vendors have native applications for the wide range of devices that are now used to browse or consume content on the Internet. Most browser-based applications automatically resize themselves according to the device resolution. Many modify the way they render based on the connection speed and the capabilities of a wide range of web browsers. Most vendors offer a range of mobile ecommerce offerings, from mobile-friendly HTML (e.g., *m.website.com*) to iOS and Android applications. Tablets have a fairly wide range of native applications available. Building native user interfaces, capable of leveraging each device's functionality, pays off with conversion rates as much as 30% higher than mobile-friendly HTML.[20]

### Transfer of control from IT to business

Business users include merchandisers, marketers, and managers. In general, the more control business users have over the platform, the better, as they're closer to customers and allow IT to focus on keeping the website up and delivering on differentiating functionality. For example, athletic apparel retailers need to be able to quickly push promotions live for the winning team of a big game. Similarly, many ecommerce vendors watch social media for trends and frequently merchandise their site differently based on what people are talking about. Waiting days for changes to take effect is no longer acceptable.

Business users today often control the following:

- Page layout—page templates and the content that fills each slot
- Customer segmentation rules
- Promotions
- Prices
- Product details—description, display name, parent category
- Categorization rules—static and dynamic rules
- Images
- Text
- Search rules—boost results, bury results, redirects

---

20  David Eads, "Mobile Web Is Only Half of Retail Mobile Commerce," Mobile Manifesto (15 May 2011), *http://bit.ly/MrUEuq*.

- A/B segments
- Campaigns (email, social, print)
- Payment methods and rules
- Shipping rules and costs

Tools used by business users range from simple spreadsheets to rich drag-and-drop user interfaces.

It used to be that ecommerce applications were entirely code-driven, meaning, for example, that you had to change code in order to swap out the main image on the home page. This was largely because the industry was just getting started. So long as the application was up in production, people were generally happy. Today, most ecommerce applications are data-driven, meaning that pages are dynamically rendered based on data in a persistent datastore, like a database, as opposed to hardcoded strings or variables. With data in a database or some other persistent datastore, it's fairly easy to build a user interface that allows business users to modify it.

There's an eternal conflict between business and IT, as the two are so intertwined but often have opposing interests. The goal of business is to make money, often by driving traffic through promotional events. In theory, the goal of IT is to see the business succeed, but in reality IT is rewarded for platform availability over all else. The two sides have to work together to succeed, and to do that, incentives must be fully aligned.

### Improvements in underlying technology

Since the beginning, ecommerce has greatly benefited from a virtuous cycle of investment and growth. That continues to this day, with daily advances made in the technology that underlies ecommerce. We'll discuss many of these advances throughout the rest of the book, but broadly this technology includes the following:

- Cloud computing
- Content Delivery Networks
- Domain name system (DNS)
- Load balancers
- Web servers
- Application servers
- Applications themselves and the frameworks used to build them
- Virtual machines
- Operating systems
- Hardware

- Cache grids
- Network infrastructure
- Databases
- Increased bandwidth at all layers

Every single layer has substantially improved since the beginning of ecommerce. These improvements have not been generally reflected in today's ecommerce deployment architectures.

# Changing Face of Retail

Retail around the world is quickly changing, with the Internet and globalization the two driving forces behind these changes. Like globalization before it, the Internet has proven to be an incredibly disruptive force. The consulting firm McKinsey & Company published a startling chart ranking the revenues of the top 10 retailers in the US in 1990 versus 2012, shown in Figure 1-6.[21]

---

21 "How retailers can keep up with consumers", October 2013, McKinsey & Company, *http://www.mckin sey.com/insights*. Reprinted by permission.

US revenues, $ billion

■ New to top 10 in 2012
▨ Dropped out of top 10 by 2012

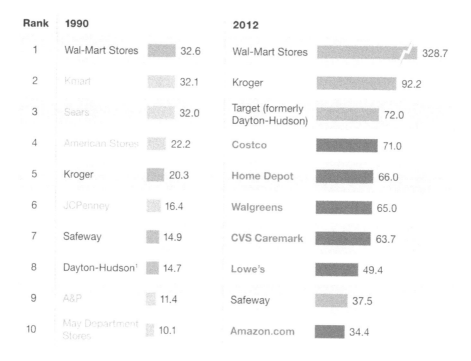

| Rank | 1990 | | 2012 | |
|------|------|------|------|------|
| 1 | Wal-Mart Stores | 32.6 | Wal-Mart Stores | 328.7 |
| 2 | Kmart | 32.1 | Kroger | 92.2 |
| 3 | Sears | 32.0 | Target (formerly Dayton-Hudson) | 72.0 |
| 4 | American Stores | 22.2 | Costco | 71.0 |
| 5 | Kroger | 20.3 | Home Depot | 66.0 |
| 6 | JCPenney | 16.4 | Walgreens | 65.0 |
| 7 | Safeway | 14.9 | CVS Caremark | 63.7 |
| 8 | Dayton-Hudson¹ | 14.7 | Lowe's | 49.4 |
| 9 | A&P | 11.4 | Safeway | 37.5 |
| 10 | May Department Stores | 10.1 | Amazon.com | 34.4 |

¹Dayton-Hudson changed its name to Target in 2000.

Source: *Stores*: US Securities and Exchange Commission filings; McKinsey analysis

*Figure 1-6. Top ten largest retailers in the US in 1990 versus 2012*

Of the top 10 largest retailers in the US in 1990, only four remained on the list in 2012. What's notable is that Amazon.com is now on the list at number 10, with its revenues quickly growing as traditional retail revenue declines.

The graphs in Figures 1-7 and 1-8 illustrate the problems facing traditional retailers.

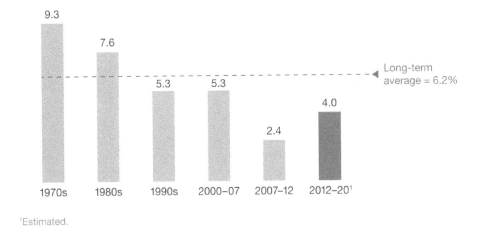

**US retail-sales growth,** compound annual growth rate (CAGR), %

9.3 | 7.6 | 5.3 | 5.3 | 2.4 | 4.0

Long-term average = 6.2%

1970s    1980s    1990s    2000–07    2007–12    2012–20[1]

[1]Estimated.

*Figure 1-7. US retail sales growth has declined since the 1970s[22]*

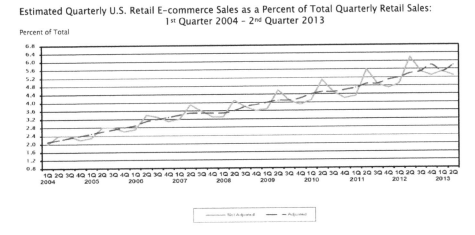

Estimated Quarterly U.S. Retail E-commerce Sales as a Percent of Total Quarterly Retail Sales:
1st Quarter 2004 – 2nd Quarter 2013

Percent of Total

*Figure 1-8. US ecommerce sales have risen steadily[23]*

Traditional retailers with physical stores that don't also excel in ecommerce are doomed to extinction. Very few of today's top 10 retailers will continue to remain in

---

22 *http://bit.ly/1g4tbGB*

23 *http://www.census.gov/retail/mrts/www/data/pdf/ec_current.pdf*

their present positions 10 or even 20 years from today. While this list is specific to the US, the principles are the same for other countries around the world.

Let's take Borders as an example. At its peak in 2003, it had 1,249 physical retail stores.[24] By the time it filed for bankruptcy in 2011, it was down to 399 stores. When faced with mounting pressure from pure play ecommerce vendors, Borders decided to outsource its entire ecommerce operation to Amazon.com in 2001.

> "In our view, that was more like handing the keys over to a direct competitor."
>
> —Peter Wahlstrom, *Morningstar*

Borders pulled out of that agreement in 2007, but it was too late. The last time it had earned a profit was 2006.[25] While Borders was investing in building out its physical stores, its competitor, Barnes & Noble, was investing in ecommerce. Barnes & Noble eventually released its own branded e-reader in 2009.

Unfortunately, many retailers suffer from what's known as *the innovator's dilemma*,[26] focusing on business as usual instead of innovating. Innovation is disruptive, both internally and externally, and it's expensive. In a world that's increasingly driven by quarterly earnings, long-term research and development isn't rewarded so much as punished by Wall Street for not "making the number." True innovation, including the adoption of ecommerce and shifting to the cloud, requires strong leadership and a commitment to investing for the future.

## Omnichannel Retailing

For traditional retailers with physical stores, ecommerce represents a big challenge to the status quo. For many decades, most retailers had just one channel: physical stores. For both retailers and customers, this was a simple model, as shown in Figure 1-9.

---

24 Mae Anderson, "Borders Closing Signals Change in Bookselling Industry," Associated Press, (20 July 2011), *http://usat.ly/1k7yw7m*.

25 Yuki Noguchi, "Why Borders Failed While Barnes & Noble Survived," NPR (19 July 2011), *http://n.pr/MrUGCy*.

26 From the book by the same name, *The Innovator's Dilemma. (http://en.wikipedia.org/wiki/The_Innovator's_Dilemma)*

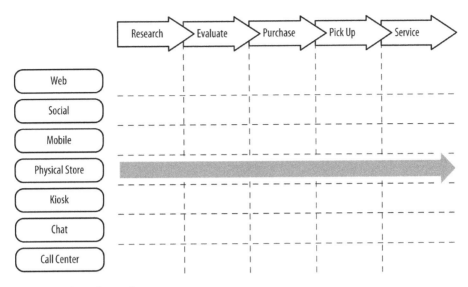

*Figure 1-9. One channel*

Most often, retailers didn't know who each customer was, as loyalty programs were still in their infancy. The customer would walk in and perhaps walk out with a product in hand. The only real influences were advertising and word of mouth. From an operations standpoint, each store was independently managed, with sales of each store easy to tabulate. If capital improvements were made to a store, it would be fairly easy to see later whether the investment was worth it. Salespeople could be paid commissions because their influence alone was likely the deciding factor in closing the sale. It was a simpler time. Today's world is much more complicated.

Dozens of channels are used for both influencing and purchasing. Customers now demand that retailers have a presence and be able to seamlessly transact across multiple channels:

- Web
- Social
- Mobile
- Physical store
- Kiosk
- Chat
- Call center

The ability to seamlessly transact across multiple channels is broadly defined as omnichannel retailing. This means reorienting from transaction and channel-focused interactions to more experience and brand-focused interactions. It's a big change. Figure 1-10 is a picture of what today's customer journey may look like.

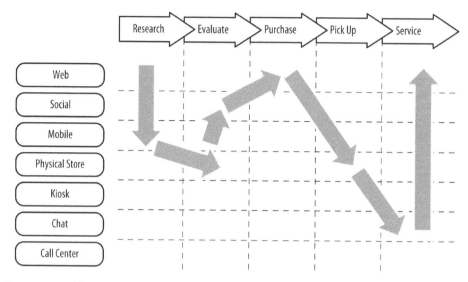

*Figure 1-10. The journey today's customers take before purchasing*

Customers constantly jump back and forth between channels, or they may even use multiple channels simultaneously—researching a product on a mobile device from a physical store. Today, the purchase process is typically some form of the following:

1. Research extensively online, leveraging social media

2. Read ratings and reviews

3. Shop for best price

4. Purchase

5. Tell people about the purchase and whether they're happy

As recently as two decades ago, only three of these seven customer touch points existed. Only one of these seven channels has existed for the first 99.3% of modern retailing. Figure 1-11 shows a breakdown of when each of these channels was first introduced.

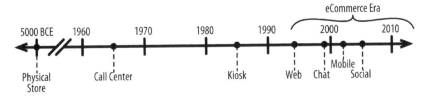

*Figure 1-11. Timeline of the introduction of channels (not to scale)*

This is only when these technologies were introduced. For example, the first modern web browser on a mobile device wasn't released until 2002, but it wasn't until the middle of 2007 that the first iPhone was released. It takes a while for these technologies to mature and become adopted by a critical mass of customers.

These changes to retailing are entirely customer-driven and have their roots in our modern consumer culture: technological advances, including the introduction of the Internet and cheap electronic devices, democratization of data, and globalization. Customers are firmly in charge. Retailers have to adapt or they will perish.

## Business Impact of Omnichannel

Many retailers with physical stores used to eye ecommerce with suspicion. Sales staff working for and managing individual stores especially feel that ecommerce is a zero sum game. They see customers coming in to look at and try on products, only to have them pull out smartphones and purchase the same product online for less, often from a different vendor.

For the first decade of ecommerce, retailers with physical stores and ecommerce just treated ecommerce as its own physical store. The cost to build an ecommerce platform was roughly the same as the cost of a physical store, and it was easier to manage ecommerce that way, given the rigidity of the backend systems. This treatment of ecommerce kept it relegated to a marginal role in most enterprises because everyone thought of it as a separate physical store, with its own growth targets, staff, and inventory. Today, ecommerce initiatives are strategic to all retailers, with the heads of ecommerce now typically reporting to the chief executive officer, as opposed to reporting to the chief marketing officer or chief information officer.

The growth of ecommerce was also constrained because of a misalignment of rewards. Individual store-level sales staff and managers were paid for sales that occurred within a physical store. As a result, many employees across an organization actively dissuaded customers from purchasing online. From a compensation perspective, an online purchase was often the same as the customer purchasing from a different retailer altogether. Now, some employees and store managers are beginning to be paid commission on ecommerce sales that occur near to their store.

Another problem is that the virtual boundaries of retailers are now wider than ever. It used to be that retailers had to respond only to customers who physically walked into a store. That's no longer the case today, as customers expect to be able to transact across multiple channels seamlessly. For example, retailers need to be able to monitor multiple social networks and quickly respond to complaints directed at them in a public forum.

Retail now is all about providing a holistic experience, as opposed to being a mere transaction. Interactions across all of these new channels count.

Now that ecommerce has been around for a while, retailers are beginning to figure things out. It'll take time, as ecommerce hasn't existed as a channel for 99.7% of retail's history. It takes time to adapt.

## Technical Impact of Omnichannel

As just discussed, omnichannel retailing has brought substantial changes to the business of retailing. But the technology is affected even more, making cloud computing such an attractive technology.

Originally, there were point-of-sale systems in stores. Then ecommerce started out as a single web-based channel with its own database. Over the years, chat, call center, mobile, and eventually social were added under the ecommerce umbrella, but these channels were mostly added from different vendors, each having their own customer profile, order database, and product catalog. Every stack was built with the assumption that it would work independently of any other software. As a software vendor, it's much easier to sell a chat platform, for example, that works standalone as opposed to only with specific ecommerce platforms. Figure 1-12 illustrates the fragmentation that arises when you have each stack functioning independently.

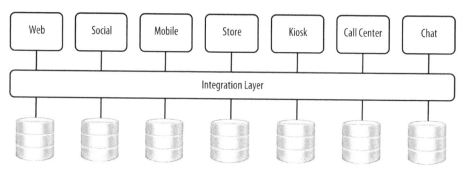

*Figure 1-12. Multichannel coupled with integration layer*

There was (and still is) so much growth in ecommerce that the revenue generated from these platforms exceeds the cost arising from suboptimal architecture and implementation. To put it another way, it's often just cheaper to throw some architects and developers at the fragmentation inherent in multichannel solutions. The problem of fragmentation is especially visible to customers between the store-based point-of-sale systems and ecommerce. The inability of these systems to speak to each other prevents most customers from buying online and picking up in a store, or adding a product in a store to an online shopping cart and then completing the order at home when the customer feels ready to make the purchase. Nothing frustrates customers more than having to re-enter data.

To combat this, retailers are beginning to build what amounts to a headless ecommerce platform using a single logical database or data store, as shown in Figure 1-13.

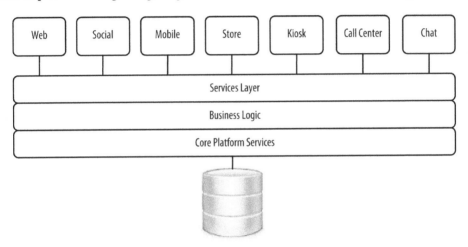

*Figure 1-13. New omnichannel-based architecture*

With this architecture, user interfaces are basically disposable, as the business logic all resides in a single layer, accessible through a services-based framework. For example, a RESTful query of:

```
http://www.website.com/ProfileLookup?profileId=12345
```

should return:

```
{
    "firstName": "Kelly",
    "lastName": "Goetsch",
    "age": 28,
        "address": {
        "streetAddress": "1005 Gravenstein Highway North",
        "city": "Sebastopol",
        "state": "CA",
        "postalCode": "95472"
    },
```

```
    "phoneNumber": [
        {
            "type": "work",
            "number": "7078277000"
        }
    ] ...
}
```

and so on. Having a single system of record makes it easy for customers to transact with you across many different channels. Multiple integrations, especially point-to-point, are painful. The various stacks are always out-of-date. There are always conflicts to resolve because a customer's data could be updated simultaneously from two or more channels. A single system of record is basically the same concept as enterprise resource planning (ERP) platforms.

Forward-looking retailers have already removed in-store point-of-sale systems in favor of tablets connecting to a single unified platform.[27] With this type of setup, it's easy for store associates to pull up customer profiles, saved orders, browsing history, and other data to help make sales.

---

## Case Study: Apple

Apple is famously a leader in omnichannel retailing, with customers having a seamless experience across multiple channels. Their leadership with omnichannel retailing has led them to have the highest sales per physical square foot in retail, double the nearest competitor.[28]

Apple's success starts at the top, in the way they approach retailing. They appoint one executive to oversee all retailing, regardless of where the sales are made. Many organizations have ecommerce roll up through the chief information officer or chief marketing officer rather than to a business leader. Having a single leader, a single organization, and a single platform makes it easy to offer a seamless experience whether in a physical retail store or online.

A cornerstone of Apple's strategy is to give its retail store employees iPads, iPods, and iPhones loaded with an interface to their ecommerce platform. Employees can approach prospective customers with the mobile device and pull up orders started online, review a customer's purchasing history, view all products offered online, schedule service appointments, and place orders. Normal point-of-sale systems simply allow customers to pay for goods, with little ability to transact.

---

27 Brian Walker, "IBM Sells POS Business to Toshiba: What It Means," Forrester (17 April 2012), *http://bit.ly/1k7yuMN*.

28 David Segal, "Apple's Retail Army, Long on Loyalty but Short on Pay," *New York Times* (23 June 2012), *http://nyti.ms/MrUGT0*.

This unified omnichannel platform is creating challenges for IT, however. As these platforms become larger and more important, scalability, availability, and performance matter even more than ever. A failure in this world knocks every channel offline, including physical stores. Outages simply cannot occur.

## Summary

In this chapter, we reviewed the substantial ways that ecommerce and retail itself are changing, along with the change in architecture that's required to support these changes. Next, we'll explore the current state of ecommerce deployment architecture to better understand how it's falling short.

# CHAPTER 2

# How Is Enterprise eCommerce Deployed Today?

Prior to ecommerce, the Web was mostly static. Web pages consisted of HTML and images—no CSS, no JavaScript, and no AJAX. SSL wasn't even supported by web browsers until late 1994. Many leading ecommerce vendors, including Amazon, eBay, Tesco, and Dell.com first came online in 1994 and 1995 with static websites. Naturally, people coming online wanted to be able to transact. Adding transaction capabilities to static HTML was a technical feat that required the following:

- Using code to handle user input and generate HTML pages dynamically
- Securing communication
- Storing data in a persistent database

Today's software and the architecture used to build these systems has largely remained the same since 1995. The innovations have been incremental at best.

 With so much money generated by ecommerce, availability has trumped all else as a driving force behind architecture.

With the rise of omnichannel retailing and the increasing demands, the current approach to architecture is not sustainable. Let's review the status quo.

# Current Deployment Architecture

Most ecommerce deployment architectures follow the legacy three-tier deployment model consisting of web, application, and database tiers, as depicted in Figure 2-1.

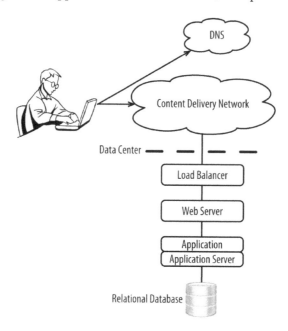

*Figure 2-1. Legacy three-tier eCommerce deployment architecture*

The web servers make up the web tier and traditionally are responsible for serving static content up to Content Delivery Networks (CDNs). The middle tier comprises application servers and is able to actually generate responses that various clients can consume. The data tier is used for storing data that's required for an application (e.g., product catalog, metadata of various types) and data belonging to customers (e.g., orders, profiles). We'll discuss this throughout the chapter, but the technology that underlies this architecture has substantially changed.

Each channel typically has its own version of this stack, with either an integration layer or point-to-point integrations connecting everything together. All layers of the stack are typically deployed out of a single data center. This architecture continues to dominate because it's a natural extension of the original deployment patterns back from the early days of ecommerce and it generally works.

Let's explore each layer in greater detail.

# DNS

DNS is responsible for resolving friendly domain names (e.g., website.com) to an IP address (e.g., 161.170.248.20). See Figure 2-2.

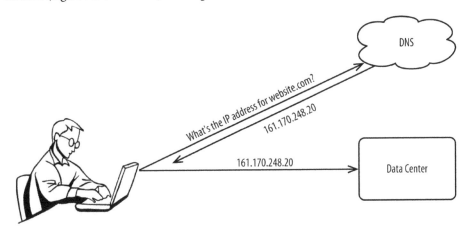

*Figure 2-2. Purpose of DNS*

DNS exists so you can remember "website.com" instead of 161.170.248.20.

When an ecommerce platform is served out of a single data center, typically only one IP address is returned because the load balancers cluster to expose one IP address to the world. But with multiple data centers or multiple IPs exposed per data center, DNS becomes more complicated because one IP address has to be selected from a list of two or more (typically one per data center). The IP addresses are returned to the client in an ordered list, with the first IP address returned the one that the client connects to first. If that IP isn't responding, the client moves down the list sequentially until it finds one that works.

Commonly used DNS servers, like BIND, work well with only one IP address per domain name. But as ecommerce has grown, there's been an increase in the use of deploying to multiple data centers in an active/active or active/passive configuration. Generally, operating from more than one data center requires the DNS server to choose between two or more IP addresses. Traditional DNS servers are capable of basic load-balancing algorithms such as round-robin, but they're not capable of digging deeper than that to evaluate the real-time health of a data center, geographic location of the client, round-trip latency between the client and each data center, or the real-time capacity of each data center.

This more advanced form of load balancing is known as *Global Server Load Balancing*, or GSLB for short. GSLB solutions are almost required now because there is more than one IP address behind most domain names. GSLB solutions can take the following forms:

- Hosted as a standalone service
- Hosted as part of a Content Delivery Network (CDN)
- Appliance based, residing in an on-premises data center

Many are beginning to move to hosted solutions. We'll discuss DNS and GSLB in greater detail in Chapter 10, but needless to say, appliance-based GSLB will no longer work when moving to the cloud. Solutions must be software based and must be more intelligent.

## Intra Data Center Load Balancing

Today's ecommerce platforms are served from hundreds or even thousands of physical servers, with only one IP address exposed to the world, as shown in Figure 2-3.

Load balancing takes place at every layer within a data center. Appliance-based hardware load balancers tend to be used today as the entry point into a data center and for load balancing within a data center. If a web server tier services traffic and sends it on to an application server tier, the web server often has load-balancing capabilities built in.

Load balancers have evolved over time from performing simple load-balancing duties to providing a full set of application control services. Even the term *load balancer* is now often replaced by most vendors with *application delivery controller*, which more accurately captures their expanding role. A few of those advanced features are as follows:

- Static content serving
- Dynamic page caching
- SSL/TLS termination
- URL rewriting
- Redirection rules
- Cache header manipulation
- Dynamic page rewriting to improve performance
- Web application firewall
- Load balancing
- Content compression

- Rate limiting/throttling
- Fast, secure connections to clouds

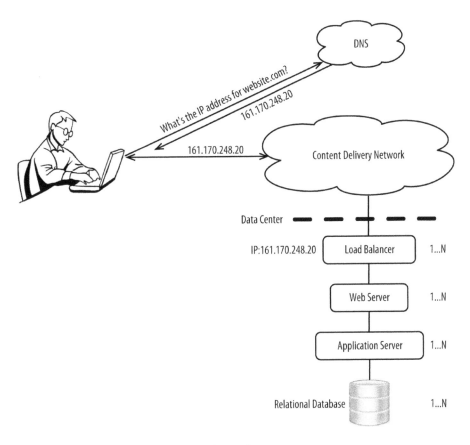

*Figure 2-3. Load-balancing points within a data center*

Load balancing in today's ecommerce platforms will have to substantially change to meet future requirements.

## Web Servers

In the early days of ecommerce, web servers were exposed directly to the public Internet, with each web server having its own IP address and own entry in the DNS record. To satisfy customers' demands for truly transactional ecommerce, Common Gateway Interface (CGI) support was added to web servers. As needs outstripped the capabilities of CGI, application servers were added behind web servers, with web servers still responsible for serving static content and serving as the load balancer for a pool of application servers.

As ecommerce usage increased and the number of web servers grew, appliance-like hardware load balancers were added in front of the web servers. Web servers can't cluster together and expose a single IP address to the world, as load balancers can. Load balancers also began to offer much of the same functionality as web servers. The line between web servers and load balancers blurred.

 Web servers are absolutely not required. In fact, their use is declining as the technology up and down stream of web servers has matured.

If web servers are used, they technically can perform the following functions:

- Serving static content
- Caching dynamic pages
- Terminating SSL/TLS
- Rewriting URLs
- Redirecting rules
- Manipulating cache headers
- Dynamic page rewriting to improve performance
- Creating a web application firewall
- Load balancing
- Compressing content

However, web servers usually just perform the following functions:

- Serving static content to a Content Delivery Network
- URL rewriting
- Redirect rules
- Load balancing

As CDNs, load balancers, and application servers have matured, functionality typically performed by web servers is increasingly being delegated to them. Table 2-1 shows what modern application servers, web servers, load balancers, and Content Delivery Networks are each capable of.

*Table 2-1. Capabilities of modern application servers, web servers, load balancers, and Content Delivery Networks*

| Function | Application servers | Web servers | Load balancers | Content Delivery Networks (when used as reverse proxy) |
|---|---|---|---|---|
| Serving static content | X | X | X | X |
| Caching dynamic pages | N/A | X | X | X |
| Terminating SSL | X | X | X | X |
| URL rewriting | X | X | X | X |
| Redirect rules | X | X | X | X |
| Manipulating cache headers | X | X | X | X |
| Dynamic page rewriting to improve performance | X | X | X | X |
| Web application firewall | | X | X | X |
| Load balancing | N/A | X | X | X |
| Clustering to expose single Virtual IP Address (VIP) | N/A | X | X | N/A |
| Content compression | X | X | X | X |
| Rate limiting/throttling | | | X | X |

Given that application servers, load balancers, and Content Delivery Networks are required, web servers are becoming increasingly marginalized, with their use on the decline among major ecommerce vendors. The real problem is that web servers greatly complicate elasticity. Deployment architecture with web servers looks something like Figure 2-4.

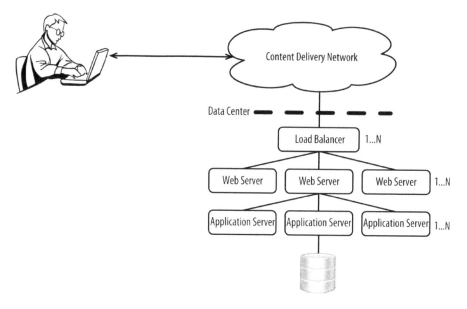

*Figure 2-4. Deployment architecture with web servers*

Adding a new application server requires the following:

1. Provisioning hardware for the new application server
2. Installing/configuring the new application server
3. Deploying the application to the application server
4. Registering the application server with the web server or load balancer

If you need to add more web server capacity because of the increased application server capacity, you need to then do the following:

1. Provision hardware for the new web server.
2. Install/configure the new web server.
3. Register the new web server with the load balancer.

It can take a lot of work and coordination to add even a single application server. While some web server and application server pairs allow you to scale each tier independently, you still have to worry about dependencies. If you add many application servers without first adding web servers, you could run out of web server capacity. The order matters.

It's often easier to eliminate the web server tier and push the responsibilities performed there to the CDN, load balancer, and application server. Many load balancers auto-detect new endpoints, making it even easier to add and remove new capacity quickly. That architecture looks like Figure 2-5.

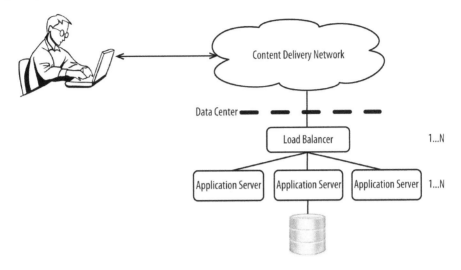

*Figure 2-5. Deployment architecture without web servers*

By flattening the hierarchy, you gain a lot of flexibility. Web servers can still add value if they're doing something another layer cannot.

## eCommerce Applications

The "e" is quickly being dropped from "ecommerce" to reflect the fact that there is no longer such a clear delineation between channels. Some retailers today are unable to report sales by channel because their channels are so intertwined. As discussed in Chapter 1, this one channel, called omnichannel, is serving as the foundation of all channels. Examples of channels include the following:

- Web
- Social
- Mobile
- Physical store
- Kiosk
- Chat
- Call center

On one extreme, you'll find that each channel has its own vertical stack, including a database, as shown in Figure 2-6.

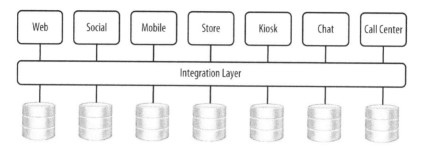

*Figure 2-6. Multichannel architecture featuring an integration layer*

With this model, each channel is wired together with each other channel through liberal use of an integration layer. This is how ecommerce naturally evolved, but it suffers from many pitfalls:

- A lot of code needs to be written to glue everything together.
- Channels are always out of sync.
- Differences in functionality leave customers upset (e.g., promotions online don't show up in in-store point-of-sale systems).
- Testing the entire stack is enormously complicated because of all of the resources that must be coordinated.
- The same customer data could be updated concurrently from two or more channels, leading to data conflicts and a poor experience.

Over the past few years, there's been a trend toward buying or building complete platforms, with one logical database and no integrations between channels, as shown in Figure 2-7.

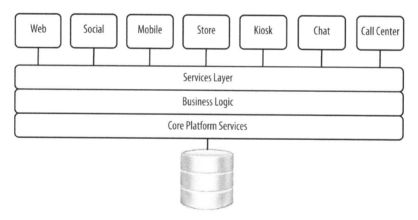

*Figure 2-7. Omnichannel architecture*

Obviously, this takes time to fully achieve but is clearly the direction that the market is heading in. And it makes perfect sense, given the rise in omnichannel retailing and ever-increasing expectations.

Support of true omnichannel retailing is now *the* competitive differentiator for commercial ecommerce platforms.

## Application Servers

Application servers, also known as *containers*, form a critical role in today's ecommerce platforms. They provide the runtime environment for ecommerce applications and provide services such as HTTP request handling, HTTP session management, connections to the database, authentication, directory services, messaging, and other services that are consumed by ecommerce applications.

Today's application servers are very mature, offering dozens of features that simplify the development, deployment, and runtime management of ecommerce applications. Over the years, they've continued to mature in the following ways:

- More modular architecture, starting up only the services required by the application being deployed
- Faster, lighter architectures
- Tighter integration with databases, with some vendors offering true bidirectional communication with databases
- Full integrations with cache grids
- Improved diagnostics
- Easier management

Application servers continue to play a central role in today's ecommerce platforms.

## Databases

Databases continue to play an important role in modern ecommerce architecture. Common examples of data in an ecommerce application that need to be stored include orders, profiles, products, SKUs, inventory, prices, ratings and reviews, and browsing history. Data can be stored using three high-level approaches.

## Fully normalized

Normalized data has a defined, rigid structure, with constraints involving data types, whether each column is required, and so on. Here's how you would define a very simple product table for a relational SQL database:

```
CREATE TABLE PRODUCT
(
        PRODUCT_ID  VARCHAR(255) NOT NULL,
        NAME    VARCHAR(255) NOT NULL,
        DESCRIPTION  CLOB NOT NULL,
        PRIMARY KEY(PRODUCT_ID)
);
```

To retrieve the data, you would execute a query:

```
SELECT * FROM PRODUCT;
```

and get back these results:

| PRODUCT_ID | NAME | DESCRIPTION |
|---|---|---|
| SK3000MBTRI4 | Thermos Stainless King 16-Ounce Food Jar | Constructed with double-wall stainless steel, this 16-ounce food jar is virtually unbreakable, yet its sleek design is both eye-catching and functional… |

This format very much mimics a spreadsheet. With data in a normalized format, you can execute complex queries, ensure the integrity of the data, and selectively update bits of data. Relational databases are built for the storage and retrieval of normalized data and have been used extensively for ecommerce.

Traditional relational databases tend to be ACID compliant. ACID stands for:[1]

*Atomicity*
> The whole transaction either succeeds or fails.

*Consistency*
> The transaction is committed without violating any integrity constraints (e.g., data type, whether column is nullable, foreign key constraints).

*Isolation*
> Each transaction is executed in its own private sandbox and not visible to any other transaction until it is committed.

*Durability*
> A committed transaction will not be lost.

---

1 Wikipedia, "ACID," (2014), *http://en.wikipedia.org/wiki/ACID*.

---

Most ecommerce applications use both a vertically and horizontally scaled ACID-compliant relational database for the core order and profile data. Relational databases used to be a primary bottleneck for ecommerce applications, but as that technology has matured, it is rarely the bottleneck it once was, provided appropriate code practices are followed. Application-level caching (both in-memory and to data grids) has helped to further scale relational databases.

## NoSQL

An increasingly popular alternative to relational databases are *key/value* or *document* stores. Rather than breaking up and storing the data in a fully normalized format, the data is represented as XML, JSON, or even a binary format, with the data available only if you know the record's key. Implementations vary widely, but collectively these are known as *NoSQL* solutions. Here's an example of what might be stored for the same product in the preceding section:

```
{
    "name": "Thermos Stainless King 16-Ounce Food Jar",
    "description": "Constructed with double-wall stainless steel, this 16-
        ounce food jar is virtually unbreakable, yet its sleek design is both
        eye-catching and functional...", ...
}
```

NoSQL is increasingly used for caching and storing nonrelational media, such as documents and data that don't need to be stored in an ACID-compliant database. NoSQL solutions generally sacrifice consistency and availability in exchange for performance and the ability to scale in a distributed nature. Product images, ratings and reviews, browsing history, and other similar data is very well suited for NoSQL databases, where ACID compliance isn't an issue.

NoSQL is increasingly beginning to find its place in large-scale ecommerce. The technology has real value, but it's going to take some time for the technology and market to mature to the level of relational databases. Relational databases have been around in their modern form since the 1970s. NoSQL has been around for just a few years.

We'll discuss ACID, BASE, and related principles in Chapter 10.

## Fully denormalized

Historically, a lot of data was stored in plain HTML format. Merchandisers would use WYSIWYG editors and save the HTML itself, either in a file or in a database. These HTML fragments would then be inserted into the larger pages to form complete web pages. Data looked like this:

```
<h2>Thermos Stainless King 16-Ounce Food Jar</h2>

<div id="product_description">
Constructed with double-wall stainless steel, this
16-ounce food jar is virtually unbreakable, yet its
sleek design is both eye-catching and functional...
</div>
```

One of the many disadvantages of this approach is that you can't reuse this data across channels. This will work for a web page, but how can you get an iPhone application to use this? This approach is on the decline and shouldn't be used anymore.

## Hosting

A key consideration for ecommerce success is the hosting model. Hosting includes at a minimum the physical data center, racks for hardware, power, and Internet connectivity. This is also known as *ping, power, and pipe*. Additionally, vendors can offer computing hardware, supporting infrastructure such as networking and storage, and various management services with service-level agreements.

> From a hosting standpoint, the cloud is much more evolutionary than revolutionary. It's been common for years to not own the physical data centers that you operate from. The hardware used to serve your platform and the networks over which your data travels are frequently owned by the data center provider. The cloud is no different in this regard.

Let's look at today's common hosting models, shown in Table 2-2.

*Table 2-2. Today's common hosting models*

| Attribute | Self-hosted on-premises | Self-hosted off premises | Colocation | Fully managed hosting | Public Infrastructure-as-a-Service |
|---|---|---|---|---|---|
| Who owns data center | You | You | Colo vendor | Hosting vendor | IaaS vendor |
| Physical location of data center | Your office | Remote | Remote | Remote | Remote |
| Who owns hardware | You | You | You or colo vendor | You or managed hosting vendor | IaaS vendor |
| Dedicated hardware | Yes | Yes | Yes | Probably | Maybe |
| Who builds infrastructure | You | You | You or colo vendor | Hosting vendor | IaaS vendor |
| Who provisions infrastructure | You | You | You or colo vendor | Hosting vendor | IaaS vendor |
| Who patches software | You | You | You or colo vendor | Hosting vendor | IaaS vendor |
| Accounting model | CAPEX | CAPEX | CAPEX | OPEX | OPEX |

It's rare to find an enterprise-level ecommerce vendor that self-hosts on premises. That used to be the model, but over the past two decades there has been a sharp movement toward fully managed hosting and now public Infrastructure-as-a-Service. Large, dedicated vendors offer much better data centers and supporting infrastructure for ecommerce. It doesn't take much to outgrow an on-premises data center. These dedicated vendors offer the following features:

- Highly available power through multiple suppliers and the use of backup generators
- Direct connections to multiple Internet backbones
- High security, including firewalls, guards with guns, physical biometric security
- Placement of data centers away from flood planes, away from areas prone to earthquakes, and near cheap power
- Advanced fire suppression
- High-density cooling

Dedicated vendors offer far and above what you can build on premises in your own data center, for substantially less cost. Some of these data centers are millions of square feet.[2] The marginal cost these vendors incur for one more tenant is minuscule, allowing them to pass some of that savings along to you. Economies of scale is the guiding principle for these vendors.

Most of these vendors offer services to complement their hardware and infrastructure offerings. These services include the following (in ascending order of complexity):

- Power cycling
- Management from the operating system on down (including patching)
- Shared services such as storage and load balancing
- Management from the application sever on down (including patching)
- Management from the application(s) on down
- Ongoing application-level development/maintenance

Platform-as-a-Service and Software-as-a-Service is what Infrastructure-as-a-Service vendors have built on top of their infrastructure in an attempt to move up the value chain and earn more revenue with higher margins.

---

2 Forbes, "The 5 Largest Data Centers in the World," *http://onforb.es/1k7ywo2*.

Anything that you cannot differentiate on yourself should be outsourced. This is now especially true of computing power.

# Limitations of Current Deployment Architecture

Present-day ecommerce deployment architecture is guided by decades' old architecture patterns, with availability being the driver behind all decisions. People are often incentivized for platform availability and punished, often with firings, for outages. An outage in today's increasingly omnichannel world is akin to barring customers from entering all of your physical retail stores. Since physical retail stores are increasingly using a single omnichannel ecommerce platform for in-store point-of-sale systems, an outage will actually prevent in-store sales, too. Keeping the lights on is the imperative that comes at the cost of just about everything else.

Current deployment architecture suffers from numerous problems:

- Everything is statically provisioned and configured, making it difficult to scale up or down.
- The platform is scaled for peaks, meaning most hardware is grossly underutilized.
- Outages occur with rapid spikes in traffic.
- Too much time is spent building infrastructure as opposed to higher value-added activities.

Cloud computing can overcome these issues. Let's explore each one of these a bit further.

## Static Provisioning

Most ecommerce vendors statically build and configure environments. The problem with this is that ecommerce traffic is inherently elastic. Traffic can easily increase by 100 times over baseline. All it takes is for the latest pop star to tweet about your brand to his or her 50 million followers, and pretty quickly you'll see exponential traffic as others re-tweet the original tweet. The world is so much more connected than it used to be. Either you have to scale for peak or you risk failing under heavy load. The cost of failing often outweighs the cost of buying a few more servers, so servers are over-provisioned, often by many times more than is necessary.

Static provisioning is bad because it's inefficient. You can't scale up or down based on real-time demand. This leads to ecommerce vendors scaling for peaks as opposed to scaling for actual load. Because nobody wants to get fired, everybody just wildly over-provisions in an attempt to maintain 100% uptime. Over-provisioning leads to serious issues:

- Wasted data center space, which is increasingly expensive
- Unnecessary cost, due to data center and human cost
- Focus away from core competency—whether that's selling the latest basketball shoe or selling forklifts

Most ecommerce vendors have to statically provision because their ecommerce platforms don't lend themselves to scaling dynamically. For example, many ecommerce platforms require ports and IP addresses to be hardcoded in configuration files. The whole industry was built around static provisioning. The cloud and the concept of dynamic provisioning is a recent development.

## Scaling for Peaks

Many ecommerce vendors simply guess at what their peaks will be and then multiply that by five in order to size their production environments. Hardware is statically deployed, sitting idle except for the few hours of the year where it spikes up to 20% utilization. The guiding factor has been to have 100% uptime, as downtime leads to unemployment. Then hardware must be procured for development and test environments, which are hardly ever used.

When you put together all of the typical environments needed, Table 2-3 shows the result, where 100% represents the hardware needed to support actual peak production traffic.

*Table 2-3. Cumulative amount of traffic required across ecommerce environments*

| Environment | % of production (actual peak traffic) | Cumulative % |
|---|---|---|
| Production—Typical utilization | 10% | n/a |
| Production—Actual peak | 100% | 100% |
| Production—Actual peak + Padding/Safety factor | 500% | 500% |
| Production—Clone of primary environment | 500% | 1000% |
| Staging—Environment 1 | 50% | 1050% |
| Staging—Environment 2 | 50% | 1100% |
| Staging—Environment 3 | 50% | 1150% |
| QA—Environment 1 | 25% | 1175% |
| QA—Environment 2 | 25% | 1200% |
| QA—Environment 3 | 25% | 1225% |

| Environment | % of production (actual peak traffic) | Cumulative % |
| --- | --- | --- |
| Development—Environment 1 | 10% | 1235% |
| Development—Environment 2 | 10% | 1245% |
| Development—Environment 3 | 10% | 1255% |

This is truer for larger vendors than it is for smaller vendors, who tend to not have the money to build out so many environments.

Because traffic can be so prone to rapid spikes, many ecommerce vendors multiply their actual expected peak by five so that peak consumes only 20% of the CPU or whatever the limiting factor is. Then most set up a mirror of production in a different physical data center for disaster recovery purposes or as a fully active secondary data center. On top of production, there are multiple preproduction environments, all being some fraction of production. Each branch of code typically requires its own environment. This amounts to a lot of hardware!

Let's apply this math to an example, shown in Table 2-4. An ecommerce vendor needs 50 physical servers to handle actual production load at peak.

*Table 2-4. Example of how many servers there are*

| Environment | % of production (actual peak traffic) | Servers |
| --- | --- | --- |
| Production—Actual peak | 100% | 50 |
| Production—Actual peak + Padding/Safety factor | 500% | 250 |
| Production—Clone of primary environment | 500% | 250 |
| Staging—Environment 1 | 50% | 25 |
| Staging—Environment 2 | 50% | 25 |
| Staging—Environment 3 | 50% | 25 |
| QA—Environment 1 | 25% | 13 |
| QA—Environment 2 | 25% | 13 |
| QA—Environment 3 | 25% | 13 |
| Development—Environment 1 | 10% | 5 |
| Development—Environment 2 | 10% | 5 |
| Development—Environment 3 | 10% | 5 |
| Total | | 629 |

A total of 629 physical servers are required across all environments.

With normal production traffic, only five servers are required (10% of actual peak of 50 servers = 5). Development and QA environments are rarely used, with the only customers being internal QA testers. Staging environments are periodically used for load tests and for executives to preview functionality, but that's about it. Figure 2-8 shows just how underutilized hardware often is.

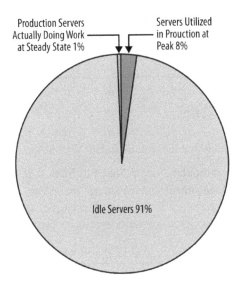

*Figure 2-8. Utilized versus unutilized hardware*

A remarkable 1% of total servers (5 out of 629) are actually being utilized at steady state in this example. Just moving preproduction environments would save an enormous amount of money.

## Outages Due to Rapid Scaling

Because the stack is so underutilized, rapid spikes in traffic often bring down entire platforms. Load tests use carefully crafted *ramp-up* times, which guide how quickly virtual customers are added. After each ramp period, there's always a period where the platform is allowed to stabilize. Stabilizing, also known as *leveling*, is done to allow the system time to recover from having a lot of load thrown at it. Load tests often look something like Figure 2-9.

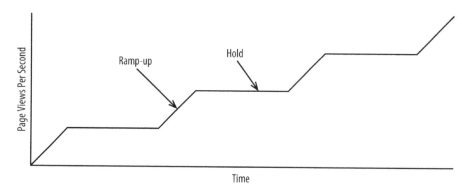

*Figure 2-9. Traffic from load test*

But in reality, traffic often looks like Figure 2-10.

Successful social media campaigns, mispriced products (e.g., $0.01 instead of $100), email blasts, coupons/promotions, mentions in the press, and important product launches can drive substantial traffic in a short period of time to the point where it can look like a distributed denial-of-service attack. Platforms don't get "leveling" periods in real life.

---

## Case Study: Dell's Price Mishap

Dell's Taiwanese subsidiary, *www.dell.com.tw*, accidentally set the price of one of its 19-inch monitors to approximately $15 USD instead of the intended price of approximately $148 USD. The incorrect price was posted at 11 PM locally. Within eight hours, 140,000 monitors were purchased at a rate of approximately five per second.[3]

---

3 Kevin Parrish, "Dell Ordered to Sell 19-inch LCD for $15," *Tom's Guide* (2 July 2009), *http://bit.ly/MrUFhW*.

---

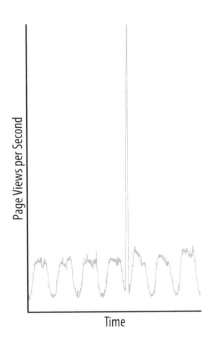

*Figure 2-10. Traffic in production*

This rapid increase in traffic ends up creating connections throughout each layer, which leads to spikes in traffic and memory consumption. Creating connections is expensive—that's why all layers use connection pooling of some sort. But it doesn't make sense to have enormous connection pools that are only a few percent utilized. Connections and other heavier resources tend to be created on demand, which can lead to failures under heavy load. Software in general doesn't work well when slammed with a lot of load.

## Summary

In this chapter, we discussed the shortcomings of today's deployment architecture, along with how the various components will need to change to support omnichannel retailing. The shortcomings discussed make a strong case for cloud computing, which we'll discuss in the next chapter.

# PART II

# The Rise of Cloud Computing

# CHAPTER 3

# What Is Cloud Computing?

*Cloud computing* is simply a new incarnation of a long-established business model: the public utility. The vast majority of households and businesses no longer invest in generating power on their own. It's faster, better, and cheaper to allow a public utility to generate it on behalf of large groups of consumers. Public utilities benefit from being able to specialize on a very limited charter while benefitting from economies of scale. Consumers have no knowledge of how to generate power, nor should they. Yet for a nominal price, any business or individual can tap into the grid (*on demand*), pull as much or as little as required (*elastic*), and pay for only the amount that's actually used (*metered*).

Power is very similar to cloud computing, both in the business model used by the vendors and the benefits it provides to individual consumers.

## Generally Accepted Definition

The term *cloud* has come to encompass everything, to the point where it means nothing. The cloud has been so broadly redefined by marketers that any service delivered over the Internet is now considered part of the cloud. Services as mundane as online photo sharing or web-based email are now counted as cloud computing, depending on who you talk to.

Cloud computing is still maturing, both as a concept and in the technology that underlies it. But for the purposes of this book, cloud computing is best described by three adjectives:

*Elastic*
> For given resources to be considered part of the cloud, you must be able to increase or decrease it either automatically or on demand using self-service user interfaces or APIs. A resource can include anything you have in your data center

today—from commoditized hardware running Linux (Infrastructure-as-a-Service), to application servers (Platform-as-a-Service), up to applications (Software-as-a-Service). The "what" doesn't matter all that much; it's the fact that you can provision new resources.

*On demand*

Seeing as *elastic* is the first word used to describe the cloud, you must be able to provision a resource precisely when you need it and release it when you don't.

*Metered*

You should pay for only what you use—like power. This has enormous implications as the costs directly reflect usage and can therefore be substantially lower. Because you're renting computing power, you can also treat the costs as operational expenditures (OPEX), like power, as opposed to capital expenditures (CAPEX), like traditional hardware.

Note these are the exact same adjectives used to define power from a public utility. If a service meets all three criteria, it can generally be considered part of the cloud. Cloud solutions can be further classified by two criteria.

The first refers to how the service is made available for consumption. This is called the *service model*, and it comes down to how much value the vendor adds. Some vendors simply offer hardware, with you having to do all of the upper-stack work on your own. An example of this is a public Infrastructure-as-a-Service offering. In the opposite direction is Software-as-a-Service, which is where the vendor builds, deploys, and maintains the entire stack for you. An example of this is a Content Delivery Network. While there is a continuum from Infrastructure-as-a-Service to Platform-as-a-Service to Software-as-a-Service, each model is distinct.

The second refers to the *deployment model*, which refers to the availability of the offering. On one extreme is public, which is just as it sounds: anyone may provision its resources. The other extreme is private, where only a select group may provision. Private clouds are often built within enterprises, though their usefulness is often limited because of lack of full elasticity. Public clouds are the focus of this book.

Any cloud solution can be evaluated and classified according to the cube shown in Figure 3-1.

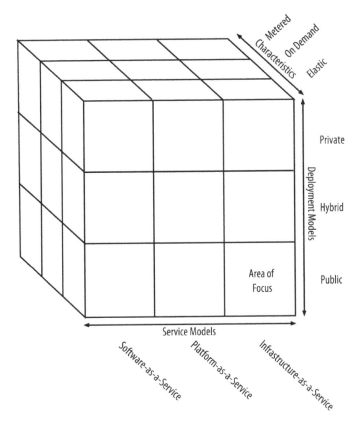

*Figure 3-1. Cloud evaluation criteria*

The focus of this book is largely public Infrastructure-as-a-Service. Let's explore the adjectives further, followed by service models and, finally, deployment models.

## Elastic

*Elasticity* refers to the ability to increase or decrease resources arbitrarily. For example, you should be able to provision more hardware for your application server tier in advance of a social media campaign or even in real-time response to a social media campaign. As traffic from the campaign tails off, you should be able to decrease your hardware to match your lower baseline of traffic. Going back to the power analogy, stadiums are able to pull as much as they please from the grid during a large event.

Elasticity is *the* defining characteristic of cloud.

*Resources* can be seen as any physical hardware or software. Any hardware or software deployed in support of an ecommerce application is technically a resource. Resources must generally be provisioned in the same ratio, though not necessarily in tandem. For example, the proportion of application servers to cache grid servers should generally remain the same, assuming the platform is scalable. More on scalability in Chapter 8.

*Provisioning* refers to the ability to acquire new hardware or software resources. Provisioning should be able to occur automatically or on demand using self-service user interfaces or APIs. The best provisioning is done automatically, either in reaction to or preferably in anticipation of increased demand. The next chapter is devoted exclusively to auto-scaling.

## On Demand

While elasticity refers to the ability to increase or decrease resources arbitrarily, *on demand* refers to the ability to provision *at any time*. You shouldn't have to order new hardware, sign a purchase order, or call up a vendor to get more capacity.

 While elasticity is the defining characteristic of cloud, it is predicated on the ability to provision at any time. Traditional noncloud deployments could technically be considered elastic because you can add more capacity; it just takes weeks or even months. *On-demand* refers to the ability to provision *at any time*.

Like power generation, cloud computing generally works because consumers of the respective services have their peaks at different times. Individual consumers are around the world in different time zones, in different verticals, running different workloads. Resource utilization should remain fairly constant for the cloud vendor but may vary greatly for individual consumers. For example, you will use a lot more resources on Black Friday or Boxing Day than on a Sunday morning in January. Should all individual consumers try to provision a large quantity of resources simultaneously, there wouldn't be enough resources available for everyone. This is formally defined as *over-subscription*, meaning the same resources are promised to multiple tenants. The business models for cloud vendors (and public utilities) work because of this principle.

Many workloads in a public Infrastructure-as-a-Service cloud do not have to be executed at a given time. Among workloads, ecommerce is unique in that a customer is waiting on the other end for an HTTP request to be executed. You can't defer the execution of an HTTP request. Many cloud workloads are batch and can be executed whenever. To even out overall demands on a cloud, some vendors offer the ability to bid on unused computing capacity in an auction format. On Black Friday, when ecommerce applications require a lot of processing power, the demands for resources would be very high and the bid price of spare capacity would also be very high. Workloads that are not time sensitive can then run on, say, Christmas day, when demands on the entire system and the prices are likely to be very low. This allows consumers of cloud resources to get lower prices while allowing the vendors to even out their traffic and purchase less overall hardware than would otherwise be necessary. A great analogy is congestion pricing for freeways, where tolls increase as more people are on the roads.

In addition to being able to provision resources, resources should be provisioned in a timely manner. It should take only a few minutes to provision.

## Metered

Another central tenet of the cloud is the ability to pay for what you use. If you provision a server for three hours, you should pay for only the three hours you actually use it. Paying for resources you haven't provisioned isn't cloud computing. Going back to the power analogy, you pay only for the power you use. The price per kilowatt-hour is known, and you can look at your meter or online to see how much power you've consumed. It would be ludicrous to pay for your peak power utilization of the year for the entire year, yet that's how most ecommerce resources are paid for today. You scale for peaks and pay for those resources the entire year.

A requirement to charging for the resources actually consumed is the ability to accurately measure. Table 3-1 lists the common usage metrics.

*Table 3-1. Common usage metrics for metering/charge-back*

| Resource | Usage metrics |
|---|---|
| Global Server Load Balancing (GSLB) | DNS lookups |
| Content Delivery Network (CDN) | HTTP requests, bandwidth |
| Load balancing | HTTP requests, bandwidth, time |
| Software-as-a-Service | HTTP requests, bandwidth, time, application-specific metrics like orders per day |
| Platform-as-a-Service | HTTP requests, bandwidth, time |
| Infrastructure-as-a-Service | Number of physical servers, capabilities of each server, time |

Unit costs should be the same or less as you add each instance. In other words, you should pay the same or less per unit as you consume more.

As disruptive as the cloud is from a technology standpoint, it's even more disruptive and potentially advantageous to the finance people. Traditional hardware that's purchased up front is treated as a CAPEX, which is a fixed cost that must be paid for up front and depreciated over a period of years. An OPEX, like power, is paid for incrementally, when value is actually realized.

Cost matched with value looks like Figure 3-2.

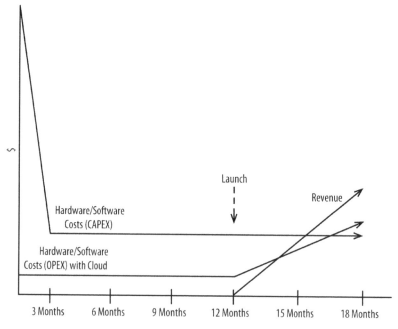

*Figure 3-2. Hardware/software costs—CAPEX versus OPEX*

Most other businesses require large sums of capital before they can start earning revenue. Think of retail, healthcare, manufacturing, software, and telecommunications —which all require large sums of capital to be invested before they earn a dollar. While this is partially true of ecommerce, at least the large static infrastructures of the past are no longer necessary.

The cloud is much more than just technology. It's a fundamental change to the economics of IT.

# Service Models

*Service models* come down to how much value the vendor adds. Each layer provided allows the vendor to add more value. Figure 3-3 shows the three most common service models.

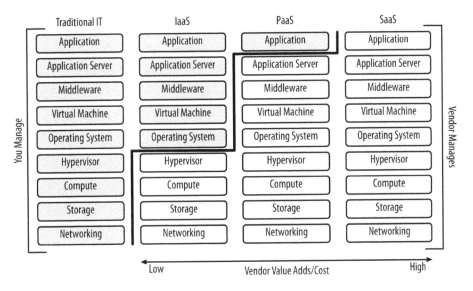

Figure 3-3. *Vendor value adds and their cost*

Vendors are always trying to move up the value chain—that is, adding more value to more layers of the stack so they can generate higher margins and increase their revenue per customer. Vendors that move up the value chain toward Software-as-a-Service offerings can charge higher margins while offering better service at a better price than what you would be able to do yourself. The vendors generally save you money and make some money themselves through labor specialization (it helps if you can hire the world's top experts in each specialization) and economies of scale (you can benefit from automation and higher purchasing power). This desire to move up the value chain is why most Infrastructure-as-a-Service vendors now have Platform-as-a-Service and Software-as-a-Service offerings that complement their core Infrastructure-as-a-Service offerings. Most vendors don't fit neatly into one category, as often each vendor has multiple offerings.

# Case Study: Amazon Web Services

Amazon first started its foray into the cloud in 2006 with EC2, its public Infrastructure-as-a-Service offering. It quickly added complementary services, from storage to load balancing. Since 2010, Amazon.com's flagship ecommerce platform has been hosted on its own cloud offerings.

In 2011, Amazon announced its Platform-as-a-Service offering, named Beanstalk. Beanstalk vertically integrates a host of offerings across Amazon's portfolio:

- Amazon Elastic Cloud Compute (Amazon EC2)
- Amazon Simple Storage Service (Amazon S3)
- Amazon Simple Notification Service (Amazon SNS)
- Amazon CloudWatch
- Amazon Elastic Load Balancing

Customers pay for the underlying Amazon services they use, but there is no additional fee for Beanstalk itself.[1] Customers pay for an additional five or more Amazon services with Beanstalk that they might otherwise not use. The alternative to Platform-as-a-Service (five vertically integrated Amazon services) is often just Infrastructure-as-a-Service (EC2). Customers get a fully vertically integrated platform, and Amazon is able to earn more revenue. It works for everyone.

It's best to determine all of the services you'll need to deliver your ecommerce platform and then decide which ones you can perform better than your competition. For example, you *could* provision some bare Linux servers from an Infrastructure-as-a-Service vendor, install a web server, and serve static content from there. Or you could outsource this to an actual Content Delivery Network. Content Delivery Networks can serve static content better, faster, and cheaper than you can, in addition to providing other added value that you could not.

Anything that you can't do better than your competition should be outsourced when possible, preferably to a vendor that has the highest offerings up the value chain.

Let's explore these models further, in order of value added by the vendor (highest value listed first).

---

1 Amazon Web Services, "AWS Elastic Beanstalk Pricing," *http://aws.amazon.com/elasticbeanstalk/pricing/*.

# Software-as-a-Service

In *Software-as-a-Service* (SaaS), vendors offer a service as opposed to the raw platform or hardware required to deliver a service. For example, DNS vendors and Content Delivery Network vendors often sell their software this way. The consumers of software delivered this way don't care how the vendor builds the service. The application server, hardware, operating system, and database don't matter so long as the service is compliant with agreed-upon service-level agreements. Service-level agreements define terms like expected availability and performance. Figure 3-4 shows what SaaS vendors offer.

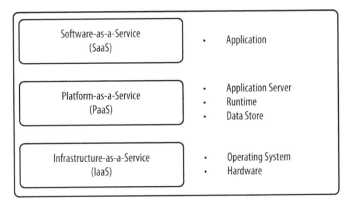

*Figure 3-4. What SaaS vendors offer*

Vendors that offer SaaS have the luxury of specializing in doing one thing exceptionally well. The platform underneath the service can be tuned and optimized specifically for a single workload. They can, in a few circumstances, make the hardware work better with the software to ensure a fully vertically integrated experience. This may be possible with PaaS or IaaS but it would require more work.

SaaS is an easy-to-deploy, cost-effective, and technically superior way of deploying standalone services such as the following:

- Global Server Load Balancing (GSLB) or DNS
- Proxying requests from the edge back to the data center running your code
- Static content serving
- Distributed denial-of-service (DDoS) attack mitigation (request scrubbing)
- Web application firewalls

SaaS doesn't always meet all of the requirements of cloud computing:

- Elastic

- On demand

- Metered

SaaS usually meets the first two but it doesn't always meet the last one. For example, many vendors offer monthly subscriptions to their services, where you can consume all you need. There are often multiyear contracts involved. While not technically cloud computing, these services should still be considered. Pragmatism should rule your decision making.

## Platform-as-a-Service

In *Platform-as-a-Service* (PaaS), vendors offer a platform you can use to deploy your own application. With the vendor responsible for the application server, runtime environment, database, and hardware, you're freed up to concentrate on your application. Many vendors also offer complementary services like integrated testing, messaging, monitoring, application modeling, and other services required to accelerate the development and deployment of applications and keep them up in production, as listed in Figure 3-5.

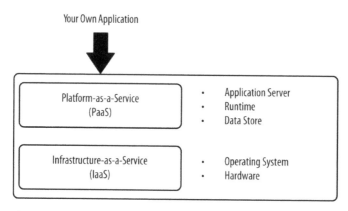

*Figure 3-5. What PaaS vendors offer*

PaaS is an entire package that you buy and build your application for. If you buy in all the way, you can save an enormous amount of time and money because the PaaS vendor does everything for you. Many vendors even set up auto-scaling for you, allowing them to monitor each tier of your application and scale up and down based on demand. But this all comes at the expense of flexibility. The experience inside the vendor's walled garden is generally very good because of tight vertical integration. But if you venture out and need something that your vendor doesn't support, you're often out of luck. For example, some PaaS vendors don't allow you to write from your application to a local filesystem. If your application needs to write to a local filesystem, you won't be able to use that vendor. This inherently leads to relying on multiple PaaS vendors, which adds complexity.

PaaS tends to work well for small applications, perhaps in support of a larger ecommerce application. For example, PaaS would be great if you wanted to build a standalone pricing engine. PaaS generally does not work well for an entire enterprise-level ecommerce application. Few ecommerce applications fit neatly inside the boundaries offered by many PaaS vendors. There are always ancillary applications, middleware, and agents of various types that must be deployed in support of an ecommerce application.

The most common challenge with PaaS is a lack of flexibility. Vendors are able to deliver the most value by standardizing on a single stack and then vertically integrating that stack. This standardization and vertical integration means, for example, you probably can't swap out the database that's provided for one you like more. It also means you can't deploy applications that don't fit neatly into their stack, like third-party monitoring agents. Either you take what's provided or you're out of luck. Vertical integration can also lead to vendor lock-in if you're not careful. Vendors are responding to these shortcomings, but you'll never have as much flexibility as you do with IaaS.

## Infrastructure-as-a-Service

In *Infrastructure-as-a-Service* (IaaS), vendors offer hardware and a hypervisor with a connection to the Internet, and that's it. You have to build out everything above the operating system, though this is often preferable because it gives you nearly total flexibility. See Figure 3-6 for what IaaS vendors offer. We'll spend Chapter 5 discussing how to rapidly build up newly provisioned servers.

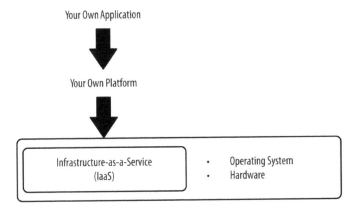

*Figure 3-6. What IaaS vendors offer*

IaaS is valuable because it gives you complete flexibility in what software you deploy and how you configure it all to work together. You can install any version of any software and configure it as you please. You'll never be stuck because a vendor you use has stopped supporting a layer of the stack used by your PaaS vendor. Because the vendor is just offering commoditized hardware, it generally costs much less than comparable PaaS or SaaS. But you have to spend more to make it work.

Look to IaaS for your core application and supporting software. Generally, only IaaS offers the flexibility required to deploy and configure an enterprise-level ecommerce platform. Specifically, consider using it for the following:

- Your core ecommerce application—the one you build or buy/customize
- Application server
- Runtime environment
- Database, like a relational or NoSQL database

Whereas IaaS is flexible and inexpensive relative to the other service models, it requires that you have the ability to implement the recommendations contained in this book. You're given some tools from vendors but you're basically on your own. For a small organization or one that isn't particularly adept at making big changes, this is a tall order.

# Deployment Models

While service models are about the value that each vendor adds, *deployment models* describe who can consume each offering. Any service model may technically be delivered using any deployment model, but in practice certain service models lend themselves better to certain deployment models. A public cloud is consumable by anybody. A private cloud is consumable by only designated organizations or individuals, and it can be deployed on or off premises. A hybrid cloud is the dynamic *bursting* to a public cloud from either a private cloud or a traditional on- or off-premises deployment.

Table 3-2 shows the attributes that these deployment models can be evaluated on.

*Table 3-2. Attributes of common deployment models*

| Criteria | Public | Hybrid | Private |
| --- | --- | --- | --- |
| Most common service models | SaaS, PaaS, IaaS | PaaS, IaaS | PaaS, IaaS |
| Who may consume | Anybody | Designated organizations/individuals | Designated organizations/individuals |
| Who owns data centers/hardware | Public cloud vendor | You + public cloud vendor | You (owned by you or a colo) |

| Criteria | Public | Hybrid | Private |
|---|---|---|---|
| Control | Low | Medium | High |
| Who manages stack | Public cloud vendor | You + public cloud vendor | You |
| Accounting model | OPEX | OPEX (for public cloud) + CAPEX (for private cloud) | CAPEX |

The definitions of each deployment model are fairly simple, but the implications can be substantial. Let's discuss further.

## Public Cloud

A *public cloud* is exactly what it sounds like: it's public. Anybody may consume its services. By definition, a public cloud is owned and operated by a third party in data centers belonging to or under contract by the vendor. In other words, the data centers aren't yours. Public cloud vendors typically operate out of many different data centers, with consumers of the service able to choose where they want to provision their resources.

Vendors offering public clouds benefit greatly from economies of scale. They can buy vast quantities of hardware, bandwidth, and power, and then build advanced automation on top of their stack. This allows them to deliver their software, platform, or infrastructure to you faster, better, and cheaper than you can. Public cloud vendors, especially IaaS vendors, also benefit by signing up a wide range of customers and ending up using the resources for different purposes at different times. This allows the resources to be oversubscribed. Higher oversubscription means less cost to you.

A public cloud is often used when large amounts of resources must be marshaled. For example, large-scale weather simulations may use thousands of servers but only for a few hours. It doesn't make sense for a university to buy a few thousand machines and use them for only a few hours a year. Or in the case where you get hit with a distributed denial-of-service attack and need to handle 1,000 times your traffic—that's where public clouds excel. It is for the exact same reason that public clouds excel for ecommerce.

Elasticity is a defining characteristic of public clouds. Cloud vendors provide easy-to-use APIs to scale up or down the use of a platform or infrastructure. Or in the case of SaaS, you can consume as much as you need and then pay for what you actually use. That elasticity and the ability to consume vast amounts of resources is important for workloads like ecommerce.

Public clouds offer their services to anyone, so security tends to be a concern. Depending on the service model, your data may be colocated with other tenants. Your data may be traversing countries that can intercept it. You can't physically see and touch the servers on which your sensitive data is traversing. Security can definitely be a concern, but as we'll discuss in Chapter 9, public clouds can make it *easier* to be secure.

## Hybrid Cloud

A *hybrid cloud* is a combination of traditional on or off-premises deployment that bursts to a public cloud. "Build the base, rent the peak" is the phrase most often used to describe a hybrid cloud. What's key about a hybrid is the bursting component—not whether the part of your environment that you directly oversee and manage is a private cloud. Hybrid clouds are often used in the following scenarios:

- Software or hardware is unable to be deployed in a cloud for technical reasons. For example, you may need a physical appliance, or an application may not work well in a virtualized environment. With this model, you could, for example, keep your backend in-house and put your more variable frontend in a public cloud.

- You want to keep sensitive data under your control on hardware that's yours, with your own badged employees serving as administrators.

- Software is unable to be deployed in a cloud for commercial reasons. For example, you may be using software whose licensing doesn't work well with a cloud.

 For the purposes of this book, the *frontend* is defined as a user interface and the *backend* is defined as server-side code that contains business logic.

A hybrid cloud is great for ecommerce, where you have a steady baseline of traffic yet want to scale dynamically for peaks. You save money, gain flexibility, yet retain full control over your sensitive data. Not everybody will deploy a full ecommerce platform out to a public cloud. A hybrid model is sometimes desired because the core of the platform holding the sensitive data can remain under your firm control, while the nonsensitive parts of the application can be deployed out to a cloud.

While a step in the right direction and a good option for many, hybrid clouds aren't perfect. Hybrid clouds require that you break your application into two pieces: the piece that's managed in-house and the piece that's deployed out to a public cloud. Splitting an existing application in two pieces isn't easy, but the benefits can easily outweigh the costs. We'll discuss this further in Chapter 11.

## Private Cloud

A *private cloud* is basically a public cloud that is limited to your own organization. While typically deployed on hardware that you own in your own data center, it can also be deployed on hardware that you don't own in a colo. To be a private cloud, it has to meet the requirements of cloud computing: elastic, on demand, and metered. Traditional static deployments of hardware and software don't meet the definition of cloud computing. Likewise, the use of virtualization doesn't make it a private cloud either, as we'll discuss in Chapter 6.

To build a private cloud and have the econommics work out, you need a large pool of software that you can deploy to this private cloud. With only one application (say, ecommerce) deployed to a private cloud, you have to buy enough hardware to handle your peak, and by doing that, you've cancelled all of the benefits of cloud computing. With varied workloads, a private cloud becomes more worthwhile, but only if each workload has its peak at different times. If you're a retailer and you use a private cloud for all of your retail applications, you're going to quickly run out of capacity on Black Friday. To solve that, you have to buy a lot more hardware than you need at steady state and let it sit idle for all but a few hours of the year, which defeats the purpose of cloud computing.

A private cloud is often used for consolidation within large enterprises. If the different workloads you have deployed to a private cloud each have their peaks at different times throughout the day, week, month, or year, you could end up saving money. But, again, if your workloads all have their peaks at the same time, you just incur unnecessary overhead.

A private cloud is used primarily for three reasons:

- You have many workloads to consolidate.
- You're especially security conscious and don't yet trust public clouds to be secure (see Chapter 9).
- You want to "try cloud computing at home" before going out to a public cloud.

Unless you have many workloads to consolidate, a private cloud doesn't offer a strong value proposition.

# Hardware Used in Clouds

Clouds are often comprised of commoditized x86 hardware, with the commoditized components assembled by off-brand manufacturers or even assembled in-house. Commodity hardware is used because it's cheap and general-purpose. The hardware is cheap because it's produced in enormous volumes and assembled by manufacturers who add very little value (cost) to it. The hardware used in clouds is meant to be nearly disposable. In the classic cost/quality/fit-for-purpose trade-off, cost is the deciding factor.

While commodity hardware is most often used in cloud computing, it need not be a defining feature of cloud computing. Cloud computing is defined as elastic, on demand, and metered. *Commodity hardware* is not among those three attributes.

The ecommerce use case is fairly unique among cloud workloads. If you're sequencing DNA in the cloud, for example, it doesn't matter whether you sequence 300 bases a second or 400. But in ecommerce, milliseconds matter because a real (potentially) paying customer is waiting on the other end for that response. Many clouds offer different types of hardware optimized for different workloads. Besides commodity, clouds now offer hardware optimized for the following:

- Memory
- Computing
- GPU
- Storage
- Networking

You may, for example, want to deploy your ecommerce application on hardware optimized for computing, and your database on hardware optimized for fast access to storage. The hardware you choose is a trade-off between performance and cost, with your architecture sometimes mandating specialized hardware. Vendors also offer general-purpose small, medium, and large instances, with cost, memory, and computing power rising in tandem.

## Hardware Sizing

The vertical scalability of software on any given hardware is always limited. It's hard to find software that will deliver the same throughput (e.g., HTTP requests per second) for CPU core number 1 and for CPU core number 64. Software always performs optimally when deployed across a certain number of CPU cores. For example, the graph in Figure 3-7 shows the marginal vertical scalability of a hypothetical single Java Virtual Machine (JVM).

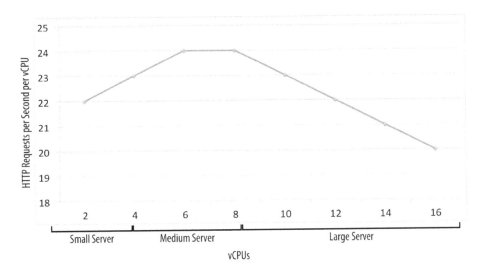

*Figure 3-7. Marginal vertical scalability of a hypothetical single JVM*

At the lower end of the x-axis, you'll find that a JVM doesn't deliver as much throughput as it could because the limited CPU and memory is consumed by the overhead of starting up each JVM and performing garbage collection. JVMs, like all software, have runtime overhead. At the high end of the x-axis, you'll suffer from thread contention as too many threads are competing to lock on the same objects, or you'll run out of CPU as your garbage collection algorithm works exponentially harder.

So long as you're meeting your necessary service-level agreements, pick the instance type that offers the lowest price per the metric that makes the most sense for each workload. For example, calculate the number of HTTP requests per second each instance type can generate and then divide that by the number of virtual CPUs, or vCPUs. That should lead you to data similar to Table 3-3.

*Table 3-3. Calculations required to find optimal server size*

| Server size | Cost per hour | vCPUs | HTTP requests/second | Cost/100 HTTP requests/second |
|---|---|---|---|---|
| Small | $0.15 | 4 | 92 (4 vCPUs × 23 HTTP requests/sec) | $0.163 |
| Medium | $0.25 | 8 | 192 (8 vCPUs × 24 HTTP requests/second) | $0.130 |
| Large | $0.50 | 16 | 320 (16 vCPUs × 20 HTTP requests/second) | $0.156 |

From this simple exercise, it's clearly best to choose the medium instance type because the cost per 100 HTTP requests per second is the least. It may also make sense to choose a compute-intensive server. Perhaps the premium you're paying could be offset by the marginal capacity it offers. Do this for each of your workloads.

Cloud vendors offer many options—it's up to you to pick the most cost-effective one for each of your workloads.

## Complementary Cloud Vendor Offerings

Cloud vendors have traditionally offered PaaS and/or IaaS, with pure play vendors offering the various SaaS components as well. Most IaaS vendors have an entire portfolio of SaaS and PaaS offerings in order to appeal to different market segments and be able to upsell to their customers. Once a vendor's platform is in place, the marginal cost of a new offering is very small, as shown in Figure 3-8.

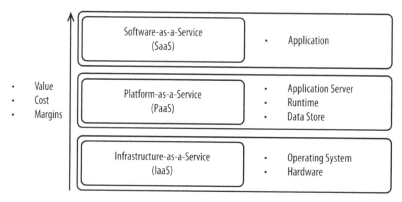

*Figure 3-8. Service models versus value/cost/margins*

The most capital-intensive part is building out the IaaS layer. That involves building, buying, or leasing data centers, as well as buying hardware. Once that's in place, building a PaaS layer is relatively easy. Once PaaS is built, SaaS is even easier because each layer builds on the layer before it.

To make these additional services more appealing, vendors vertically integrate the solutions to work together. When taken together, the ancillary services offered by each vendor create compelling solutions. Vertically integrated solutions are almost always better than individual services offered by different vendors.

Here are some examples of ancillary services offered by many vendors:

- Global Server Load Balancing (GSLB)/DNS (Chapter 10)
- Proxying requests from the edge back to the data center running your code (Chapter 7)
- Static content serving (Chapter 7)
- DDoS attack mitigation (request scrubbing) (Chapter 9)
- Web application firewalls (Chapter 9)

- Storage
- Load balancing
- Virtual private clouds within a larger public cloud (Chapter 9)
- Auto-scaling (Chapter 4)
- Monitoring (Chapter 4)
- Backup
- Databases (Chapter 8)
- Cache grids (Chapter 8)

Many of these services come with high service-level agreements and enterprise-level 24/7 support.

# Challenges with Public Clouds

Public clouds, the focus of this book, provide strong advantages as well as disadvantages. The disadvantages of public clouds often stem from what's known as the *agency dilemma* in economics, whereby the two parties (you and your public cloud vendor) have different interests and information. For example, you may lock down your environments and disallow any further changes (called a *holiday freeze*) beginning in October and ending after Christmas because you earn much of your annual revenue in the weeks before, during, and after Black Friday. With no changes to your environment, you're less likely to have outages. But a cloud vendor is unlikely to have the same incentives to avoid downtime and may decide to do maintenance when you have your annual peak. Of course, both parties have an interest in maintaining availability, but an outage on Black Friday is going to cost you a lot more than it will cost your cloud vendor. That agency problem is at the root of many of these challenges.

Let's discuss some of these issues.

## Availability

As we discussed in Chapter 2, availability is of utmost importance for ecommerce. While rare, public clouds will always suffer from server-level failures, data center–wide failures, and cloud-wide failures. Let's look at these each individually.

Server-level failures are common. It is expected that hardware will fail:[2]

---

2 Stephen Shankland, "Google Spotlights Data Center Inner Workings," CNet (30 May 2008), *http://cnet.co/ MrUH9A*.

In each cluster's [of 10,000 servers] first year, it's typical that 1,000 individual machine failures will occur; thousands of hard drive failures will occur; one power distribution unit will fail, bringing down 500 to 1,000 machines for about 6 hours; 20 racks will fail, each time causing 40 to 80 machines to vanish from the network; 5 racks will "go wonky," with half their network packets missing in action; and the cluster will have to be rewired once, affecting 5 percent of the machines at any given moment over a 2-day span, Dean said. And there's about a 50 percent chance that the cluster will overheat, taking down most of the servers in less than 5 minutes and taking 1 to 2 days to recover.

—Jeff Dean, *Google Fellow*

Cloud vendors have the same challenges that Google has. Hardware is cheap and unreliable. To compensate for the unreliability, resiliency is (or should be) built in to software through the use of clustering and similar technology. Almost without exception, you can deploy any software across two or more physical servers to minimize the impact of any one server failing.

While rare, entire data centers do go offline. For example, Hurricane Sandy took out data centers across the East Coast of the US in 2012. Natural disasters and human error (including cable cuts) are often to blame. No data center should be seen as immune to going entirely offline. This is why most ecommerce vendors have an off-site replica of production, either in an active/passive or active/active configuration across two or even more data centers (discussed in Chapter 10). To avoid these issues, most vendors group together data centers into partitions that are (supposedly) entirely separated from each other. By deploying your software across multiple partitions, you should be fairly safe.

While exceptionally unlikely, cloud-wide failures do occur. For example, a large cloud vendor recently suffered a complete worldwide outage because they forgot to renew their SSL certificate. Clouds are supposed to span multiple physical data centers and be partitioned to avoid outages propagating from one data center to another, but you can never be 100% certain that there are no dependencies between data centers. Cloud-wide outages may be due to the following:

- A reliance on shared resources, coupled with the failure of a shared resource. That resource may even be something as simple as an SSL certificate.

- Technical issues that propagate across data centers.[3]

- Operational missteps, like patching all data centers at the same time only to discover there was a bug in one of the patches applied.

- Malicious behavior, like DDoS attacks or hacking.

---

3 Matthew Prince, "Today's Outage Post Mortem," CloudFlare (3 March 2013), *http://bit.ly/1k7yxbx*.

The only way to completely protect your ecommerce platform against entire cloud-wide outages is to deploy your software across multiple clouds, though most vendors do a pretty good job of isolation. Deploying across multiple data centers and multiple clouds is covered in Chapter 10.

## Performance

Performance is always a concern for ecommerce because revenue depends so much on it. In responding to customer feedback, Google increased the number of results on its search engine result page from 10 to 50. Immediately after implementing that change, the company saw a 20% decline in page views and corresponding ad revenue. What Google didn't control for was the extra 500 milliseconds of latency introduced by the larger response. When 500 milliseconds of response time was artificially added to the standard page with 10 results, the same 20% decline in traffic (and therefore revenue) was also seen.[4] Amazon.com saw conversion rates drop 1% for every 100 milliseconds of additional response time.[5] Customers may say they want more functionality, but real-world testing has repeatedly shown that they value performance as much, if not even more than, additional functionality.

In your own data center, you can optimize performance of your hardware and software stack. Need to make 1,000 synchronous calls back to your cache grid to build a page? No problem, so long as you use specialized networking technology like Infini-Band, bypass the kernel, and have submicrosecond round-trip latency. In a cloud environment, you can't change very much. You're stuck with the stack you're given, for better or worse. Every time you have to communicate with another machine, as is increasingly common, your data takes the journey shown in Figure 3-9.

---

4  Greg Linden, "Marissa Mayer at Web 2.0," Geeking with Greg (9 November 2006), *http://bit.ly/QnOcHH*.

5  Todd Hoff, "Latency Is Everywhere And It Costs You Sales—How To Crush It," High Scalability (25 July 2009), *http://bit.ly/1hEgNOK*.

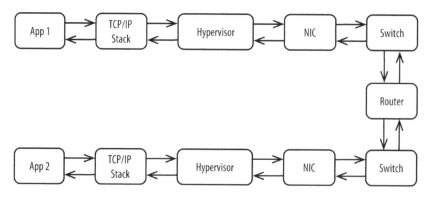

*Figure 3-9. Layers involved in making a call to a remote host*

The hardware and software used in public clouds is designed to be general-purpose because public clouds need to support so many workloads.

Now take that page with 1,000 synchronous calls to your cache grid and deploy it in a cloud with four milliseconds of latency between your application server and cache grid and you have a big problem, as shown in Figure 3-10.

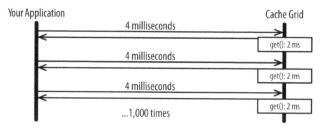

*Figure 3-10. Impact of latency with multiple calls*

Applications written to deal with latency, usually through the use of batching, shouldn't have a problem. Most software now supports the equivalent of `getAll()` calls (as opposed to simple `get()`). That all but eliminates this as a challenge, as Figure 3-11 shows.

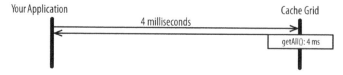

*Figure 3-11. Impact of using a `getAll()` equivalent*

## Case Study: Reddit

Reddit, an online discussion community with two billion page views per month,[6] had this issue when it moved to a public IaaS cloud.[7] Reddit was calling its cache grid, Memcached, up to 1,000 times per page view when hosted out of its own data center. In a public IaaS cloud, Reddit's latency between servers increased by 10 times, which made that old approach unusable in a cloud. The company had to batch up requests to Memcached to avoid the overhead of synchronously going back and forth to Memcached. Doing this completely eliminated the impact of the latency that its cloud vendor introduced.

## Oversubscription

Public SaaS, PaaS, and IaaS work as business models because each consumer of the respective service uses the service at roughly different times. Most shared utility-based services work like this, from power to roads to physical retail stores. Problems arise for service providers when everybody tries to use a shared resource at the same time—as when everybody turns their air conditioning on during the hottest day of the year.

Some vendors have this problem because they're used heavily by one industry. For example, Content Delivery Networks are used by nearly every major ecommerce vendor, and most ecommerce vendors have their spikes on the same few days: Black Friday (US, Brazil, China), Singles' Day (China), Boxing Day (UK, Australia), and El Buen Fin (Mexico).[8] On these few days, traffic can spike hundreds of times over the average.

To make matters worse, cloud vendors tend to have a few endpoints in each country. So El Buen Fin in Mexico, for example, taxes the few data centers each Content Delivery Network has in Mexico. Fortunately, Content Delivery Networks, as with SaaS offerings, have the benefit of you being able to hold the vendor to meeting predetermined service-level agreements. Those vendors then have to scale and have a lot of hardware sit idle throughout the year. Although you pay for it, it's not as direct of a cost as if you had the hardware sitting idle in your own data centers.

6 Todd Hoff, "Reddit: Lessons Learned From Mistakes Made Scaling To 1 Billion Pageviews A Month," High Scalability (26 August 2013), *http://bit.ly/1kmFZke*.

7 Todd Hoff, "How Can Batching Requests Actually Reduce Latency?" High Scalability (4 December 2013), *http://bit.ly/MrUHq1*.

8 Akamai Technologies, "Facts and Figures" (2014), *http://www.akamai.com/html/about/facts_figures.html*.

When looked at globally, large public IaaS vendors are relatively protected against these spikes because their customers come from various industries and run a wide range of workloads. Demand-based pricing, as discussed earlier, also helps to smooth out load.

While vendors claim you can always provision, and have a good track record of allowing customers to provision at any time, it is theoretically possible that a vendor could run out of capacity. For example, a cloud vendor could run out of capacity during a news event as people look online for more information and websites auto-scale to handle the increased demand. For example, web traffic more than doubled following Michael Jackson's death in 2009.[9]

To guard against this, various strategies may be employed, including:

- Pre-provisioning hours ahead of your big events. Traffic from special events is often predictable.
- Buying dedicated capacity. Most vendors offer this.
- Being able to provision and run smoothly across multiple data centers within the same cloud vendor's network.
- Being able to provision from multiple clouds.

You need to take proactive steps to ensure that your vendor(s) has enough capacity available to handle your peaks.

## Cost

While cloud computing is generally less expensive than traditional on-premises computing, it may be more expensive, depending on how you use it. Cloud computing excels in handling elastic workloads. Highly static workloads may or may not make sense, depending on whether your organization can cost-effectively deploy and manage hardware and software.

If you calculate the cost of a server on a public IaaS cloud over the expected useful life of a server (say, three years) and compare that to the cost to acquire the same hardware/software, the cost of a cloud-based solution is likely to be more. But you need to look at costs holistically. That hourly price you're being quoted includes the following:

- Data center space
- Power

---

9 Andy Jordan, "The Day the Internet Almost Died," *The Wall Street Journal* Online (26 June 2009), *http:// on.wsj.com/P93I93.*

- Bandwidth out to the Internet
- Software
- Supporting network infrastructure
- Patching (firmware and possibly operating system)
- All of the labor required to rack/stack/cable/maintain the hardware
- A baseline of support

These costs can be considerable. You're generally renting capacity for hours at a time to handle big spikes in traffic. The cost of building up all of that capacity in-house and then letting it sit idle for most of the year is exponentially greater than the cost you would pay to a cloud vendor. You also have to take into consideration that your organization's core competency is unlikely to be building out hardware and/or software infrastructure. Your organization is likely to be a retailer of some variety. Straying too far away from your organization's core competency is never a good thing in the longrun.

Cloud vendors often offer better prices than what you could do in-house because their core competency is delivering large quantities of resources like infrastructure. When you can specialize and offer one service exceptionally well, you do it better than an organization whose focus is elsewhere. Specifically, cloud vendors benefit from the following:

- Economies of scale—you can purchase hardware, software, and data center space at much better rates if you buy in bulk.
- Being able to hire the world's experts in various topics.
- Heavy automation—it makes sense to automate patching if you have 100,000 servers but not if you have 10, for example.
- Organizational alignment around delivering your core competency.

While most of these principles are applicable to public IaaS vendors, they apply equally to PaaS and SaaS vendors.

Cloud vendors are also able to offer flexible pricing by allowing you to rapidly scale up/down, select your preferred server type, and purchase capacity by the hour or on a fixed basis throughout the year.

For more information on the cloud, read *Cloud Architecture Patterns* by Bill Wilder (O'Reilly).

# Summary

In this chapter, we've defined cloud and its benefits, reviewed the concepts of service and deployment models, discussed complementary offerings, and covered the challenges of public clouds. In the next chapter, we'll explore auto-scaling, the enabler of cloud's central promise: elasticity.

# CHAPTER 4

# Auto-Scaling in the Cloud

## What Is Auto-Scaling?

*Auto-scaling*, also called *provisioning*, is central to cloud. Without the elasticity provided by auto-scaling, you're back to provisioning year-round for annual peaks. Every ecommerce platform deployed in a cloud should have a solution in place to scale up and down each of the various layers based on real-time demand, as shown in Figure 4-1.

An auto-scaling solution is not to be confused with *initial provisioning*. Initial provisioning is all about getting your environments set up properly, which includes setting up load balancers, setting up firewalls, configuring initial server images, and a number of additional one-time activities. Auto-scaling, on the other hand, is focused on taking an existing environment and adding or reducing capacity based on real-time needs. Provisioning and scaling may ultimately use the same provisioning mechanisms, but the purpose and scope of the two are entirely different.

The goal with auto-scaling is to provision enough hardware to support your traffic, while adhering to service-level agreements. If you provision too much, you waste money. If you provision too little, you suffer outages. A good solution will help you provision just enough, but not so much that you're wasting money.

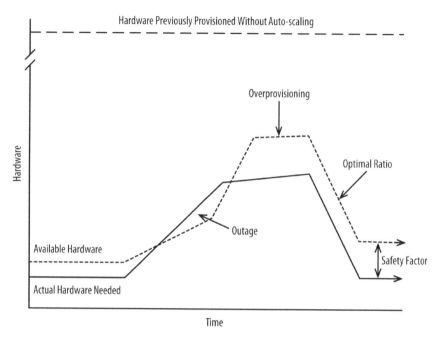

*Figure 4-1. Benefits of an auto-scaling solution*

In this chapter, we'll cover what needs to be provisioned, when to provision, followed by how to provision.

## What Needs to Be Provisioned

The focus of this chapter is provisioning hardware from an Infrastructure-as-a-Service platform because that has the least amount of provisioning built in, as shown in Figure 4-2.

When you're using Infrastructure-as-a-Service, your lowest level of abstraction is physical infrastructure—typically, a virtual server. You have to provision computing and storage capacity and then install your software on top of it. We'll discuss the software installation in the next chapter. IaaS vendors handle the provisioning of lower-level resources, like network and firewalls. Infrastructure-as-a-Service vendors invest substantial resources to ensure that provisioning is as easy as possible, but given that you're dealing with plain infrastructure, it's hard to intelligently provision as you can with Platform-as-a-Service.

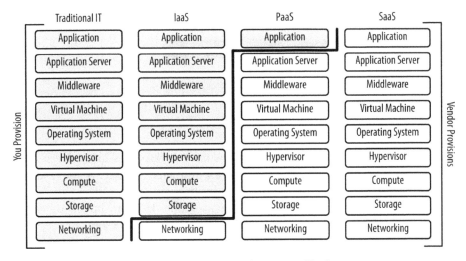

*Figure 4-2. What you and your vendor are each responsible for provisioning*

Moving up the stack, Platform-as-a-Service offerings usually have tightly integrated provisioning tools as a part of their core value proposition. Your lowest level of abstraction is typically the application server, with the vendor managing the application server and everything below it. You define when you want more application servers provisioned, and your Platform-as-a-Service vendor will provision more application servers and everything below it in tandem. Provisioning is inherently difficult, and by doing much of it for you, these vendors offer value that you may be willing to pay extra for.

Finally, there's Software-as-a-Service. Most Software-as-a-Service vendors offer nearly unlimited capacity. Think of common software offered as Software-as-a-Service: DNS, Global Server Load Balancing, Content Delivery Networks, and ratings and reviews. You just consume these services, and it's up the vendor to scale up their entire backend infrastructure to be able to handle your demands. That's a big part of the value of Software-as-a-Service and is conceptually similar to the public utility example from the prior chapter. You just pull more power from the grid when you need it. This differs from Platform-as-a-Service and Infrastructure-as-a-Service, where you need to tell your vendor when you need more and they meter more out to you.

The downside of your vendors handling provisioning for you is that you inherently lose some control. The vendor-provided provisioning tools are fairly flexible and getting better, but your platform will always have unique requirements that may not be exactly met by the vendor-provided provisioning tools. The larger and more complicated your deployment, the more likely you'll want to build something custom, as shown in Table 4-1.

*Table 4-1. Breakdown of criteria for Infrastructure-as-a-Service, Platform-as-a-Service, and Software-as-a-Service*

| Criteria | IaaS | PaaS | SaaS |
|---|---|---|---|
| Need to provision | Yes | Yes | No |
| What you provision | Computing, storage | Platform (application) | N/A |
| Who's responsible | You | Mostly vendor | Vendor |
| Flexibility of provisioning | Complete to limited | Limited | None |

Your goal in provisioning is to match the quantity of resources to the level of each resource that is required, plus any safety factor you have in place. A *safety factor* is how much extra capacity you provision in order to avoid outages. This value is typically represented in the auto-scaling rules you define. If your application is CPU bound, you could decide to provision more capacity at 25%, 50%, 75%, or 95% aggregate CPU utilization. The longer you wait to provision, the higher the likelihood of suffering an outage due to an unanticipated burst of traffic.

# What Can't Be Provisioned

It's far easier to provision more resources for an existing environment than it is to build out a new environment from scratch. Each environment you build out has fixed overhead—you need to configure a load balancer, DNS, a database, and various management consoles for your applications. You then need to seed your database and any files that your applications and middleware require. It is theoretically possible to script this all out ahead of time, but it's not very practical.

Then there are a few resources that must be fully provisioned and scaled for peak ahead of time. For example, if you're deploying your own relational database, it needs to be built out ahead of time. It's hard to add database nodes for relational databases in real time, as entire database restarts and other configuration changes are often required. A database node for a relational database isn't like an application server or web server, where you can just add another one and register it with the load balancer. Of course, you can use your vendor's elastic database solutions, but some may be uncomfortable with sensitive data being in a multitenant database. Nonrelational databases, like NoSQL databases, can typically be scaled out on the fly because they have a shared-nothing architecture that doesn't require whole database restarts.

Each environment should contain at least one of every server type. Think of each environment as being the size of a development environment to start. Then you can define auto-scaling policies for each tier. The fixed capacity for each environment can all be on dedicated hardware, as opposed to the hourly fees normally charged. Dedicated hardware is often substantially cheaper than per-hour pricing, but hardware requires up-front payment for a fixed term, usually a year. Again, this should be a fairly small footprint, consisting of only a handful of servers. The cost shouldn't be much.

# When to Provision

Ideally, you'd like to perfectly match the resources you've provisioned to the amount of traffic the system needs to support. It's never that simple.

The problem with provisioning is that it takes time for each resource to become functional. It can take at least several minutes for the vendor to give you a functioning server with your image installed and the operating system booted. Then you have to install your software, which takes even more time. The installation of your software on newly provisioned hardware is covered in the next chapter.

Once you provision a resource, you can't just make it live immediately. Some resources have dependencies and must be provisioned in a predefined order, or you'll end up with an outage. For example, if you provision application servers before your messaging servers, you probably wouldn't have enough messaging capacity and would suffer an outage. In this example, you'd have to add your application servers to the load balancer only after the messaging servers have been fully provisioned. The trick here is to provision in parallel, and then install your software in parallel, but add your application servers to the load balancer as a last step.

Provisioning takes two forms:

*Proactive provisioning*
Provisioning ahead of time when you expect there will be traffic

*Reactive provisioning*
Provisioning in reaction to traffic

Reactive provisioning is what you should strive for, though it comes with the risk of outages if you can't provision quickly enough to meet a rapid spike in traffic. The way to guard against that is to overprovision (start provisioning at, say, 50% CPU utilization, assuming your application is CPU bound) but that leads to waste. Likewise, you could provision at 95% CPU utilization, but you'll incur costs there, too, because you'll suffer periodic outages due to not being able to scale fast enough. It's a balancing act that's largely a function of how quickly you can provision and how quickly you're hit with new traffic.

# Proactive Provisioning

In *proactive provisioning*, you provision resources in anticipation of increased traffic. You can estimate traffic based on the following:

- Cyclical trends
  - Daily
  - Monthly
  - Seasonally
- Active marketing
  - Promotions
  - Promotional emails
  - Social media campaigns
  - Deep price discounts
  - Flash sales

If you know traffic is coming and you know you'll get hit with more traffic than you can provision for reactively, it makes sense to proactively add more capacity. For example, you could make sure that you double your capacity an hour before any big promotional emails are sent out.

To be able to proactively provision, you need preferably one system to look at both incoming traffic and how that maps back to the utilization of each tier. Then you can put together a table mapping out each tier you have and how many units of that resource (typically uniformly sized servers) are required for various levels, as shown in Table 4-2.

*Table 4-2. Example of resources that must be provisioned at each tier*

| Resource | 10,000 concurrent customers | 20,000 concurrent customers | 30,000 concurrent customers |
| --- | --- | --- | --- |
| Application servers | 5 | 10 | 15 |
| Cache grid servers | 3 | 6 | 9 |
| Messaging servers | 2 | 4 | 6 |
| NoSQL database servers | 2 | 4 | 6 |

Ideally, your system will scale linearly. So if your last email advertising a 30% off promotion resulted in 30,000 concurrent customers, you know you'll need to provision 15 application servers, 9 cache grid servers, 6 messaging servers, and 6 NoSQL database servers prior to that email going out again. A lot of this comes down to process. Unless you can reliably and quickly reactively provision, you'll need to put safeguards in place to ensure that marketers aren't driving an unexpectedly large amount of traffic without the system being ready for it.

The costs of proactive provisioning are high because the whole goal is to add more capacity than is actually needed. Traffic must be forecasted, and the system must be scaled manually. All of this forecasting is time-consuming, but compared to the cost of an outage and the waste before the cloud, the costs are miniscule.

## Reactive Provisioning

*Reactive provisioning* has substantial benefits over proactive provisioning and is what you should strive for. In today's connected world, a link to your website can travel across the world to millions of people in a matter of minutes. Celebrities and thought leaders have 50 million or more followers on popular social networks. All it takes is for somebody with 50 million followers to broadcast a link to your website, and you're in trouble. You can forecast most traffic but not all of it. The trend of social media–driven spikes in traffic will only accelerate as social media continues to proliferate.

In addition to avoiding outages, reactive provisioning has substantial cost savings. You provision only exactly what you need, when you need it.

Reactive provisioning is built on the premise of being able to accurately interrogate the health of each tier and then taking action if the reported data warrants it. For example, you could define rules as shown in Table 4-3.

*Table 4-3. Sample rules for provisioning*

| Tier | Metric | Threshold for action | Action to be taken |
|---|---|---|---|
| Application servers | CPU utilization | 50% | Add 5 more |
| Cache grid servers | Memory | 50% | Add 3 more |
| Messaging servers | Messages per second | 1,000 | Add 3 more |
| NoSQL database servers | CPU utilization | 50% | Add 2 more |

By adding more capacity at 50%, you should always have 50% more capacity than you need, which is a healthy safety factor. We'll get into the *how* part of provisioning shortly.

Sometimes your software's limits will be expressed best by a custom metric. For example, a single messaging server may be able to handle only 1,000 messages per second. But how can you represent that by using off-the-shelf metrics, like network utilization and CPU utilization? Your monitoring tool will most likely allow you to define custom metrics that plug in to hooks you define.

# Auto-Scaling Solutions

There are many auto-scaling solutions available, ranging from custom-developed solutions to solutions baked into the core of cloud vendors' offerings to third-party solutions. All of them need to do basically the same thing as Figure 4-3 shows.

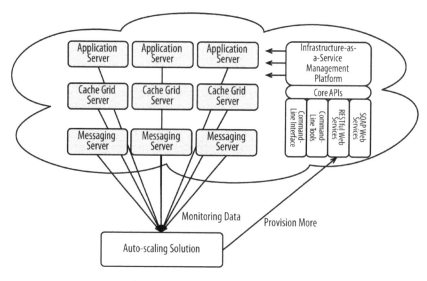

*Figure 4-3. How an auto-scaling solution works*

While these solutions all do basically the same thing, their goals, approach, and implementation all vary.

Any solution that's used must be fully available and preferably deployed outside the cloud(s) that you're using for your platform. You must provide full high availability within each data center this solution operates from, as well as high availability across data centers. If auto-scaling fails for any reason, your platform could suffer an outage. It's important that all measures possible are employed to prevent outages.

# Requirements for a Solution

The following sections show broadly what you need to do in order to auto-scale.

### Define each tier that needs to be scaled

To begin with, you need to identify each tier that needs to be scaled out. Common tiers include application servers, cache grid servers, messaging servers, and NoSQL database servers. Within each tier exist numerous instance types, some of which can be scaled and some of which cannot. For example, most tiers have a single admin server that cannot and should not be scaled out. As mentioned earlier, some tiers are fixed and cannot be dynamically scaled out. For example, your relational database tier is fairly static and cannot be scaled out dynamically.

### Define the dependencies between tiers

Once you identify each tier, you then have to define the dependencies between them. Some tiers require that other tiers are provisioned first. An earlier example used in this chapter was the addition of more application servers without first adding more messaging servers. There might be intricate dependencies between the tiers and between the components within each tier. Dependencies can cascade. For example, adding an application server may require the addition of a messaging server that may itself require another NoSQL database node.

### Define ratios between tiers

Once you've identified the dependencies between each tier, you'll need to define the ratios between each tier if you ever want to be able to proactively provision capacity. For example, you may find that you need a cache grid server for every two application servers. When you proactively provision capacity, you need to make sure you provision each of the tiers in the right quantities. See "Proactive Provisioning" for more information.

### Define what to monitor

Next, for each tier you need to define the metrics that will trigger a scale up or scale down. For application servers, it may be CPU (if your app is CPU bound) or memory (if your app is memory bound). Other metrics include disk utilization, storage utilization, and network utilization. But, as discussed earlier, metrics may be entirely custom for each bit of software. What matters is that you know the bottlenecks of each tier and can accurately predict when that tier will begin to fail.

### Monitor each server and aggregate data across each tier

Next, you need to monitor each server in that tier and report back to a centralized controller that is capable of aggregating that data so you know what's going on across the whole tier, as opposed to what's going on within each server. The utilization of any given server may be very high, but the tier overall may be OK. Not every server will have perfectly uniform utilization.

### Define rules for scaling each tier

Now that all of the dependencies are in place, you need to define rules for scaling each tier. Rules are defined for each tier and follow standard if/then logic. The *if* should be tied back to tier-wide metrics, like CPU and memory utilization. Lower-utilization triggers increase safety but come at the expense of overprovisioning. The *then* clause could take any number and any combination of the following:

- Add capacity
- Reduce capacity
- Send an email notification
- Drop a message onto a queue
- Make an HTTP request

Usually, you'll have a minimum of two rules for each tier:

1. Add more capacity
2. Reduce capacity

Figure 4-4 shows an example of how you define a scale-up rule.

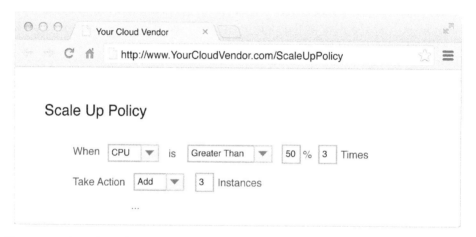

*Figure 4-4. Sample scale-up rule*

And the corresponding scale-down rule is shown in Figure 4-5.

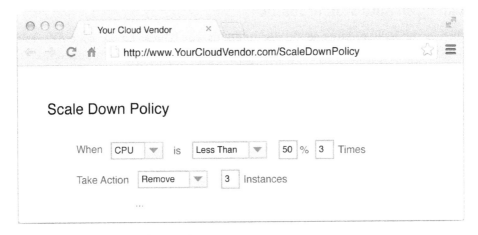

*Figure 4-5. Sample scale-down rule*

If there are any exceptions, you should be notified by email or text message, so you can take corrective action.

Your solution should offer safeguards to ensure that you don't provision indefinitely. If the application you've deployed has a race condition that spikes CPU utilization immediately, you don't want to provision indefinitely. Always make sure to set limits as to how many servers can be deployed, as shown in Figure 4-6.

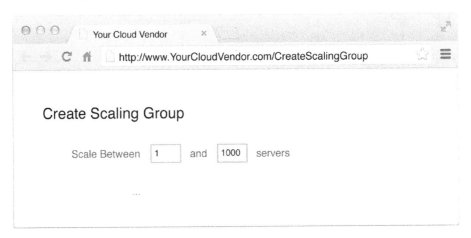

*Figure 4-6. Minimum and maximum server counts*

Revisit this periodically to make sure you don't run into this limit as you grow.

# Building an Auto-scaling Solution

Whether you build or buy one of these solutions, you'll be using the same APIs to do things like provision new servers, de-provision underutilized servers, register servers with load balancers, and apply security policies. Cloud vendors have made exposing these APIs and making them easy to use a cornerstone of their offerings.

Means of interfacing with the APIs often include the following:

- Graphical user interface
- Command-line tools
- RESTful web services
- SOAP web services

These APIs are what everybody uses to interface with clouds in much the same way that APIs are powering the move to omnichannel. An interface (whether it's a graphical user interface, command-line tool, or some flavor of web service) is a more or less disposable means to interface with a core set of APIs, shown in Figure 4-7.

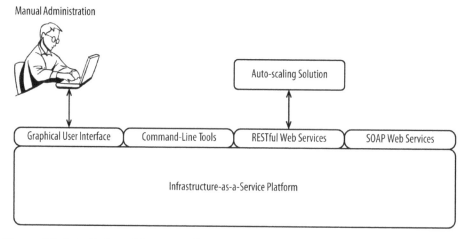

*Figure 4-7. Interfacing with auto-scaling APIs*

OpenStack is a popular open source cloud management stack that has a set of APIs at its core. All cloud vendors offer APIs of this nature. Here are some examples of how you would perform some common actions:

## Create machine image (snapshot of filesystem)

```
// HTTP POST to /images
{
    "id":"production-ecommerce-application-page-server",
    "name":"Production eCommerce Application Page Server",
}
```

## Write machine image

```
// HTTP PUT to /images/{image_id}/file
Content-Type must be 'application/octet-stream'
```

## List flavors of available images

```
// HTTP GET to /flavors
{
    "flavors": [
        {"id": "1", "name": "m1.tiny"},
        {"id": "2", "name": "m1.small"},
        {"id": "3", "name": "m1.medium"},
        {"id": "4", "name": "m1.large"},
        {"id": "5", "name": "m1.xlarge"}
    ]
}
```

## Provision hardware

```
// HTTP POST to /{tenant_id}/servers
{
    "server": {
        "flavorRef": "/flavors/1",
        "imageRef": "/images/production-ecommerce-application-page-server",
        "metadata": {
            "JNDIName": "CORE"
        },
        "name": "eCommerce Server 221",
    }
}
```

## De-provision hardware

```
// HTTP POST to /{tenant_id}/servers/{server_id}
```

You can string together these APIs and marry them with a monitoring tool to form a fairly comprehensive auto-scaling solution. Provided your vendor exposes all of the appropriate APIs, it's not all that challenging to build a custom application to handle provisioning. You can also just use the solution your cloud vendor offers.

## Building versus Buying an Auto-Scaling Solution

Like most software, auto-scaling solutions can be built or bought. Like any software, you have to decide which direction you want to go. Generally speaking, if you can't differentiate yourself by building something custom, you should choose a prebuilt solution of some sort, whether that's a commercial solution sold by a third-party vendor or an integrated solution built into your cloud. What matters is that you have an extremely reliable, robust solution that can grow to meet your future needs.

Table 4-4 shows some reasons you would want to build or buy an auto-scaling solution.

*Table 4-4. Reasons to build or buy auto-scaling solution*

| Build | Buy |
| --- | --- |
| Your IaaS vendor doesn't offer an auto-scaling solution. | You want to get to market quickly. |
| You want more functionality and control than what a pre-built solution can offer. | Your IaaS vendor offers a solution that meets your needs. |
| You want to be able to provision across multiple clouds. | A third-party vendor offers a solution that meets your needs. |
| You have the resources (finances, people, time) to implement something custom. | You don't have the resources to implement something custom. |

Generally speaking, it's best to buy one of these solutions rather than build one. Find what works for you and adopt it. *Anything* is likely to be better than what you have today.

For more information on auto-scaling, read *Cloud Architecture Patterns* by Bill Wilder (O'Reilly).

# Summary

In this chapter we discussed the importance of auto-scaling solutions, how they work, and whether you should build or buy one.

Once you've implemented an auto-scaling solution, the next step is to install software on the hardware that you provision from an auto-scaling solution.

# CHAPTER 5

# Installing Software on Newly Provisioned Hardware

The adoption of Infrastructure-as-a-Service requires a fundamental change to how software is installed and configured on newly provisioned servers. Most organizations manually install and configure software on each server. This doesn't work when you're quickly provisioning new servers in response to real-time traffic. Servers need to be serving HTTP requests or doing other work within minutes of being provisioned. They also need to be configured accurately, which is something humans have difficulty doing reliably.

 You can skip this chapter if you're using only Platform-as-a-Service or Software-as-a-Service because they do all this for you. This is what you're paying them a premium for over Infrastructure-as-a-Service.

In this chapter, we'll discuss how to build, maintain, and monitor self-contained modular stacks of software. These stacks are called *deployment units*.

## What Is a Deployment Unit?

When you provision capacity with Infrastructure-as-a-Service, you get raw hardware with your choice of an image. But before you can do anything with the hardware, you need to install and configure software so it can handle HTTP requests or serve whatever purpose it's destined for, as shown in Figure 5-1.

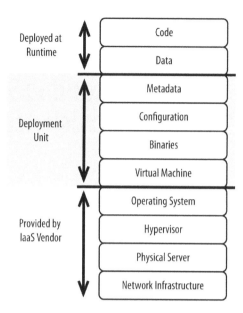

*Figure 5-1. Scope of a deployment unit*

Specifically, this requires installing a base image and/or doing the following:

1. Installing software from binary distributions (virtual machine, application server, caching server)

2. Configuring each of the pieces of software to work together (e.g., telling your application servers where the database is listening)

3. Setting environment variables (e.g., enabling huge pages, TCP/IP stack tuning)

4. Defining metadata (e.g., environment-specific search initialization variables)

Every environment has numerous server types. Common server types include these:

*eCommerce server*
    ecommerce application + application server + virtual machine

*Cache server*
    Cache grid + application server + virtual machine

*Messaging server*
    Messaging system + application server + virtual machine

*Service bus server*
    Service bus + application server + virtual machine

*Order management server*
    Order management system + application server + virtual machine

*Search engine server*
    Search engine

*Database server*
    Database node

Each of these servers is unique, requiring potentially different binaries, configuration, and so on. What matters most is that you can build up a freshly provisioned bit of hardware within minutes and without human interaction. A single stack that is able to be deployed on a single operating system instance is considered a deployment unit for the purposes of this book.

# Approaches to Building Deployment Units

Individual units can be built numerous ways, ranging from snapshots of entire systems (including the operating system) to scripts of various types that can be used to build each system from source. There are broadly three ways of building out individual servers. Let's review each approach.

## Building from Snapshots

Public Infrastructure-as-a-Service vendors all offer the ability to snapshot servers. These snapshots (also called *images*) are basically byte-level disk copies along with some metadata that can then be used as the basis for building a new server (Figure 5-2). That snapshot is installed directly on top of a hypervisor, giving you the ability to quickly build servers. You can also define bootstrap scripts that execute when the server is started up. These scripts can change network settings, update hostnames, start processes, register with the load balancer, and perform other tasks required to make the server productive.

Common snapshot formats used by Infrastructure-as-a-Service vendors include Open Virtualization Format (OVF), RAW, ISO, and Amazon Machine Image (AMI). Again, all of these are basically byte-level disk copies along with some metadata. Individual vendors sometimes have their own proprietary formats, some of which can be used with other vendors (as is the case with AMI).

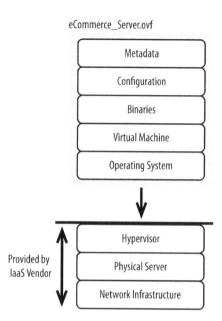

*Figure 5-2. Contents of a snapshot*

You can build libraries of these snapshots and then specify which snapshot you want to build your server from when you provision your new server. The snapshot-based approach works well for the following:

*Quickly building servers*

The time from when you provision the hardware to when it's useful is governed by how quickly the bytes can be written to a filesystem. It typically takes no more than a few minutes before a server is built with the machine image of your choice. This is helpful when you need to scale up very quickly because of an unanticipated spike in traffic.

*Capturing intricate changes*

Some software requires intricate installations. There may be lengthy configuration files, changes to file permissions, and special operating system users. It's rare that you can simply install an applications server from binary and deploy a package of code to it.

*Being able to test*

Like code, snapshots can be tested for functionality, security, and performance.

*Archiving audit trails*

You can easily archive snapshots for auditing and compliance purposes. If there was ever an incident, you could quickly go back and show the state of each server in an environment.

A downside of this approach is that it has no ability to handle patching and routine maintenance on its own. Without the introduction of software that handles this, you'll have to do the following:

1. Apply changes to live systems.
2. Snapshot each of the live servers that runs a unique image.
3. Swap out the images on each of the affected live servers.

Or you'll have to apply the updates manually to each server, which probably isn't even feasible. More on this topic in "Lifecycle Management".

## Building from Archives

While a snapshot is a clone of an entire live operating system and its contents, an archive (e.g., *.tar*, *.zip*, *.rar*) is a collection of directories and files. You provision new resources from an Infrastructure-as-a-Service vendor and then extract the directories and files on to your local filesystem. The archive can contain scripts or other means required to change file permissions, configure the software to run in your environment, and so on. Compression may also be included to reduce the amount of data that must be transferred. The contents of an archive are depicted in Figure 5-3.

This approach works by being able to isolate the changes you make to a base filesystem image. In other words, all of the changes you make to a base filesystem should be captured either in the directories and files in your archive or through a manual script that can be replayed after the files are written. If you install all of your software under a single root directory (e.g., */opt/YourCompany*), it's pretty easy to archive that root directory.

Once you provision a new server, you'll have to get the archive to that new server, extract it to the local filesystem, and run any scripts you need to generally initialize the environment. Since you can't do this manually, it's a great idea to create a bootstrap script to pull the latest archive and extract it. You can bake this bootstrap script into a snapshot, which you can use as the baseline for new servers.

This approach works best for software shipped in zip distributions or software that can be fully installed under a given root (e.g., */opt/YourCompany*). Applications that sprawl files across a filesystem, set environment variables, or change file permissions, do not work well as you have to capture the changes made and then replay them manually in a script. Most software today is shipped through a zip distribution or is able to be fully installed under a given root, so it shouldn't be an issue.

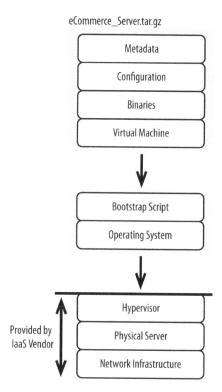

*Figure 5-3. What's capable of being included in an archive*

This approach can be better than the snapshot-based approach because you're dealing with relatively small archives all self-contained under a root (e.g., */opt/YourCompany*). As with the snapshot-based approach, the downside is having no real ability to handle patching and routine maintenance. We'll discuss an alternative in "Lifecycle Management".

## Building from Source

Rather than installing software and then taking a snapshot of a whole server or a directory, you can build an entire stack of software from source. *Source* in this case refers to actual source code or precompiled binaries. This approach involves scripting out your environments, including what must be installed, in what order, and with what parameters. An agent installed on an operating system then runs the script, downloading, installing, and configuring as required (see Figure 5-4).

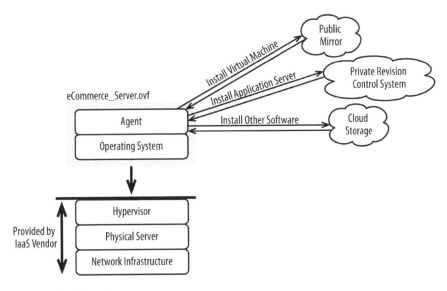

*Figure 5-4. Building from source*

Numerous commercial and open source products on the market allow you to:

- Download binaries
- Execute installers
- Detect failures in installations
- Configure software (e.g., updating properties/XML files)
- Issue arbitrary commands to the operating system
- Push arbitrary files
- Execute scripts and report the output
- Define hierarchal relationships between components with either declarative or procedural dependency models
- Execute the same script across different platforms and operating systems

All of these activities are typically done through a lightweight agent installed on each server, with the agent communicating with a central management server either within or outside of an Infrastructure-as-a-Service cloud. Here's how you would install JDK 8 using Chef, a popular configuration management tool:

```
# install jdk8
java_ark "jdk" do
    url 'http://download.oracle.com/otn-pub/java/jdk/8-b132/jdk-8-linux-x64.bin'
    checksum  'a8603fa62045ce2164b26f7c04859cd548ffe0e33bfc979d9fa73df42e3b3365'
    app_home '/usr/local/java/default'
```

```
    bin_cmds ["java", "javac"]
    action :install
end
```

For more information, please read *Learning Chef* by Seth Vargo and Mischa Taylor (O'Reilly).

Many software vendors have contributed to these projects to make it exceptionally easy to install their products. Of course, shell scripting is always an option, but that is far more challenging because it lacks so many of the capabilities of purpose-built solutions.

Many of these systems have full support for scripting, allowing you to customize the installation of each product. For example, you can see how many vCPUs are available and then change how many threads you allocate to a load balancer. You can fine-tune your software to run well on its target server. When you snapshot a live system, it's just that: a static snapshot. Building from source is the most robust approach but it adds substantial overhead to the development and deployment process. For this to work properly, you need to build out fairly lengthy scripts, even for simple environments. It's a lot of work to maintain them, especially for software that's complex to install.

> If you have to SSH into a server to do anything manually, your automation has failed.

# Monitoring the Health of a Deployment Unit

Regardless of whether your servers are in a public Infrastructure-as-a-Service cloud or in your own data centers managed by your own administrators, the health of each deployment unit must be thoroughly interrogated. Individual deployment units should be considered disposable. The health of a deployment unit is best evaluated by querying the uppermost stack of software, as shown in Figure 5-5.

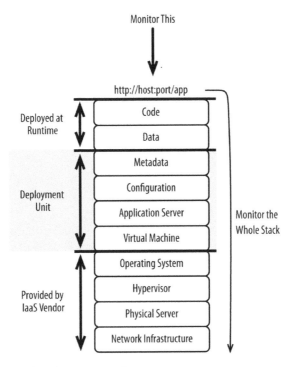

*Figure 5-5. What needs to be monitored*

Bad servers should be immediately pulled from the load balancer to prevent customers from having a poor experience. This is especially important with cloud environments where there may be interference from noisy neighbors.

Traditional health checking has been very superficial, with its scope limited to the health of individual components (e.g., filesystem, memory, network, CPU) and whether the specified HTTP port responds to a TCP ping (see Figure 5-6).

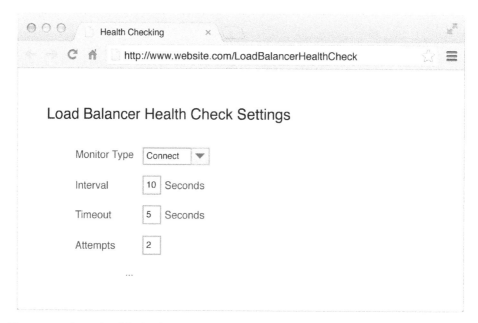

*Figure 5-6. Basic health check*

This is of no use: an application server could respond to a TCP ping, with, for example, an HTTP 500 error because the application server couldn't establish a connection to the database. Testing TCP pings tests only the lower levels of the stack, not whether anything is actually working.

A better, and perhaps the most common approach is shown in Figure 5-7.

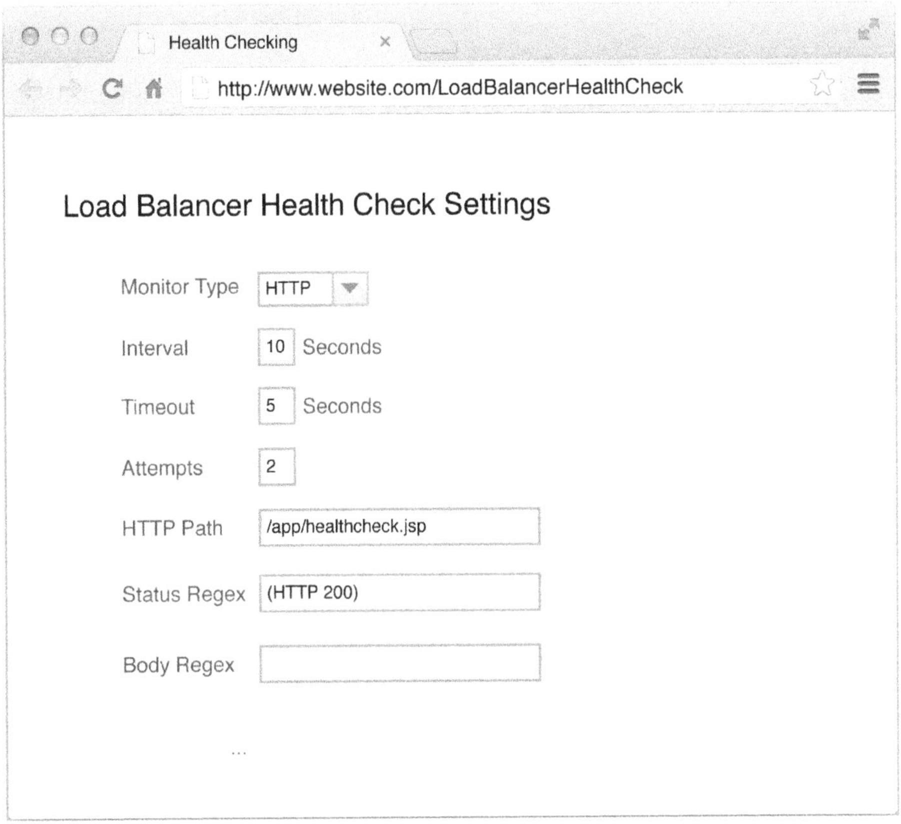

*Figure 5-7. Better health check*

With this approach, you're verifying that the home page or another functionally rich page actually responds with an HTTP 200 response code. This is slightly better, but it can't evaluate the health of the entire application and the services (e.g., database, cache grid, messaging) required to fully deliver the entire application. Home pages, for example, tend to be fairly static and heavily cached.

The most comprehensive way of health checking is to build a dynamic page that exercises the basic functionality of an application. If all tests are successful, it writes PASS. If there was an error, it writes FAIL. Then, configure the load balancer to search for an HTTP 200 response code and PASS. Figure 5-8 shows how you configure your load balancer.

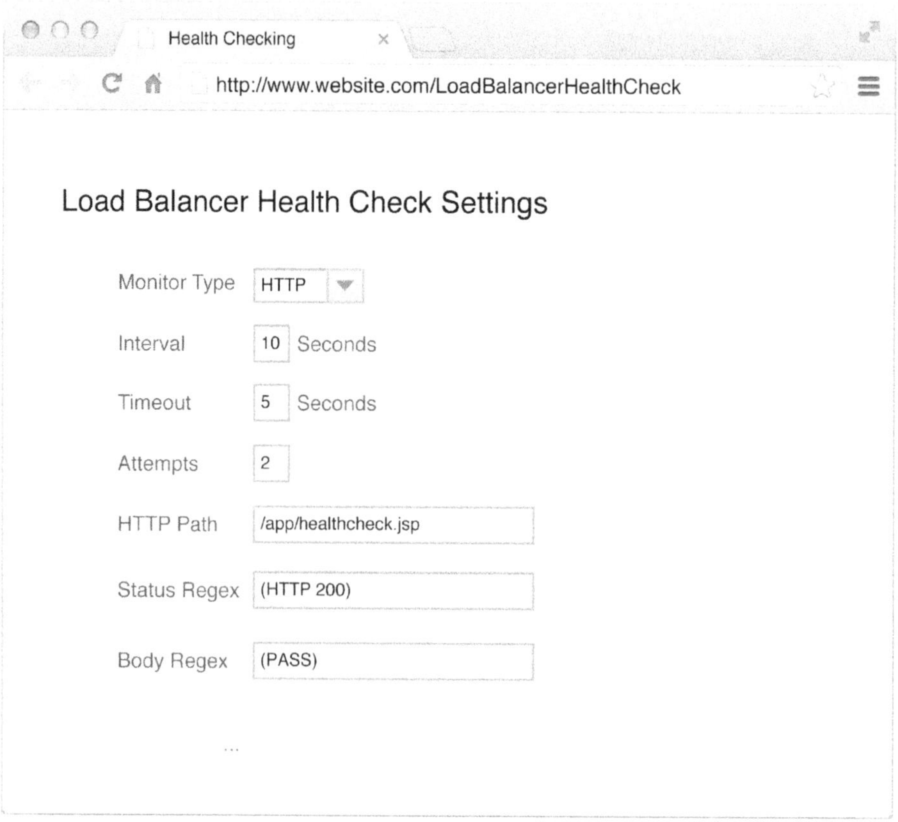

*Figure 5-8. Best health check*

Tests performed on this page can include:

- Querying the cache grid for a product
- Adding a product to the shopping cart
- Writing a new order to a database and then deleting it
- Querying the service bus for inventory availability
- Executing a query against the search engine

These few tests are far more comprehensive than any arbitrary page or URL you select. It's very important that the load balancer you choose has the ability to look at both the HTTP response header and the body of the response.

This monitoring is not to take the place of more comprehensive system-level monitoring—rather, it's to tell the load balancer whether a given unit is healthy enough to continue serving traffic. Standard system-level monitoring is required and expected, though outside the scope of this book.

Make sure you don't overdo your health checking, as frequent monitoring can add work to your system without providing a clear benefit.

# Lifecycle Management

Every one of your servers has its own stack of software, patches, configuration, and code. Once a server is provisioned and built, it must be updated as you make changes to the baseline. Being able to quickly push updates to production helps to ensure that servers stay up, making it easier to debug problems, all while reducing labor costs. In addition, you will likely have to be able to push through emergency configuration and security-related changes (Figure 5-9).

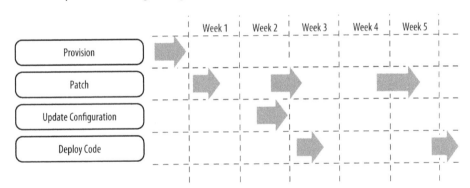

*Figure 5-9. Lifecycle of each server*

Often a single logical change (e.g., applying a patch or deploying new code) requires executing many, if not all, of the following actions:

- Updating files on a filesystem
- Arbitrarily executing commands against a shell script and monitoring the results
- Making configuration changes (through updating configuration files or executing commands through the shell)

All running servers, as well as your reference snapshot if you use a snapshot-based approach, must be updated as you advance your baseline of software, patches, configuration, and code. Again, you can't do this by hand, so you have to automate the process.

The approach outlined in "Building from Source" is often used for both initial installation and ongoing lifecycle management. Because an agent is always running on each server, you can push any files or make any configuration changes you want. You can even use it for deploying new builds. But the snapshot-based approaches (either full images or archives) lack agents. They're static snapshots and therefore need supplemental software to handle a lifecycle.

Once you do pick a solution and start to use it, make sure you stage your changes and test them with a limited set of customers before you roll the changes out across an entire environment. You can just apply the changes to a handful of servers, monitor their health, and then roll out the changes across the entire environment. Or if your changes are more substantial, you can even build a separate parallel production environment and instruct your load balancer to direct a small amount of traffic to the new environment. When you're satisfied with the results, you can have your load balancer cut all of your traffic over to your new production environment and then decommission your old servers. This can get very complicated, but the payoff can be substantial.

## Summary

In this chapter we discussed three approaches for installing software on hardware, followed by how to monitor each stack of software. While building and monitoring deployment units is a fundamental prerequisite to adopting cloud, virtualization is perhaps even more of a basic building block.

# CHAPTER 6

# Virtualization in the Cloud

Virtualization is a key enabler of cloud computing but it is not part of the cloud itself. As previously discussed, the cloud is defined by the following three attributes: elastic, on demand, and metered. Virtualization itself isn't one of those three attributes but it does help to enable all three.

 Virtualization is a key enabler of the cloud but it is not the cloud itself.

Virtualization in its various forms enables the following:

*Partitioning*
> Vendors don't make any money if they can't pack a lot of their customers on each physical server. Many vendors offer virtualized servers with as little as one physical hardware thread. There are typically two hardware threads per physical CPU core, 12 cores per processor, and two processors per physical host. That means a single commodity machine can be divided into 48 servers, each capable of being rented out to an individual or organization. Density is how vendors make their money.

*Isolation*
> Given that partitioning hardware is required to make business models work, isolation is required to keep individual partitions from interfering with each other. You wouldn't want a CPU-intensive workload like DNA sequencing to interfere with your application server's ability to respond to HTTP requests. You can provision whole servers from many Infrastructure-as-a-Service vendors, just as you would secure fractional slices of physical servers.

*Portability*

Virtualization has tooling that makes it easy to take snapshots of live running systems. These snapshots, as we discussed in the last chapter, can be used as the starting point when provisioning new hardware. Everything is fully encapsulated in these snapshots, making them fully portable across other servers within a cloud or even across clouds.

*Workload shifting*

With virtualization serving as an abstraction layer over the hardware, some cloud vendors offer the ability to move live running virtual machines from one physical host to another. Sometimes your cloud vendor even does this for you automatically while performing maintenance or as the hardware is experiencing a fault of some sort.

Isolation and portability benefit ecommerce most. Isolating workloads on shared hardware is a necessity, given the sensitive nature of the data involved with ecommerce. Portability is a key enabler of building deployment units very quickly, as you can work with predeveloped snapshots instead of having to build up each system from scratch.

While virtualization has benefits, it also has drawbacks that have wide-ranging implications for your deployment architecture. Let's review the different forms of virtualization and the implications of each.

# What Is Virtualization?

*Virtualization* is more of a concept than an actual implementation of any given technology. Virtualization offers you the ability to partition a physical server into many smaller servers, with each virtual server isolated from other virtual servers on the same physical server. The technology behind virtualization has been around since the beginning of the mainframe days. At its core, there's typically an abstraction layer called a hypervisor that is responsible for splitting up a system's resources and making them available to guests.

There are three broad approaches to virtualization, which we'll cover in the following sections.

# Full Virtualization

In *full virtualization*, the hypervisor is installed directly on bare metal. The hypervisor allocates the server's physical resources (CPU, memory, disk, NIC) to virtualized servers. Operating systems are installed directly on the virtual servers, with the physical resources allocated to each virtual server being the only resources each virtual server has access to.

The advantage of this approach is that you don't have to make any changes to the operating system. You can install any operating system the underlying hardware supports and not have to make any changes. Each operating system is entirely oblivious to the other operating systems on the same physical server. This type of hypervisor lends itself well to public Infrastructure-as-a-Service clouds. Examples of full virtualization include Xen Hardware Virtual Machine, Linux KVM, and Microsoft Hyper-V. Figure 6-1 shows how full virtualization carves up each physical machine.

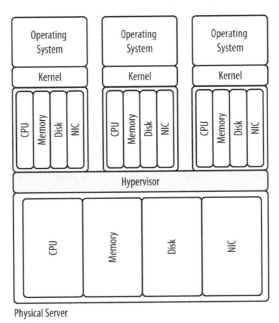

*Figure 6-1. Full virtualization*

Full virtualization is best when you need to support many different operating systems, especially those that do not support a limited form of virtualization known as *paravirtualization*. Most clouds support both full virtualization and paravirtualization.

Full virtualization suffers from performance degradation because all physical resources must be accessed through the hypervisor. The performance of full virtualization is starting to be improved through the use of hardware virtual machine (HVM) extensions to x86 processors that make it easier for the guest operating system to bypass the hypervisor and use the CPU directly. But paravirtualization takes things a step further and allows more native access to many resources.

# Paravirtualization (Operating System–Assisted Virtualization)

Traditional full virtualization requires that every system call be trapped by the hypervisor and passed back to the physical host. Depending on the workload, performance can be dramatically worse than if the operating system was not running on top of a hypervisor. In _paravirtualization, the kernel works cooperatively with the hypervisor to pass through certain calls directly to the underlying hardware. Calls such as those for memory management, time keeping, and interrupt handling are often passed right through from the guest to the host.

 While the term *paravirtualization* may be new to many readers, the concepts and even much of the technology have been in use for decades. Almost all operating systems bypass the hypervisor in *some* way.

Paravirtualization, shown in Figure 6-2, requires that the kernel be substantially modified so it can work with the hypervisor. Most modern Linux kernels, along with some Unix kernels, support paravirtualization, so you probably won't ever have to do any of this work on your own.

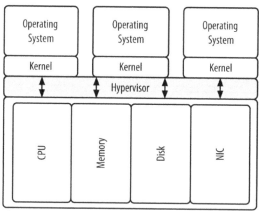

*Figure 6-2. Paravirtualization*

Paravirtualization is great because you get isolation offered by full hardware virtualization, yet you get nearly the performance of operating system–level virtualization. So long as your Infrastructure-as-a-Service and kernel vendors support it, paravirtualization is the best approach. They incur the costs of making the kernel and hypervisor work together, and you reap the rewards of better performance than full virtualization with nearly no overhead. Common implementations include Xen and VMware.

Paravirtualization is now the most prevalent virtualization option offered by public Infrastructure-as-a-Service vendors.

## Operating System Virtualization

In *operating system virtualization*, a very light hypervisor is installed on the operating system itself (see Figure 6-3). With this approach, guest operating systems share the kernel of the parent operating system. The kernel offers each guest operating system its own caged sandbox so that processes cannot interfere with each other. Some forms of operating system virtualization offer resource throttling so a given guest cannot consume more than a specified amount of system resources. This approach is entirely dependent on what the operating system you're using supports.

This technology has been around since the days of mainframes and continues to be used today. Today's well-known incarnations include FreeBSD Jails, Solaris Containers/Zones, and Linux Containers (LXC).

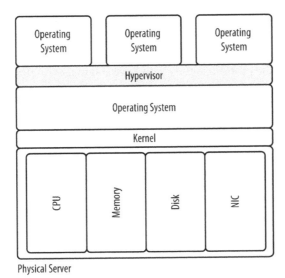

*Figure 6-3. Operating system virtualization*

The following sidebar contains a humorous explanation of operating system virtualization.

# Linux Containers (LXC), Explained

Think of every process on the machine as being like a five-year-old. If you have a bunch of them, they're eventually going to start fighting. Ever seen five-year-olds fight? It's stupid:

"He's standing near me, and I don't like it!"

"I don't want her to make that noise!"

In the context of a process on Linux, you can think of this as two server processes both wanting to listen on the same port, or writing a config file to the same place. And here you are, thinking, "Grow up and share. If you can't handle this, wait till your first interaction with the DMV."

But they will never share, because they're five years old. They'll just whine at each other to the point where you have to physically separate them just to preserve your own sanity.

One way to physically separate a dozen five-year-olds is to build a dozen houses, and give them each a house. This is like running a separate physical machine for each process. Yes, it solves the problem, but it's expensive and wastes resources.

So then you try a virtual machine within one physical host. If we're talking about separating five-year-olds, this is like turning one house into a bunch of apartments, one for each five-year-old. This allows for maximum configurability. Each five-year-old can set the thermostat at whatever temperature is comfortable. Sure, they don't have as much space as they would if they had the whole house, but at least they're contained. They're not really aware of each other, but generally, they're happy.

But if you're Mom and Dad, this is just silly. Do you really need one separate kitchen for each five-year-old? No, that's overkill. One kitchen is enough. Do five-year-olds really need to set the thermostat as they please? No, they're five. Plus, I'm the parent, I pay the heating bill, and the thermostat isn't going over 57 degrees all winter.

So what's the solution?

You give each kid a magic pair of glasses that let them see everything but each other. They're all walking around the house, aware only of their own existence. Ah, but what if they both want to play with the same toy? Simple, buy the same toy for each kid. A lot easier than building a house for each kid. In reality, they're going to conflict over only a very small number of things in the house, so you can replicate those things, and the five-year-olds will be none the wiser.

This is what LXC is. It lets processes think they have complete run of the machine, but a very lightweight hypervisor keeps them separate. They're all still running in the same kernel, but they don't know it. An LXC container is a collection of files that represents the minimum set of "toys" the processes might fight over. It's a bit more advanced, though. You can, for example, run a Red Hat LXC container inside an Ubuntu kernel. As long as your processes don't have explicit expectations about the kernel, you're fine. And most of the time, processes don't have such expectations.[1]

This approach is becoming increasingly popular because of the performance it offers relative to running an operating system natively on physical hardware, while still providing enough isolation between tenants. With operating system virtualization, you have full native access to the CPU, memory, disk, NIC, and so forth, because you're relying on a shared kernel that itself is natively accessing the physical resources. With full virtualization, you have to go through your guest kernel and then through a hypervisor before you can access any physical resources. There is potentially a lot of overhead when every operation must pass through the hypervisor.

With operating system virtualization, depending on how you configure it, you could allow the guests to cooperatively share resources, thus enabling higher density.

Platform-as-a-Service vendors have embraced operating system virtualization because they have no need to support a wide range of operating systems. These vendors tend to pick one operating system and standardize on it. You can pack many guests on a single physical host, because the overhead of each guest is so small. The performance is also much better than with some of the heavier virtualization techniques, while allowing for varying levels of isolation between guests.

# Summary of Virtualization Approaches

Virtualization of various forms will continue to be used by cloud vendors for the foreseeable future. The vendors need to be able to pack multiple guests on a single physical host to make their business model work. At the same time, cloud users need to have isolation between their workloads and other workloads running on the same physical host.

The trend has been away from full isolation, in which everything is virtualized to lighter-weight solutions like paravirtualization, which is now the standard for most Infrastructure-as-a-Service vendors. Paravirtualization is a great trade-off between full hardware virtualization and operating system virtualization. It is also supported by most Linux kernels, so it's fairly easy to deploy now. Most vendors offer two or three virtualization solutions, so you get to pick which one works best for you.

Table 6-1 shows a quick review of the approaches to virtualization.

---

1 Ted Dziuba (2013), adapted from *http://bit.ly/MrUJ13*.

*Table 6-1. Review of approaches to virtualization*

| Attribute | Full virtualization | Paravirtualization | Operating system virtualization |
|---|---|---|---|
| Used by | IaaS, PaaS, SaaS | IaaS, PaaS, SaaS | PaaS, SaaS |
| Hypervisor installed | On bare metal | On bare metal | On operating system |
| Isolation between guests | Complete | Complete | Variable; complete to limited |
| Performance overhead | High | Low | Virtually none |
| Kernels per physical server | Multiple; each guest has its own | Multiple; each guest has its own | One; guests share |
| Kernel modifications required | No | Yes | Yes |
| Support for multiple guest operating systems | Yes | Limited | No |
| Common implementations | Xen HVM, VMware | Xen PV, VMware | FreeBSD Jails, Solaris Containers/Zones, and Linux Containers |

These approaches to virtualization are increasingly blending together. You have to research your vendor's implementation of each of these approaches to find out exactly what, for example, paravirtualization means to your vendor.

# Improving the Performance of Software Executed on a Hypervisor

The difference between the three high-level approaches come down to how many resources must be accessed through the hypervisor. With full virtualization, everything must be accessed through the hypervisor. With operating system virtualization, nothing passes through the hypervisor. Table 6-2 shows the three approaches to virtualization and whether each resource must be accessed through the hypervisor.

*Table 6-2. Must access physical resources through the hypervisor*

| Resource | Full virtualization | Paravirtualization | Operating system virtualization |
|---|---|---|---|
| CPU | Yes (except if HVM extensions in x86 processors are used) | Maybe | No |
| NIC | Yes | Maybe | No |
| Memory | Yes | No | No |
| Disk | Yes | No | No |
| BIOS/motherboard | Yes | No | No |
| Interrupts/timers | Yes | No | No |

Full virtualization and paravirtualization are likely to suffer from some performance degradation because access to some physical resources must pass through a hypervisor. That will always take longer than natively accessing those resources.

As we discussed in Chapter 3, the single biggest hindrance to server-side performance is the number of calls to remote systems. It's increasingly common to call out to multiple remote systems to assemble a single page. Figure 6-4 shows the systems most shopping cart pages have to call out to before they can be rendered.

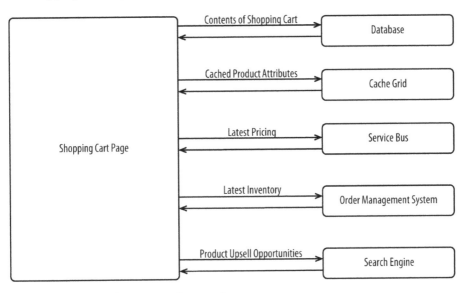

*Figure 6-4. Services often required to render a cart page*

There are likely to be a number of calls out to each one of these remote systems, with each call being synchronous. As we discussed in Chapter 3, each call out to a third party requires that the potentially dozens or hundreds of packets representing the HTTP request and HTTP response travel over the path shown in Figure 6-5.

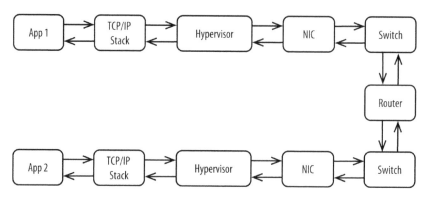

*Figure 6-5. Intermediary required for host-to-host communication*

A single page may require 50 of these synchronous calls. The real performance problem comes not from the time it takes for each system to respond to these calls but generally from the overhead associated with going back and forth.

> Performance problems in ecommerce are almost always due to making *too many* calls rather than the response time of any given call.

Overhead comes in two forms:

- Network latency
- Latency incurred on each physical server

Virtualization is in large part responsible for the latency incurred on each server. Traversing TCP/IP stacks on each guest operating system turns out to be much slower if the guest operating system has to pass through a hypervisor to access the CPU, memory, and NIC. It's best to bypass the hypervisor as much as possible, provided there is adequate separation between virtual servers. If you have to use a full hypervisor for some reason, try to bypass it for anything related to HTTP request handling through techniques like single-root I/O virtualization (SR-IOV). SR-IOV, which is now supported by many cloud vendors, allows your NIC to be presented to your guest virtual servers as if it was a physical device. Any calls from your virtual server to your NIC bypasses the hypervisor entirely.

# Summary

In this chapter, we reviewed how virtualization is an enabler of cloud computing, but is not a defining attribute. We then reviewed the three basic approaches to virtualization and covered techniques used to improve performance. Next, we'll discuss Content Delivery Networks.

# CHAPTER 7

# Content Delivery Networks

*Content Delivery Networks*, known as CDNs, are large distributed networks of servers that accelerate the delivery of your platform to your customers, provide security, assign customers to a data center if you operate more than one, provide throttling, and a host of other value adds. Their role in modern large-scale ecommerce is ubiquitous and often a necessity.

The largest CDN in the world has 137,000 servers in 87 countries.[1] Servers belonging to CDNs are often colocated directly in ISP/backbone vendors' data centers and plugged directly into their high-speed networks. Chances are, a CDN has servers within a few milliseconds of where you live. It's because of this proximity to customers that CDNs are often called *edge computing*. Often CDNs are entirely transparent to your customers.

An example of the value CDNs offer is in their acceleration of HTML-based web pages.

> For most web pages, less than 10%–20% of the end-user response time is spent getting the HTML document from the web server to the web browser. If you want to dramatically reduce the response times of your web pages, you have to focus on the other 80%–90% of the end-user experience.
>
> —Steve Souders, *High Performance Websites*

Figure 7-1 shows a breakdown of the time it takes to load the home page of a popular US-based ecommerce website for an anonymous customer.

---

1 Akamai Technologies, "Facts and Figures," (2014) *http://www.akamai.com/html/about/facts_figures.html*

# Backend

- 1 HTTP Request
- 35.1 KB
- 211 MS

# Frontend

- 163 HTTP Requests
- 1.7 MB
- 8.78 S

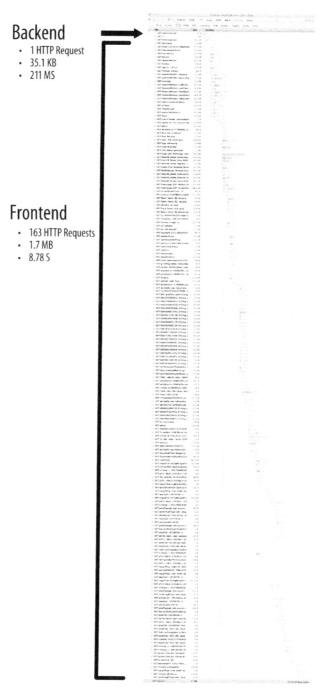

*Figure 7-1. Frontend versus backend HTTP requests for SamsClub.com home page*

Waiting for a server-side response accounts for just 2.4% of the total page view time. This is very representative of most ecommerce web pages. CDNs are responsible for delivering the remaining 97.6% in this example. CDNs can also accelerate the delivery of the server-side response, as we'll discuss later in the chapter. CDNs play an increasingly important role when transitioning to the cloud.

> While CDNs have long been associated with delivering websites (HTML, images, CSS, JavaScript), their role has greatly expanded to the point where they're now crucial to delivering entire platforms.

Let's look at their multifaceted roles and how they can improve your customers' experience.

# What Is a CDN?

CDNs first started to be used in the late 1990s to deliver static content at scale. At the time, most eCommerce websites were delivered from in-house corporate data centers belonging to eCommerce vendors. Serving large amounts of static content requires an enormous amount of Internet bandwidth and specialized network infrastructure that was prohibitively expensive and complicated. A side effect of delivering all of this content was that performance improved. Improved performance leads to improved customer satisfaction, higher conversion rates, and increased brand loyalty. As performance became more important to the customers of CDNs and of eCommerce customers in particular, CDN vendors shifted their attention to improving performance.

For a while, CDNs were basically web servers serving up static content. Their value proposition was that they provided availability and scale by offloading static content and delivering it from machines near the end user. Over time, CDN vendors have evolved their offerings to:

- Proxy HTTP requests back to your data centers (called an *origin*), effectively taking your platform off the Internet by forcing all HTTP requests through the CDN first.
- Optimize delivery of content through advanced functionality like content prefetching, network optimization, compression, image resizing, geolocation, and modifying the HTML of pages to improve rendering and browser performance.
- Cache entire responses (including HTML pages) at the edge, such as the home page for anonymous customers.
- Cache API calls at the edge. Responses are typically XML or JSON.

- Offer value adds like a web application firewall, protection against distributed denial-of-service attacks, and a full Global Server Load Balancing solution.
- Reduce the CPU usage by multiplexing HTTP connections and keeping the connections alive for longer periods of time.

 An *origin* is a term used by Content Delivery Network vendors to refer to the data center(s) that actually generate the content that the Content Delivery Network serves. This typically means the data centers where you have your application servers.

## Are CDNs Clouds?

CDNs are clouds, albeit a lesser form of clouds. To be considered part of the cloud, an offering must be described by the following three adjectives:

- Elastic
- On demand
- Metered

CDNs always meet the first and second requirement but not always the third. Some vendors permit the use of their services only with contracts that last a year or longer.

 Fixed long-term contracts are common ways of paying CDN vendors and therefore may technically not be considered cloud computing. Pragmatism should rule your decision making. Go for the best vendor, regardless of how they bill you.

With their core business now being fairly mature, CDNs are moving down into the space traditionally owned by cloud vendors. Cloud vendors are also moving up into the CDN space as they seek to offer their customers full vertically integrated solutions and increase their share of their customers' technology spending. All technology vendors seek to provide their customers with one-stop, full vertically integrated solutions, as opposed to point products/services.

The real difference between CDNs and Infrastructure-as-a-Service vendors is that CDNs still don't *originate* the content they're serving. They just accelerate the delivery of content originated elsewhere. Infrastructure-as-a-Service vendors originate content and can accelerate its delivery to some degree. While there's a lot of overlap, both still do fundamentally different things.

For more information on Content Delivery Networks and optimization, read Steve Souders' *High Performance Websites* and *Even Faster Websites* (O'Reilly).

# Serving Static Content

The first and original value proposition of CDNs is that they almost entirely eliminate latency. When you pull up your favorite ecommerce website, you make a single HTTP request to *http://www.walgreens.com*. In response to your request, you'll get an HTML file that's probably under 100 kilobytes in size (*http://bit.ly/1g4biId*). If that was it, you wouldn't need a CDN. The average latency between Tokyo and London is only 242 milliseconds.[2] That latency could be tolerated for one HTTP request.

Web browsers have to make hundreds of HTTP requests. When your web browser gets the HTML back from the origin, it will parse it to find out what other content it needs to fetch to make the page render:

```
<script type="text/javascript" src='/gomez-tag.js'></script>
<script type="text/javascript" src='http://img.website.com/scripts/mbox.js'>
</script>
<link rel="shortcut icon" type="image/x-icon" href="/favicon.ico"/>
<script type="text/javascript" src="http://www.website.com/scripts/common.js">
</script>
<script type="text/javascript" src="http://img.website.com/scripts/menu.js">
</script>
```

Each of these includes requires an HTTP request, at least until the object is cached locally on the client's web browser. The number of HTTP requests can range from dozens to several hundred. Table 7-1 shows a random sampling of the page weight and number of HTTP requests needed from the top 100 largest ecommerce websites in the US.

*Table 7-1. Page weight and number of HTTP requests for a sample of large ecommerce websites in the US*

| Website | Page weight | Number of HTTP requests |
| --- | --- | --- |
| *http://www.chicos.com* | 2.4 MB | 187 |
| *http://www.1800flowers.com* | 1.5 MB | 213 |
| *http://www.jcrew.com* | 1.9 MB | 92 |
| *http://www.walgreens.com* | 870 KB | 92 |
| *http://www.samsclub.com* | 2.2 MB | 166 |
| *http://www.shutterfly.com* | 2.5 MB | 362 |
| *http://www.lowes.com* | 1.7 MB | 187 |

---

2 AT&T, "Global Network Latency Averages," (2014) *http://www.akamai.com/html/technology/dataviz2.html.*

| Website | Page weight | Number of HTTP requests |
|---|---|---|
| http://www.ebay.com | 2.9 MB | 176 |
| http://www.hsn.com | 2.1 MB | 178 |
| http://www.staples.com | 3.2 MB | 277 |
| **Mean** | **2.1 MB** | **193** |

The problem with loading all of these objects in under a few seconds is that web browsers load objects in serial batches of roughly 10 HTTP requests. Let's look at an example. Using the mean number of HTTP requests from the preceding sample, a customer in Los Angeles accessing a website served from New York would incur roughly one additional second of overhead due to the latency between the two data centers, as shown in Figure 7-2.

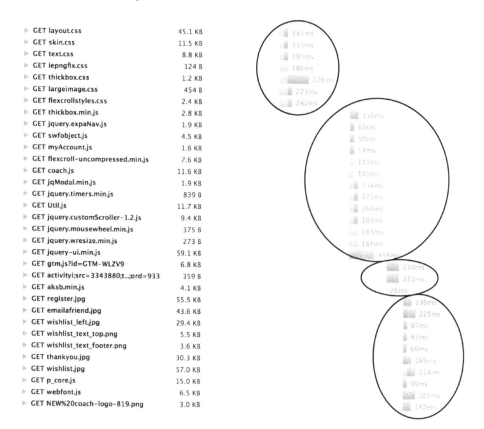

*Figure 7-2. Browsers making HTTP requests in batches*

This gets even worse for websites that are served to audiences on high latency net-works, such as those not physically near to the origin, cellular networks, etc. This doesn't include the time it takes for the origin to actually generate the response. It can take one second or more just to generate the HTTP response for a dynamic page.

Without a CDN, loading a page consists of what's shown in Figure 7-3.

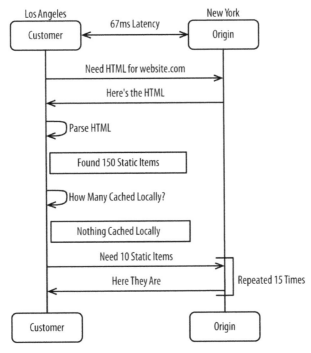

*Figure 7-3. Page rendering without Content Delivery Network*

Now, let's see what happens when you use a CDN, as in Figure 7-4.

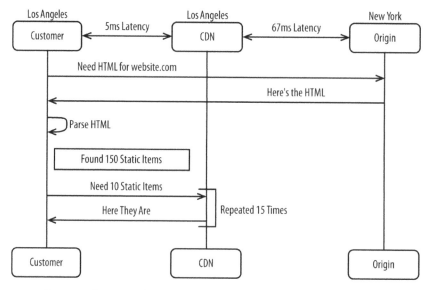

*Figure 7-4. Page rendering with Content Delivery Network*

As you can see, only one HTTP request incurs the 67-millisecond overhead. The remaining 150 HTTP requests are served directly from the customer's local CDN data center in Los Angeles. The latency is almost entirely eliminated. It is this principle that allows websites to be served from one data center to a global audience. Assuming the same 15 round-trips back to the origin data center to render a page, a website served from London to Tokyo with 260 milliseconds of latency would incur 3.9 seconds of overhead just due to latency. When you factor in the time it takes to render the HTML, serve the static content, and so forth, response times of 6+ seconds are to be expected. In addition to substantially reducing latency, the static content is downloaded faster because the packets must travel a shorter distance across fewer network hops. With average home pages exceeding 2 MB, clients have to download a lot of data very quickly.

The business advantages of this are clear: larger, more interactive pages can be delivered with less latency than if you didn't use a CDN.

# Serving Dynamic Content

The technology behind serving static content is fairly straightforward. CDNs build dozens or even hundreds of data centers and serve up static content from web servers in their data centers under their own domain (e.g., *http://www.website.com/images*) or a subdomain of yours (e.g., *http://images.website.com*). It used to be that images had to be served from *http://customer.cdn-vendor.com*. Content is accelerated primarily because it's so close to customers.

To move beyond static content delivery, CDN's can act as a proxy in front of your entire website. This approach requires your DNS record to point to the CDN vendor and have all traffic pass through the CDN (Figure 7-5).

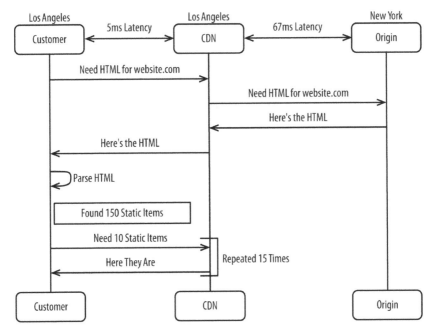

*Figure 7-5. Content Delivery Network as a reverse proxy*

With this approach, your DNS record actually points to your CDN vendor. Requests for *http://www.website.com* go *through* your CDN. The benefits of this are enormous to performance and security. Let's explore the different things this enables in the following sections.

## Caching Entire Pages

The vast majority of HTTP requests are for static content. Of the average 151 HTTP requests involved to render a page for the first time, the first HTTP request is for the HTML of the page. Until the web browser loads and parses that HTML, none of the other 150 subsequent HTTP requests are made. In other words, it is on the critical path. The requests for HTML need not always get passed back to the origin, because most of the time the HTML is always the same for a given set of input parameters. For example, HTTP requests made by anonymous customers for a home page (e.g., *http://www.website.com*) are likely to return the exact same HTML unless you employ some advanced targeting based on a user's geography.

The vast majority of traffic to an ecommerce platform is cacheable because of what's known as the *ecommerce traffic funnel*, as shown in Figure 7-6.

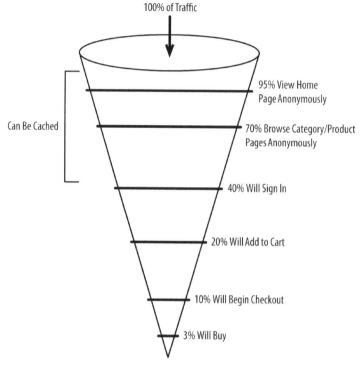

100% of Traffic

Can Be Cached

95% View Home Page Anonymously

70% Browse Category/Product Pages Anonymously

40% Will Sign In

20% Will Add to Cart

10% Will Begin Checkout

3% Will Buy

*Figure 7-6. ecommerce traffic funnel*

This doesn't even include traffic from nonhuman bots, which now accounts for 48% of all web traffic.[3] All responses to bots can be served directly from a CDN. The remaining HTTP requests depicted in this funnel are from anonymous customers for the home page, category pages, product pages, and so forth. Again, most of those pages can be served from a CDN too. Only a relatively small fraction of total traffic is from real customers who are actually logged in. An even smaller percentage of customers actually buy anything.

Many customers visit websites with persistent login cookies. Websites welcome back customers by saying, "Welcome Back, [First Name]!" or something similar. If the personalization isn't too substantial, you can simply cache the entire HTML page on the CDN but make an AJAX callback to your origin to populate it with dynamic content, like the customer's name. Code-wise, it would look something like this:

---

3 "The Internet Is for Humans, Not Robots," The Atlantic (2015), *http://theatln.tc/1NH3XDp*.

```
<head>
    <script src="/app/jquery/jquery.min.js"></script>
    <script>
        $.ajax({url:"/app/RetrieveWelcomeMessage",success:function(result){
            // retrieves "Welcome Back, Kelly!"
            $("#WelcomeMessage").html(result);
        }});
    </script>
</head>
<body>
    <h2><div id="WelcomeMessage">Please Log In</div></h2>
    ... rest of web page
</body>
```

You can repeat this for other dynamic areas on your web page, like the "You Might Also Like" section or the main image on the home page. You could also make just one callback to your origin, with a single JSON or XML response containing all of the data required to properly personalize the page.

The advantage of this approach is that it removes loading the first HTML page from the critical path (as AJAX requests are asynchronous), yet you can still employ limited personalization. Customers get fast performance, and your origin is barely touched. It's a great approach that's discussed further in Chapter 11.

A slight variation is to cache different versions of each page in a CDN. CDNs are all capable of looking more deeply into the HTTP request at fields such as your source IP address, user agent, URL parameters, and cookies. This information can then be used by CDNs to discover facts like these:

- Whether the customer is logged in
- Web browser/user agent
- Physical location (sometimes accurate to zip + 4 within the US or post code outside the US)
- Internet connection speed
- Locale
- Operating system
- Screen dimensions
- Flash support
- Capabilities supported by each device

If you have variations of your pages based on these attributes, you can just store each variation in a CDN and have it pull the right version of the page for each customer. For example, a retailer selling online internationally could have country-specific versions of each home page, with each locale having its own copy. That would save dozens, if not hundreds, of milliseconds in just latency while allowing for the pages to be heavier and more dynamic.

Even many search result pages can now be cached. For large eCommerce platforms, 20% of search terms account for 80% of the traffic. So long as you can pull out the search parameters and put them in the URL, you can cache the pages. Search result pages require URLs like *search.jsp?query=shirt&size=xl&onsale=true*. This trick can result in even more of your platform being served directly from a CDN.

## Pre-fetching Static Content

Some pages just cannot be statically cached. For example, checkout pages are inherently dynamic and cannot be easily cached. When used as a reverse proxy, CDNs can speed up the delivery of the static content for all pages. Around 150 of an average of 151 HTTP requests to initially load a page are for static content.

Because the HTTP response passes back through the CDN on its return to your customers, the CDN can parse the HTML and proactively make concurrent HTTP requests to the origin for the static content it doesn't already have. CDNs have dozens or even hundreds of data centers, and each data center generally maintains its own autonomous cache. A CDN can make all of the HTTP requests concurrently over a lightning-fast network, whereas your web browser has to make HTTP requests in batches of 10 over a slow "last mile" network before it even hits the CDN's optimized network, see Figure 7-7.

Pre-fetching is wise to use and can yield substantial benefits.

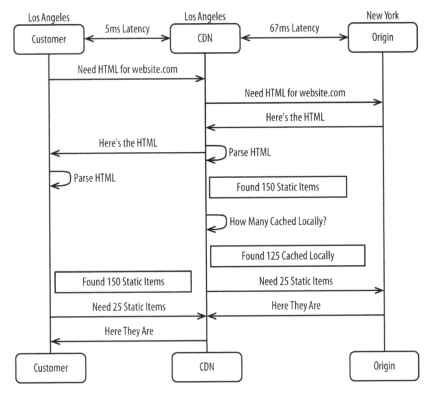

*Figure 7-7. Retrieving a web page through a CDN with pre-fetching*

## Security

CDNs are able to provide exceptional security by basically erasing your origin data center(s) from the Internet. To get to your origin, everybody must first go through the CDN. That alone provides enormous value by reducing your attack profile. *Defense in depth*, or adding security in layers, is an excellent defense against attacks. CDNs have a few tricks that they are able to employ to keep you secure.

Distributed denial-of-service attacks, whereby attackers flood your origin with traffic in an attempt to knock you offline, are a big problem. In addition to special techniques to prevent and stop distributed denial-of-service attacks, CDNs have many thousands of physical servers across dozens or even hundreds of data centers that can soak up traffic from an attack. For example, this can be helpful for US-based eCommerce vendors, as many attacks originate from Asia. The CDN's servers in Asia soak up the traffic from the attack, leaving the US servers and origin to continue serving traffic to the US and other customers around the world as normal. Also, attacks tend to target one website at a time, leaving the excess capacity in a CDN available to handle the onslaught of traffic from an attack. CloudFlare famously handled 118 gigabits of data per second,[4] despite being a fairly small CDN relative to its competitors.

Most ecommerce platforms have some form of distributed denial-of-service attack mitigation in place, whether from a dedicated Software-as-a-Service vendor or a CDN.

It is exceptionally rare these days that attackers are able to gain root access to your operating system. Use of CDNs and other intermediaries, coupled with strong firewalls, has largely prevented those attacks. Attacks like SQL injection (forcing the database to execute your own arbitrary SQL), cross-site scripting (which allows sessions and the permissions tied to them to be stolen), and code injection (executing your own arbitrary code) are far more likely. For example, SQL injection is a common vulnerability:

```
<%
  String userId = request.getParameter("userId");
  String query = "SELECT * FROM user where userId=" + userId + "'";
  Statement st = conn.createStatement();
  ResultSet res = st.executeQuery(query);
%>
```

Setting `userId` to 12345 or 1=1 by executing the URL *&productId=12345'%20or %20'1%3D1* will lead to an application printing the details of every single user in the database without explicitly compromising any systems.

Many CDNs have full web application firewalls in place to inspect the HTML and evaluate it for vulnerabilities. For example, any parameter with a value of *select%20\* %20from%20credit_card* (select * from *credit_card*) should never be allowed to be passed back to the application.

When you operate a large-scale ecommerce platform, you'll find that certain bots can wreak havoc by requesting too many pages too quickly. Since most bots don't understand HTTP sessions, they'll end up creating a new HTTP session for each page view. Most CDNs allow you to blacklist by IP, user agent, subnet, and so forth.

Many CDNs also offer full compliance with common security frameworks such as FedRAMP,[5] PCI DSS,[6] HIPAA,[7] and ISO.[8] Compliance with these frameworks helps to demonstrate that these vendors can be trusted with your most sensitive data.

---

4 Matthew Prince, "The DDoS That Knocked Spamhaus Offline (And How We Mitigated It)," CloudFlare (20 March 2013), *http://bit.ly/1gAdrNp*.

5 US General Services Administration, "About FedRAMP," *http://www.gsa.gov/portal/category/102375*.

6 PCI Security Standards Council, *https://www.pcisecuritystandards.org*.

7 US Department of Health & Human Services, "Health Information Privacy," *http://www.hhs.gov/ocr/privacy/*.

8 ISO/IEC 27001—Information Security Management, *http://bit.ly/1gAdt7W*.

Security will be discussed in detail in Chapter 9.

# Additional CDN Offerings

In addition to performance and security, CDNs offer many ancillary services such as DNS and storage. CDNs are strategically placed by having a large footprint of servers around the world plugged directly into backbone networks. From that vantage point, it's easy to push other add-ons to the edge, using the considerable infrastructure they have in place.

## Frontend Optimization

The frontend code of most ecommerce websites is very poorly written. Individual developers are working on their own small page fragments, often with nobody looking at the big picture. By the time anybody cares about performance, it's usually too late to go back and fix things. Many CDNs now offer HTML rewriting (see Figure 7-8), whereby they will dynamically rewrite your HTML at the edge for each specific customer based on factors such as device type, resolution, web browser, and connection speed.

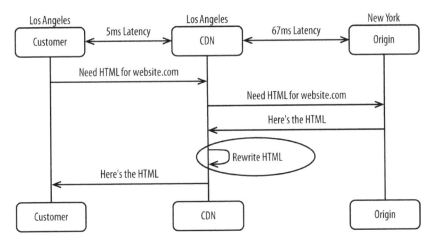

*Figure 7-8. HTML optimization performed by the CDN*

Optimizations can include the following:

- Reducing the number of HTTP requests by clubbing together CSS and Java-Script, and by inlining
- Pushing commonly referenced static items down to the web browser before the HTTP request is even made to the CDN
- Making browser-specific optimizations

- Deferring the loading of third-party JavaScript beacons (e.g., analytics and ads) until after the page has fully rendered

- Using just-in-time or on-demand image loading, which loads images as the customer scrolls

- Retrieving images from multiple subdomains to allow the web browser to download more in parallel

- DNS pre-fetching

- Reducing whitespace

- Resizing images

- Using compression

- Rewriting HTML to leverage browser-specific features

If you're unable to perform these optimizations on your own, it is highly recommended that you use these services.

## DNS/GSLB

DNS is an area that CDNs have invested heavily in, both in standard DNS hosting and more-advanced Global Server Load Balancing (GSLB). We'll discuss DNS and GSLB extensively in Chapter 10. DNS is something no ecommerce vendor should host themselves. Disadvantages of self hosting include the following:

- Cost to properly build and maintain DNS

- Challenge of deploying DNS across multiple data centers or multiple networks

- Security concerns

    — DNS is often targeted for exploits.

    — DNS can be brought down with distributed denial-of-service attacks.

    — DNS can be tricked into flooding a distributed denial-of-service attack victim with traffic.

- Latency involved, with customers querying DNS servers

Properly hosted DNS solutions, whether in a CDN or not, are able to overcome these challenges primarily through their ability to focus. Vendors who sell this service are able to hire the best experts in the world, use the best technology, and employ the best security techniques. The marginal cost of a new consumer of their service is very low, allowing them to make money while saving you money.

CDNs offer the ability to respond to DNS queries from the edge, likely just a few milliseconds away from each customer, as shown in Figure 7-9.

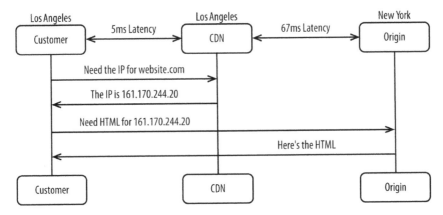

*Figure 7-9. DNS resolution with a CDN*

With traditional DNS, you may have to go cross-country or even transcontinental to retrieve an IP address (see Figure 7-10).

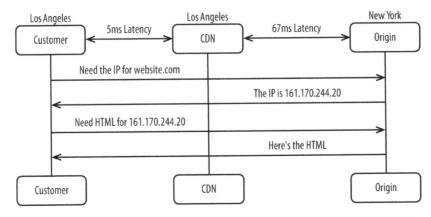

*Figure 7-10. DNS resolution without a CDN*

DNS is much more complicated than this, but as you can see, serving DNS from the edge has advantages.

In addition to mapping domain names back to IP addresses, DNS can also be used to assign customers to data centers. Each data center you're running an ecommerce platform out of generally presents one IP address to the world. If you're running out of multiple data centers, you need a way of deciding which data center each customer should be assigned to. This is called *Global Server Load Balancing* (GSLB) and it's effectively enhanced DNS.

GSLB works by constantly redirecting customers to the right data center by a combination of factors, including availability, data center capacity/utilization, arbitrary weights, and real-time performance. Again, we'll discuss GSLB and DNS in more detail in Chapter 10.

CDNs have a fairly unique advantage over traditional DNS hosting vendors, as they are able to accurately map the real-time performance of the Internet and because they have so many servers connected to so many different networks around the world. It is often the case that the fastest route between any two points is not the shortest distance-wise. Network capacity, speed, congestion, hops, and interference by governments all play a role in reducing network throughput and latency. Another advantage CDNs have is they're able to monitor the actual time it's taking each data center to respond to HTTP requests, because they're often serving as proxies.

## Throttling

Prior to cloud computing, each platform had a fixed amount of capacity it could handle without breaking. For example, if you deployed 500 servers and each server got you 10,000 concurrent customers, you knew you couldn't handle more than 5,000,000 concurrent customers. There was no use in letting anybody access your origin if you know that it won't work. CDNs offer the ability to throttle so that the 5,000,001st customer would get directed to a virtual waiting room. At a minimum, these waiting rooms offer helpful messages about the situation, including estimates as to when the site will be accessible again. Waiting rooms can also have games or even full catalogs so customers can begin shopping and then finish after your website comes back online again. Employing throttling protects your origin from overuse while keeping your customers happier than if they simply received an error message.

Traditional hardware load balancers also offer throttling, but there are two disadvantages. The first is that load balancers themselves can be overwhelmed. Like any physical system, they have their limits. It's also connected to networks and other physical infrastructure that itself can be overwhelmed. The second disadvantage is that traditional load balancers must direct overflow traffic to a waiting room page. If that page is within the same data center that's overwhelmed, there's a good chance the waiting room itself won't work. CDNs themselves can serve content directly from the edge, regardless of what's happening in your data center(s).

There may be some software that cannot scale past a certain point or software that cannot be deployed in a cloud and therefore has a fixed capacity of hardware behind it. No platform scales infinitely. For these reasons, even with the elasticity that a cloud brings, it is advised that you throttle.

# Summary

In this chapter, we discussed the multifaceted role CDNs play in today's Internet and how they can be beneficial to eCommerce. In the next part of the book, we'll focus on how to actually adopt the cloud, beginning with its architecture.

# PART III
# To the Cloud!

# CHAPTER 8

# Architecture Principles for the Cloud

Cloud computing *shouldn't* be all that challenging to adopt, provided that your organization is competent, willing to make changes, and has the resources to do it. If you've already embraced the principles found in the first two parts of this book, it shows you're both competent and willing to make changes and should therefore have few problems embracing cloud computing. More fully adopting cloud computing is an enormous undertaking, but one that can be fairly painless when done properly.

The problem with more fully using cloud computing is that it greatly exacerbates both organizational and technical deficiencies. If you're already struggling with keeping your platform up today, a cloud is almost certain to make your problems worse. On the other hand, a cloud can be equally transformational in the right hands. Cloud computing is powerful, and those who master it will have a competitive advantage for years to come.

In this chapter, we'll discuss how ecommerce is unique from an architecture standpoint, followed by how to architect ecommerce for the cloud. Extra attention will be focused on what scalability is and how to achieve it. Subsequent chapters in this part of the book will discuss how to actually adopt various forms of cloud computing.

## Why Is eCommerce Unique?

Let's explore a few of the ways ecommerce is so unique. These reasons are why eCommerce platforms are architected and deployed different than most other systems.

### Revenue Generation

With the rise in omnichannel retailing, most revenue now flows through an organization's ecommerce platform. A platform-wide outage will prevent an entire organization from taking in revenue. It's the equivalent of barring customers from entering all physical retail stores. Many organizations are now able to accurately calculate how much each second of downtime costs them in lost revenue. However, the real long-term cost of an outage is the damage caused to brand reputation. Many customers won't come back after an outage.

It is because of how important ecommerce is that most environments are wildly over-provisioned.

## Visibility

High visibility characterizes most ecommerce platforms, often serving as the public face and increasingly the back office of an organization. Every HTTP request is a reflection on that brand, just as much as the physical condition of a retail store is. Every millisecond in delayed response time reflects more poorly on that brand. A 100-millisecond response will delight customers and make a brand shine, whereas a 10-second response will upset customers and tarnish a brand.

## Traffic Spikiness

A defining feature of ecommerce is that it's subject to often unpredictable spikes in traffic that are one or two orders of magnitude larger than steady state. Most software simply wasn't built to handle enormous spikes in traffic. For example, database connection pools in application servers often cannot double or triple the size of a given connection pool instantaneously. Software was architected for a world in which it was statically deployed, with workloads being fairly steady. In today's world, capacity can be provisioned and immediately slammed with a full load of traffic. Software that is architected well is often able to handle these spikes in traffic, but not always.

## Security

Everybody is rightly concerned about security. Organizations are often liable for breaches, with even small breaches costing tens of millions of dollars, not to mention the negative publicity and loss in confidence by customers. Breaches tend to be far-reaching, with all data under management exposed. It's rare that only a subset of customer information is compromised. The introduction of cloud computing, depending on how it's used, can mean more data is more often transferred over untrusted networks and processed on shared hardware, further adding to the complexity of securing that data. We'll discuss this all further in Chapter 9.

## Statefulness

HTTP requests can be separated into two classes: those that require state and those that do not require state. State is typically represented as an HTTP session. It's a temporary storage area that's unique to a given customer and durable across HTTP requests. Shopping carts, for example, are typically stored in an HTTP session. Authentication status is also persisted for the duration of a session. The HTTP protocol is stateless by definition, but state is added on top by application servers and clients to make basic ecommerce function.

HTTP requests from anonymous customers for static non-transactional pages (e.g., home page, product detail page) generally don't require state. State generally begins when you log in or add to a cart, as Figure 8-1 shows.

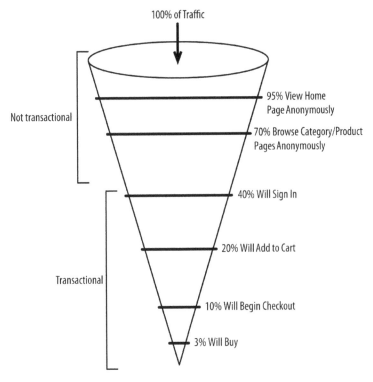

*Figure 8-1. ecommerce traffic funnel*

The challenge with ecommerce is that customers often browse anonymously for an extended period of time before they identify themselves by logging in. Most large websites force you to log in immediately (e.g., social media, email, online banking) or not at all (news, search engines, Wikipedia). When you log in to an ecommerce website, you have to merge everything that happened throughout the session with the data that's been persisted about the customer. For example, personalization may be employed to trigger a discount on all Nike shoes after viewing 10 Nike shoes and not purchasing anything. An anonymous customer who has viewed eight pairs of Nike shoes would not trigger the discount. But what happens when that anonymous user logs in to an account that has already registered four Nike page views? The promotion would then be triggered after the anonymous customer profile and logged-in customer profile have been successfully merged.

We'll discuss this more in Chapter 10, but another issue is the problem of multiple concurrent logins for the same account. What happens if a husband and wife are both logged in to the same account, making changes to the same order and customer profile in the database at the same time? With one data center, this isn't a problem, because you're sharing one logical database. But what happens when you're using public Infrastructure-as-a-Service for hosting, and you span your ecommerce platform across two data centers with each data center having its own database?

Maintaining state across HTTP requests most often means that a given customer must be redirected to the same data center, load balancer, web server (if used), and application server instances. Maintaining this stickiness requires extra attention that many other applications don't have to deal with.

# What Is Scalability?

Strictly speaking, scalability is the ability of a system to increase its output (for example, concurrent users supported or HTTP requests per second) by adding more inputs (for example, an additional server). To be *perfectly scalable*, your inputs must always equal your outputs in the same proportion. For example, if your first server delivers you 200 page views per second, your 1,000th server should deliver you 200 page views per second as well. If your first server delivers 200 page views per second and your 1,000th server delivers 20 page views per second, your system has a scalability problem.

All layers of the stack must be equally scalable, from DNS down to storage. We will discuss two forms of scalability: scaling up (vertical) and scaling out (horizontal).

## Throughput

*Throughput* refers to the amount of work or capacity that a unit of input (e.g., server, cache grid node, database node) or an entire system can support. Common examples of metrics used to represent throughput include the following:

- Page views per second
- Transactions per second
- Concurrent customers

Don't confuse throughput with overall system-wide scalability, as the two are independent of each other. The throughput of an individual unit of input (e.g., an application server) may be low, but so long as you can continually get the same level of marginal output (e.g., page views per second) as you increase the number of inputs, your system is scalable.

# Scaling Up

*Scaling up*, otherwise known as *vertical scalability*, is increasing the output (e.g., page views per second) of a fixed unit of input (e.g., an application server running on 8 cores). When you have increased an application server's output from 200 page views per second to 250 page views per second, you have scaled up that resource. Scaling up (Figure 8-2) can be performed by optimizing (caching more, making code more efficient, and so forth) or adding more physical resources (e.g., going from 8 vCPUs to 12). This is in contrast to scaling out, where the page views per second would be increased by adding another application server instance.

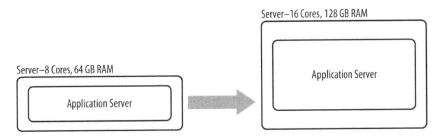

*Figure 8-2. Scaling up*

No software is truly infinitely scalable. At some point, you start to get diminishing returns. For example, Apache historically hasn't scaled well beyond more than a handful of physical cores. You would get more total throughput by running four instances of Apache on a single 32 CPU core server than you would if you ran one instance of Apache on that same server. Some software must be scaled up because of constraints in its architecture. Often times, old backend systems don't scale out very well because they were designed for an era where CPUs had only one core. Multicore CPUs are a fairly modern invention.

## Case Study: The C10K Problem

In 2003, a developer named Dan Kegel published a web page stating that modern web servers should be able to handle 10,000 concurrent clients.[1] He termed the problem *C10K*, where *C* means connections and *10K* means 10,000. His astute observation was that hardware had made great advances over the previous few years but that the ability of a web server to scale up and use that hardware had not changed. At the time, many web servers were able to support only 1,000. Dan and subsequent work proved that 10,000 concurrent connections could be sustained with changes to the operating system and web server software.

A decade later, in 2013, Robert Graham showed that modern servers could support 10 million concurrent clients.[2] Again, the solution was software.

These two initiatives showed that the bottleneck to vertical scalability was mostly software. Hardware matters, but not nearly as much as good software does.

## Scaling Out

*Scaling out*, otherwise known as *horizontal scalability*, is increasing output (e.g., page views per second) of a system by adding more inputs (e.g., more application servers running on more hardware). An example of scaling out a resource is adding a server, as opposed to increasing the memory or processing power of an existing server (see Figure 8-3).

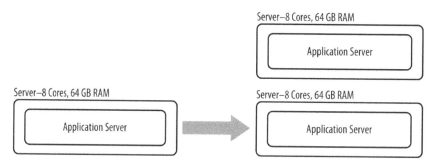

*Figure 8-3. Scaling out*

If the marginal input (e.g., an additional server) equals the marginal output (e.g., page views per second), you have a perfectly scalable system. If additional units of input

---

1  Dan Kegel, "The C10K Problem," (5 February 2014), *http://www.kegel.com/c10k.html*.

2  Robert Graham, "C10M," *http://c10m.robertgraham.com*

(e.g., physical servers) equal fewer and fewer units of output (e.g., page views per second), the system isn't scalable. Figure 8-4 applies equally to both individual units as well as the entire system.

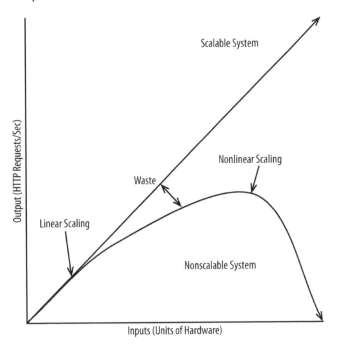

Figure 8-4. Linear versus nonlinear scaling

# Rules for Scaling

While scaling out is an absolute necessity, scaling up is important too. The more you scale up, the less you have to scale out and the lower your marginal costs. You can avoid a whole class of problems by better architecting your system to drive more throughput out of each server. Modern commodity x86 servers can handle 10 *million* concurrent HTTP connections due to the lockless event loop-based architectures favored by newer web servers/load balancers like nginx and Node.js. Apache is now able to support more than a few thousand concurrent HTTP requests on a single commodity server, but that's largely due to hardware advancements and some tuning. The massive increase in throughput of these newer web servers is purely a function of their better architecture.

Scaling software comes down to two principles. The first is to allow each system to do the work it needs to do with as few impediments as possible. Calls to remote systems are fine, provided they don't block. Threads that are blocked kill both throughput and performance. Avoiding threads where possible eliminates the problem of blocking threads. A second and even more potent barrier to scalability is the human side of technology. Hiring the right people will pay dividends for decades to come and could make the difference between your company's success or failure. Individual people are only vertically scalable to a certain point. Scaling out and scaling up of your staff is required for success.

The following section will discuss each of the following principles:

- Convert synchronous to asynchronous
- Reduce locking
- Simplify
- Remove state
- Cache intelligently
- Hire the right people
- Plan, plan, plan
- Size properly
- Use the right technology

For more information on this topic, read *The Art of Scalability* by Martin L. Abbott and Michael T. Fisher (Addison-Wesley Professional).

# Technical Rules

### Convert synchronous to asynchronous

In synchronous processing, the execution of one task (e.g., an application server generating an HTTP response) is dependent upon the execution of one or more other tasks (e.g., querying a database). A common example of this is an email confirmation being sent synchronously following an order submission. Assuming transactions are being properly used, the successful placing of an order is entirely dependent upon something as frivolous as an SMTP server's availability and performance. With proper decoupling of these two systems, an order would be placed as normal, but instead of synchronously sending the message, it would be dumped in a queue and delivered asynchronously to an available SMTP server.

Synchronous calls to any system put it in the critical path, making the entire system's scalability dependent upon the least scalable resource. For example, your order management system may struggle to handle traffic from your busiest days of the year. If you're connecting synchronously to your order management system, the scalability of your *entire* platform will be dependent upon the scalability of that one system. In an omnichannel world, where all channels use the same backend systems, some of your systems will not be able to scale. Any activity that's not directly tied to generating revenue or doesn't require an instantaneous response should be performed asynchronously so it doesn't interfere with generating revenue.

---

## Case Study: Node.js

Traditional web and application servers work on the concept of threads, whereby a single HTTP request will tie up a single thread until the response is fully generated. Everything is executed synchronously. With a traditional web and application server combination, this means each web server thread waits for the application server's response and each application server's thread waits for responses from various databases, cache grids, third-party systems, and so forth. Threads spend a lot of time blocked, waiting to do something. Threads are expensive, as each one requires dedicated memory. This model was built for a world in which customers passively downloaded static web pages.

Node.js is a JavaScript-based framework that serves as both the web server and client-side development framework. The two work together to offer full bidirectional communication between the web server and client, along with an asynchronous execution model that eschews threads. By not using threads, each instance of Node.js can support a million or more concurrent connections. The way it works is that HTTP requests come in and, as backend systems each do their work (e.g., an inventory lookup, a request to load product details via an HTTP request with a REST response), the response is incrementally pushed to the client. This allows the web browser to begin rendering the response in parallel while the response is actually being generated.

---

In any platform, but especially in a cloud, databases can serve as a bottleneck. Databases tend to be heavily used in ecommerce because applications are so stateful. Outside the cloud, databases are deployed to dedicated hardware backed by high-grade storage with high-speed networking gear connecting the components of the system. In a public Infrastructure-as-a-Service cloud, you have very little control over your environment. You can't optimally tune much outside the operating system and you're dealing with hardware and networks that are shared by many tenants. While cloud vendors do take great precautions to isolate traffic, it's never perfect. To prevent databases from being the bottleneck, you can use a write-back cache for all or a subset of your writes. This means that your application uses a cache as the system of record, with the cache reading and writing back to the database asynchronously (see Figure 8-5).

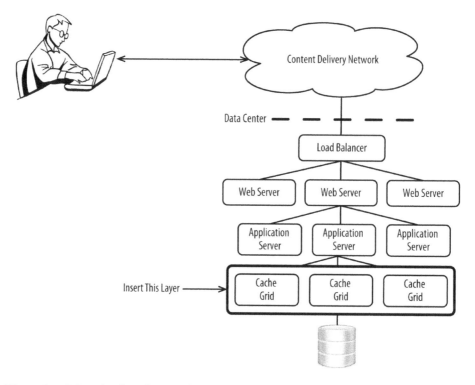

*Figure 8-5. Write-back cache to reduce database load*

Figure 8-6 shows a sequence diagram.

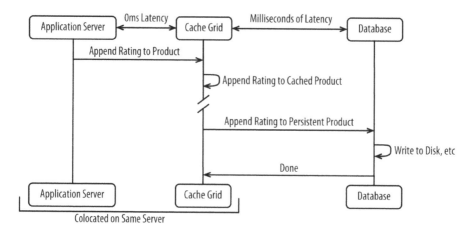

*Figure 8-6. Generating a response with a write-back cache*

This can allow your system to scale up and out while improving the performance. To customers, the write happens instantaneously to local cache, which allows the response to be generated instantaneously. While this may not be suitable for something important like inventory, it is perfectly suitable for things like product reviews, customer profile updates, cart updates—anything where the source system being out-of-date by a few milliseconds doesn't matter. We'll discuss some options for running your database in a cloud in Chapter 11.

The most scalable platforms have completely decoupled their frontends from backends. All calls from the frontend to the backend are asynchronous, with queueing introduced to allow the backend to disappear for periods of time. With the backend down, the frontend continues to accept revenue.

### Reduce locking

By definition, work (e.g., HTTP requests) in an ecommerce platform is executed concurrently across multiple threads. These can be threads in a managed runtime environment, threads in a database, or threads in a cache grid. Web servers and load balancers typically don't lock very much and they are increasingly moving away from threading, so there aren't issues there.

There are objects that need to be updated by a large number of threads simultaneously. A great example of this is when millions of people are trying to buy the latest smartphone the minute it is available for sale. Inventory across an entire platform typically comes down to updating one record in a centralized cache grid, in a database row, and so forth. Without proper concurrency, your database and application server threads can end up waiting too long to update, causing a cascading lockup across your entire platform. This is a common cause of outages.

Blocking can also occur within a single process, inhibiting its ability to scale up. Your application may have a few common *hot* objects that are locked by each request-handling thread. When you have too many threads, each thread has to wait longer to lock, and eventually it becomes too long, and you can't scale up anymore. Blocking can be a quick way to limit your ability to scale out and up. It should therefore be avoided at all cost.

You can largely eliminate locking by using some common sense when architecting your system. Let's go back to the inventory example. With a traditional database-backed cache, each update of the inventory requires what's shown in Figure 8-7.

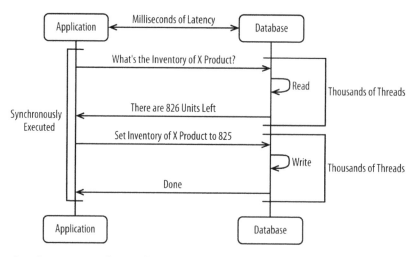

*Figure 8-7. Steps required to update inventory*

Rather than reading the inventory all the time, you can set *low-inventory* flags or allot a batch of inventory to each instance if there's a lot of inventory available. For updating inventory, you can instead make simple increment and decrement calls to a cache grid or similar in-memory system that uses a lockless data structure. The call could be as simple as this:

```
http://www.website.com/InventoryUpdate?productId=X&value=-1&securityToken=ABC123
```

You could even execute the call asynchronously if you know you have enough inventory to last for a while.

By simply telling your inventory management system to increment or decrement, you avoid having to read the object, set its value, and wait for the database to commit it to disk. It's just much faster.

Every programming language has the concept of lockless data structures. Internally, these data structures may use more-efficient nonblocking OS-level techniques, like compare and swap. Using these data structures greatly reduces thread contention within a single process and allows for much greater scaling up.

## Simplify

Your architecture should be as simple as possible. Simplicity begets scalability. This covers a wide range of topics, including these:

*Removing tiers from your platform*
    Removing web servers.

*Simplifying configuration*
> Changing IP addresses to hostnames, removing hostnames entirely, eliminating singletons, and so forth.

*Removing unnecessary wrappers/envelopes*
> Switching from SOAP to SOA, not using SSL/TLS when it is not truly necessary, and so forth.

*Building discrete interfaces between your systems*
> This allows you to decouple your systems better. Discrete interfaces can be written to and from a service bus and similar technologies.

Simplification must be built in from the beginning. It's very hard to go back to simplify old code. Build it properly from the start by hiring the right people and making simplicity a top goal.

## Remove state from individual servers

As mentioned earlier in this chapter, state is a temporary storage area that's unique to a given customer and durable across HTTP requests. Shopping carts, authentication status, promotions, and so on all depend on state. State is always going to be a fixture given the nature of ecommerce.

Maintaining state across HTTP requests most often means that a given customer must be redirected to the same data center, load balancer, web server (if used), and application server instance. When you're rapidly adding and removing servers in a cloud through auto-scaling, you can't always guarantee that a given server is going to be available. Servers in a cloud are by nature ephemeral. Forcing a customer to log in again because the state was lost after a server was de-provisioned is not acceptable.

> Servers in a cloud are by nature ephemeral. Don't store state in them.

State has substantial technical implications for a few reasons:

- State can be heavy, typically in terms of memory utilization. Nothing kills your ability to scale up like having 1 MB sessions.

- Maintaining state for ecommerce requires that it be persisted on the server side and made available to any application server that requests it. Again, servers can quickly go up and down. If you de-provision a server, the customer shouldn't know.

- States must be merged. As discussed earlier in the chapter, customers browse anonymously, all the while accumulating state. When the customer logs in, that session state must be merged with the persistent state that is durable across HTTP sessions.

To minimize the harmful effects of state, keep the following rules in mind:

- State should be as light as possible—a few kilobytes at most. Anything not important should be left out.

- State should be relegated to as few systems as possible. While it makes sense for your application server to care about state, your application's call to a standalone inventory management service should probably be stateless. Go through every remote call you're making and confirm whether state is truly required.

- State should be avoided unless it is necessary. For example, search engine bots crawling your website have no concept of sessions and will create a brand new HTTP session with every page view. Either prevent the HTTP session from being created in the first place or consider invalidating HTTP sessions created by search engine bots (which can be identified by user-agent string) after each HTTP request. Likewise, anonymous customers pulling up the home page probably don't need a session either.

The big question is where state should be stored. Traditionally, application servers have been responsible for HTTP session lifecycle management. Applications deployed to the application servers add data to the session. Then you may choose to replicate the HTTP session or not. Replication can be entirely in-memory, through a database, through a cache grid, or by almost any other means of moving around data between processes.

To mitigate the overhead of maintaining state on the server side, it would be natural to push it to the client (e.g., web browser, mobile application), as is common with many other workloads. This is frequently accomplished with web browsers through the use of cookies or HTML 5. But in an omnichannel world, that doesn't work well because you're using so many different channels, each requiring client and version-specific means to represent state. Because HTTP is stateless by definition, it's up to each client to implement state. For example, web browsers use cookies, whereas Android applications use a Java-based API with a native persistence mechanism. Some clients don't even support the ability to persist data between HTTP requests. Because of the variety of clients and their ever-changing APIs, it's best to let the application server continue to manage state. Don't assume clients even support something as rudimentary as cookies.

Applications and application servers should be configured to persist state to a distributed system, like a NoSQL database or cache grid. You can then serve an HTTP request out of any server with access to the NoSQL database or cache grid.

## Cache as much as possible, as close to the client as possible

Caching is exceptionally important for ecommerce because customers demand the absolute best available performance. At the same time, caching can save enormous computing resources by making it possible to scale up individual servers much further than would otherwise be possible. The value offered by the multibillion-dollar Content Delivery Network (CDN) industry over the past decade has been almost exclusively their ability to cache content.

The rule with caching is that it's best to cache as much as possible, as close to the end-customer as possible. The closer you cache, the less each intermediary system between the customer and the source system actually generating the content has to work. Figure 8-8 shows a list of what you can cache where.

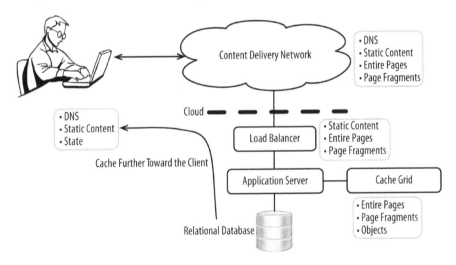

*Figure 8-8. Cache as much as possible, as close to the end customer as possible*

If you have a proper architecture in place, your system's bottleneck should be on the CPUs running the application server. Memory, storage, networking, and other layers formerly were the bottlenecks, but now it tends to be the CPUs running the application server. Executing the code to generate pages is what consumes most of the CPU. Most pages are constructed using fragments, as shown in Figure 8-9.

*Figure 8-9. Cacheable static page fragments*

While an entire page may have too much content to be cacheable in an intermediary layer, individual page fragments themselves are dynamic. For example, this entire fragment shown in Figure 8-10 is unlikely to change.

*Figure 8-10. Navigation bar*

Rather than constantly executing code to generate a page fragment that you know will never change, you can instead cache the execution of that fragment, passing in variables. Most web frameworks have the ability to cache fragment includes, with input parameters being cache keys.

To cache a fragment, you would take the equivalent of:

```
<jsp:include page="/menu_bar.jsp" />
```

and convert it to:

```
<jsp:include page="/menu_bar.jsp">
    <jsp:param name="anonymous" value="false" />
    <jsp:param name="user_segment" value="bay_area_male_engineer" />
    <jsp:param name="locale" value="us_EN" />
</jsp:include>
```

With the `anonymous`, `user_segment`, and `locale` parameters forming a key, you can simply create copies of each combination and cache the HTML. It is easier to include a pre-cached block of HTML than execute the thousands of lines of code that go into generating HTML from source. Fragments should be cached wherever possible.

Caching is one of the most fundamental principles in computer science and should be used liberally.

### Use the right technology

Technology is an incredibly fashion-driven industry, with decisions on which technology to use often driven by what's fashionable instead of what's pragmatic. People confuse using new, unproven technology with innovation, when the two are almost entirely unrelated. Innovation should come from how you use technologies to achieve business objectives as opposed to the technologies themselves. While new technology has its place, you should always balance the marginal benefits a new technology provides with the following characteristics of more-established options:

- Maturity
- Availability of skills in the market
- Support
- Ongoing maintenance
- How well it can be monitored

For example, using a new programming language may allow you to write 10% less code, but if you can't find an IDE or developers, is the 10% really worth it? Probably not. Yet decisions like this are made all the time, often due to the "it won't scale" excuse. But scalability is far more about how you use the technology than about the technology itself.

It's generally best to outsource or use well-established technology for any part of your system that you don't do faster/better/cheaper than your competitors. This principle is exactly why ecommerce should be deployed to a cloud. Innovate on the implementation and/or development of your ecommerce application. Build beautiful and functional user interfaces. Tie in with physical stores by providing functionality such as real-time, store-level inventory, and pricing. Support a wide range of clients. Make it fast and highly available. Leave the development of the building blocks (e.g., hardware, software, services) to technology vendors or the open source community.

Make sure you have a process in place to evaluate the technology that's selected. Individuals selecting technology may not have a view of the overall cost of using a given technology. Spend time delivering on your core competency—not in building commoditized components.

# Nontechnical Rules

### Hire the right people

Broadly, you need architects and developers to deliver a high-quality platform. Of course, there are many more supporting roles involved, but you need people to design (architects) and you need people to implement (developers).

Architects are responsible for the design of your entire system, from how and where the code is deployed, all the way down to method-level design. Architecture has changed over the past two decades, from designing systems from scratch to leveraging building blocks. Building blocks today are cloud services (Software-as-a-Service, Platform-as-a-Service, Infrastructure-as-a-Service), web development frameworks, and software products such as cache grids. Very few of these building blocks existed even a decade ago. You had to build everything you wanted by hand. Architects now have many more options available—which is good if you know what you're doing, but bad if you don't. The job has shifted more from the *how* to the *what*. It's a fundamental change—one that requires hiring a few very high-skilled architects, as opposed to a large number of average or below-average architects. You just don't need that many people today.

The entire ecosystem that developers work within has substantially matured over the past decade. Programming languages, web development frameworks, tooling, and runtimes all have the effect of allowing developers to write less code, with higher quality, in less time than ever before. One good developer now has the productivity of 10 or more average developers.[3] With modern tooling, a good developer may be even more productive than that. Modern developers just don't write all that much low-level code. Those "reverse a linked list on a white board" interview questions are useless at best, as a good developer should simply call a method to do the sorting. Most developers today should be writing *glue code*, which amounts more to leveraging web development frameworks and using prebuilt libraries than writing a lot of code from scratch. Code that's written must be commented, unit tested, QA tested, performance tested, and maintained. All of that costs time and money. Good developers *shouldn't* be writing much code, and the code itself should be simple and clearly documented. It shouldn't take a computer science degree to understand what most code does.

---

3 Andy Oram and Greg Wilson, *Making Software*, (O'Reilly).

Good developers also need to have a strong awareness of where and how their code is executed. That's not just the job of an architect.

While basic computer science skills are often required, it's more important for architects and developers to be able to communicate with stakeholders, collaborate with colleagues, advocate for positions, figure things out independently, and generally employ soft skills rather than hard skills to advance goals. Going back to the "reverse a linked list" problem, a good developer should be able to use an IDE to find the method to call, do a quick search on the Internet to find the method, or ask the developer sitting next to him what the method is. A bad developer will implement the algorithm by hand rather than using the available tools to find the method.

While soft skills are an important requirement for success, it is enthusiasm, competence, and perseverance that are the three hallmarks of the best architects and developers. Enthusiasm and perseverance are intrinsic characteristics that can't be taught, while competence comes from experience.

It's best to build relatively small teams of highly skilled developers. A few good developers colocated can accomplish an enormous amount of work. Many of the best startups were built by a handful of people. Amazon famously uses "two-pizza teams," which means that any team should be small enough that it could be fed by two pizzas. A great way of structuring a project is to break apart your project into small teams, with each focused on delivering a service exposed by a clear interface. For example, you can assign an architect and a handful of developers to go build an inventory management system. Define the interfaces and let that team go off to build it, while coding the rest of the platform to use those interfaces. Not only are there technical advantages to breaking apart the platform, but it's easier to assign accountability, and people like owning something. When everybody owns everything, nobody ends up actually owning anything.

When hiring, it's all about quality as opposed to quantity.

Hire the best, organize them into small teams, delineate responsibility clearly, and work to remove impediments to people doing their jobs.

### Collaboration with lines of business

All too often, important business decisions are made by IT in isolation, based on invalid or outdated assumptions. Communication must be frequent, bidirectional, and without intermediaries. It can take the form of in-person meetings, emails, instant messages, and even text messages. Any medium is fine. Building a platform that doesn't meet the needs of business is an enormous waste of time and energy. It's a collaborative effort.

Service-level agreements (SLAs) must be defined for every aspect of the system. This includes server-side and client-side response times, how much the system must be available, how long it should take to recover from an outage (recovery time objective), and how much data loss is acceptable during an outage (recovery point objective). Higher SLAs means higher cost. For example, if the requirement is to never have any platform downtime, you'll have to deploy your platform to multiple geographic zones across multiple cloud vendors. That gets complicated and expensive. It's always a tradeoff. What matters is that these numbers are jointly agreed upon and there is accountability when objectives are not met.

Any event that could drive substantial traffic to your platform (e.g., flash sales, coupons, exceptional discounts) needs to be planned ahead of time. With ecommerce platforms available to the whole world, plus the speed at which messages can travel through social media, you can quickly get besieged with traffic. While proper use of a cloud should allow the system to automatically scale up to meet the increased demand, it's good for high-visibility events to scale up ahead of time for extra safety. Whenever possible, there should be a robust approval system in place so that IT signs off on marketing campaigns.

For example, it's easy to accidentally embed the cookie identifier from your current session (e.g., `;jsessionid=0000000fec3dff553fc1532a937765d43fc42836ed3f8894`) in the URL of a link you send out to customers in an email campaign. You can scale out your environment as much as you please, but if you embed your session identifier, all customers will hit the same server if you have session stickiness.

To help IT understand how their decisions are affecting business, it's great to quantify how much effect various IT metrics have on revenue. For example, calculate how much each minute of downtime costs in lost revenue or how much each additional millisecond of page-loading time negatively impacts revenue. Quantifying these costs helps to put the decisions people make into perspective. It changes the whole way of thinking. For example, a 20-minute outage for maintenance doesn't seem like much to most IT administrators, but knowing that outage costs $300,000 in lost revenue would make anyone think of ways to reduce the length of the outage or eliminate it entirely.

Increasingly, ecommerce platforms are so important that they're being deployed to multiple data centers and even different cloud vendors to ensure that the platform is as available as possible. That's what we'll discuss in Chapter 10.

# CHAPTER 9

# Security for the Cloud

In today's world, sensitive data used by ecommerce is strewn across dozens of systems, many of which are controlled by third parties. For example, the most sensitive of ecommerce data, including credit cards and other personally identifiable information (often abbreviated PII) routinely passes through Content Delivery Networks before being sent to third-party fraud-detection systems and then ultimately to third-party payment gateways. That data travels securely across thousands of miles over multiple networks to data centers owned and managed by third parties, as depicted in Figure 9-1.

 What cloud computing lacks in direct physical ownership of assets, it offers in more control—which is more important.

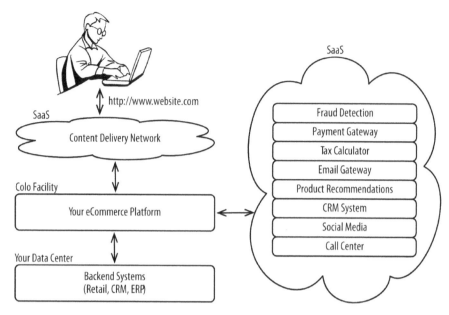

*Figure 9-1. Use of SaaS within ecommerce platforms*

It's highly unlikely that you even own the data center or the hardware you serve your platform from, as most use a managed hosting service or a colo. Your data is already out of your physical possession but is firmly under your control. Control is far more important than possession. The adoption of Infrastructure-as-a-Service or Platform-as-a-Service for the core ecommerce platform is an incremental evolution over the current approach. Next to legacy backend systems, your ecommerce platform is the last to be deployed out in a cloud. Eventually, those legacy systems will be replaced with cloud-based solutions. It's only a matter of time.

The unfounded perception is that clouds are inherently insecure, when in fact they can be more secure than traditional hosting arrangements. Clouds are multitenant by nature, forcing security to be a forethought rather than an afterthought. Cloud vendors can go out of business overnight because of a security issue. Cloud vendors go out of their way to demonstrate compliance with rigorous certifications and accreditations, such as the Payment Card Industry Data Security Standard (PCI DSS), ISO 27001, Federal Risk and Authorization Management Program (FedRAMP), and a host of others.

Cloud vendors have the advantage of being able to specialize in making their offerings secure. They employ the best experts in the world and have the luxury of building security into their offerings from the beginning, in a uniform manner. Cloud vendors have also invested heavily in building out tools that you can use to make your deployments in their clouds more secure. For example, many vendors offer an identity and access management suite that's fully integrated with their offerings as a free value add. The ability to limit access to resources in a cloud in a fine-grained manner is a defining feature of cloud offerings.

The use of a cloud doesn't absolve you of responsibility. If your cloud vendor suffers an incident and it impacts your customers, you're fully responsible. But cloud vendors spend enormous resources staying secure, and breaches are many times more likely to occur as a result of your code, your people, or your (lack of) process.

# General Security Principles

Security issues are far more likely to be caused by a lack of process or to be a consequence of a lack of process. Security encompasses hundreds or even thousands of individual technical and non-technical items. Think of security as an ongoing *system* as opposed to something you do.

 You can't ever be completely secure—you just have to be more secure than your peers so the attackers go after *them* instead of *you*.

According to a survey from Intel, respondents said 30% of threats come from within an organization and 70% of threats come from the outside.[1] Of the threats coming from the outside, Rackspace quantified them in another study as follows:[2]

- 31% of all incidents involved SQL injection exploit attempts
- 21% involved SSH brute-force attacks
- 18% involved MySQL login brute-force attempts
- 9% involved XML-RPC exploit attempts
- 5% involved vulnerability scans

These issues are equally applicable to both traditional environments and clouds; there isn't a single vulnerability in this list that is more applicable to a cloud. The tools to counter internal and external threats are well-known and apply equally (but sometimes differently) to the cloud. What matters is that you have a comprehensive system in place for identifying and mitigating risks. These systems are called *information*

---

1 Intel IT Center, "What's Holding Back the Cloud," (May 2012), *http://intel.ly/1gAdtVB*.

2 Rackspace, "Reference Architecture: Enterprise Security for the Cloud," (2013), *http://bit.ly/1gAdwke*.

*security management systems* (ISMS). We'll quickly cover a few so you can have an understanding of what the most popular frameworks call for.

## Adopting an Information Security Management System

An information security management system (ISMS) is a framework that brings structure to security and can be used to demonstrate a baseline level of security. They can be built, adapted, or adopted. Adherence to at least one well-defined framework is a firm requirement for any ecommerce deployment, whether or not it's in the cloud. Full adoption of at least one of these frameworks will change the way you architect, implement, and maintain your platform for the better.

All frameworks call for controls, which are discrete actions that can be taken to prevent a breach from occurring, stop a breach that's in progress, and take corrective actions after a breach. Controls can take a form that's physical (security guards, locks), procedural (planning, training), or technical (implementing a firewall, configuring a web server setting).

ISO 27001 outlines a model framework, which most cloud vendors are already compliant with. Its central tenets are as follows:

*Plan*
Establish controls, classify data and determine which controls apply, assign responsibilities to individuals

*Do*
Implement controls

*Check*
Assess whether controls are correctly applied and report results to stakeholders

*Act*
Perform preventative and corrective actions as appropriate

Other frameworks include PCI DSS and FedRAMP, which all call for roughly the same plan/do/check/act cycle but with varying controls. Rely on these frameworks as a solid baseline, but layer on your own controls as required. For example, PCI DSS doesn't technically require that you encrypt data in motion between systems within your trusted network, but doing so would just be common sense.

The *check* part of the plan/do/check/act cycle should always be performed internally and externally by a qualified assessor. An external vendor is likely to find more issues than you could on your own. All of the major frameworks require third-party audits because of the value they offer over self-assessment.

For cloud vendors, compliance with each of the frameworks is done for different reasons. Compliance helps to ensure security, and most important, helps to demonstrate security to all constituents. Compliance with some frameworks, such as FedRAMP, is required in order to do business with the US government. If there ever is a security issue, cloud vendors can use compliance with frameworks to reduce legal culpability. Retailers who suffer breaches routinely hide behind compliance with PCI DSS. These frameworks are much like seat belts. Being compliant doesn't guarantee security any more than wearing a seat belt will save your life in a car crash. But there's a strong causal relationship between wearing a seat belt and surviving a car crash.

Your reasons for adopting a security framework are largely the same as the reasons for cloud vendors, except you have the added pressure of maintaining compliance with PCI DSS. PCI DSS, which we'll discuss shortly, is a commercial requirement imposed by the credit card industry on those who touch credit cards.

Let's review a few of the key frameworks.

## PCI DSS

The *Payment Card Industry Data Security Standard* (PCI DSS) is a collaboration between Visa, MasterCard, Discover, American Express, and JCB for the purpose of holding merchants to a single standard. A merchant, for the purposes of PCI, is defined as any organization that handles credit card information or personally identifiable information related to credit cards. Prior to the introduction of PCI DSS in 2004, each credit card issuer had its own standard that each vendor had to comply with. By coming together as a single group, credit card brands were able to put together one comprehensive standard that all merchants could adhere to.

While protecting credit card data is obviously a priority, personally identifiable information extends far beyond that. PII is often defined as "any information about an individual maintained by an agency, including (1) any information that can be used to distinguish or trace an individual's identity, such as name, social security number, date and place of birth, mother's maiden name, or biometric records; and (2) any other information that is linked or linkable to an individual, such as medical, educational, financial, and employment information."[3] Even IP addresses are commonly seen as PII because they could be theoretically used to pinpoint a specific user. The consequences of disclosing PII, whether or not related to credit cards, is usually the same.

---

3 Erika McCallister, et al., "Guide to Protecting the Confidentiality of Personally Identifiable Information," National Institute of Standards and Technology (April 2010), *http://1.usa.gov/1gAdwAK*.

PCI DSS is not a law, but failure to comply with it brings consequences such as fines from credit card issuers and issuing banks, and increased legal culpability in the event of a breach.

The PCI DSS standard calls for adherence to 6 objectives and 12 controls, as Table 9-1 demonstrates.[4]

*Table 9-1. PCI DSS control objectives and requirements*

| Control objectives | Requirements |
| --- | --- |
| Build and maintain a secure network and systems | 1) Install and maintain a firewall configuration to protect cardholder data |
| | 2) Do not use vendor-supplied defaults for system passwords and other security parameters |
| Protect cardholder data | 3) Protect stored cardholder data |
| | 4) Encrypt transmission of cardholder data across open public networks |
| Maintain a vulnerability management program | 5) Protect all systems against malware and regularly update antivirus software or programs |
| | 6) Develop and maintain secure systems and applications |
| Implement strong access control measures | 7) Restrict access to cardholder data by business need to know |
| | 8) Identify and authenticate access to system components |
| | 9) Restrict physical access to cardholder data |
| Regularly monitor and test networks | 10) Track and monitor all access to network resources and cardholder data |
| | 11) Regularly test security systems and processes |
| Maintain an Information Security Policy | 12) Maintain a policy that addresses information security for all personnel |

Validation of compliance is performed annually by a third-party qualified security assessor (QSA). PCI DSS is not intended to be extremely prescriptive. Instead, it's meant to ensure that merchants are adhering to the preceding principles. So long as you can demonstrate adherence to these principles, QSAs will generally sign off. If your QSA won't work with you to understand what you're doing and how you're adhering to the stated objectives of PCI DSS, you should find another QSA. All of the major cloud vendors have achieved the highest level of PCI DSS compliance and are regularly audited. Cloud computing in no way prohibits you from being PCI compliant.

---

4 PCI Security Council, "Requirements and Security Assessment Procedures," (November 2013), *https://www.pcisecuritystandards.org/documents/PCI_DSS_v3.pdf*.

---

Cardholder data is defined as the credit card number, but also data such as expiration date, name, address, and all other personally identifiable information that's stored with the credit card. Any system (e.g., firewalls, routers, switches, servers, storage) that comes in contact with cardholder data is considered part of your cardholder data environment.

Your goal with PCI DSS should be to limit the scope of your cardholder data environment. One approach is to limit this scope by building or using a credit card processing service that is independent of the rest of your environment. If you build a service, you can have a separate firewall, load balancer, application server tier, database, and VLAN, with the application exposed through a subdomain such as *https://pci.website.com*, with an IFrame submitting cardholder data directly to that service. Only the systems behind that service would be considered in the scope of your cardholder data environment and thus subject to PCI DSS. All references to cardholder data would then be through a randomly generated token. We'll discuss this in an edge-based approach shortly.

While PCI DSS is very specific to ecommerce, let's explore a more generic framework.

## ISO 27001

*ISO 27001* describes a model information security management system, first published in 2005 by the International Organization for Standardization (ISO). Whereas PCI is a pragmatic guide focused on safeguarding credit card data, you're free to choose where ISO 27001 applies and what controls you want in place.

Compliance with ISO 27001 is sometimes required for commercial purposes. Your business partners may require your compliance with the standard to help ensure that their data is safe. While compliance does not imply security, it's a tangible step to show that you've taken steps to mitigate risk. Compliance with ISO 27001 is very similar to the famed ISO 9000 series for quality control, but applied to the topic of information security. As with ISO 9000, formal auditing is optional. You can adhere to the standard internally. But to publicly claim that you're compliant, you need to be audited by an ISO-approved third party.

In addition to the plan/do/check/act cycle we discussed earlier, ISO 27001 allows you to select and build controls that are uniquely applicable to your organization. It references a series of controls found in ISO 27002 as representative of those that should be selected as a baseline:

*Information security policies*
    Directives from management that define what security means for your organization and their support for achieving those goals

*Organization of information security*
How you organize and incentivize your employees and vendors, who's responsible for what, mobile device/teleworking policies

*Human resource security*
Hiring people who value security, getting people to adhere to your policies, what happens after someone leaves your organization

*Asset management*
Inventory of physical assets, defining the responsibilities individuals have for safeguarding those assets, disposing of physical assets

*Access control*
How employees and vendors get access to both physical and virtual assets

*Cryptography*
Use of cryptography, including methods and applicability, as well as key management

*Physical and environmental security*
Physical security of assets, including protection against manmade and natural disasters

*Operations management*
Operational procedures and responsibilities including those related to backup, antivirus, logging/monitoring, and patching

*Communications security*
Logical and physical network controls to restrict the flow of data within networks, nontechnical controls such as nondisclosure agreements

*System acquisition, development, and maintenance*
Security of packaged software, policies to increase the software development lifecycle, policies around test data

*Supplier relationships*
Policies to improve information security within your IT supply chain

*Information security incident management*
How you collect data and respond to security issues

*Information security aspects of business continuity management*
Redundancy for technical and nontechnical systems

*Compliance*
Continuous self-auditing, meeting all legal requirements

While not complete, this list should provide you with an idea of the scope of ISO 27001 and 27002.

# FedRAMP

Whereas PCI DSS is focused on safeguarding credit card data and ISO 27001 is about developing a process for information security, *FedRAMP* was specifically designed to ensure the security of clouds for use by the US government. (G-Cloud is the UK's equivalent.) FedRAMP is a collaboration among government agencies to offer one security standard to cloud vendors. Cloud vendors simply couldn't demonstrate compliance with each federal agency's standards. Since 2011, the US government has had a formal cloud first policy. FedRAMP enables that policy by holding cloud vendors to a uniform baseline. Once a cloud vendor is certified, any US federal agency may use that vendor.

At its core, FedRAMP requires that vendors:

- Identify and protect the boundaries of their cloud
- Manage configuration across all systems
- Offer firm isolation between software and hardware assets
- Adhere to more than 290 security controls
- Submit to vulnerability scans, including code scans
- Document their approach to security
- Submit to audits by a third party

Most of the security controls come right from the National Institute of Standards and Technology (NIST) Special Publication 800-53, with a few additional controls.[5] FedRAMP certification is a rigorous, time-consuming process, but one that yields substantial benefits to all constituents. Most of the major cloud vendors have achieved compliance.

FedRAMP differs substantially from PCI DSS in that it has a broader scope. PCI DSS is focused strictly on safeguarding credit card data, because that's what the credit card issuers care about. FedRAMP was built for the purpose of securing government data, which may range from credit card numbers to tax returns to personnel files. FedRAMP is also built specifically for cloud computing, whereas PCI DSS is applicable to any system that handles credit card data.

---

5 NIST, "Security and Privacy Controls for Federal Information Systems and Organizations," (April 2013), *http://1.usa.gov/1j2786S*.

FedRAMP differs from ISO 27001 in that it's more of a pragmatic checklist, as opposed to an information security management system. To put it another way, ISO 27001 cares more about the *how*, whereas FedRAMP cares more about the *what*.

FedRAMP, like all frameworks, doesn't guarantee security. But cloud vendors that achieve this certification are more likely to be secure.

# Security Best Practices

While PCI DSS, ISO 27001, and FedRAMP differ in their purpose and scope, they all require the development of a plan and call for adherence to a range of technical and nontechnical controls. Again, cloud vendor compliance with these and similar certifications and accreditations maintains a good baseline of security, but compliance doesn't equal security by itself.

In addition to ensuring that your cloud vendor is meeting a baseline of security and developing a plan, you must take proactive steps to secure your own information, whether or not in a cloud. Let's review a few key security principles.

## Defense in Depth

Your approach to security must be layered, such that compromising one layer won't lead to your entire system being compromised. Layering on security is called *defense in depth* and plays a key role in safeguarding sensitive information, as Figure 9-2 shows.

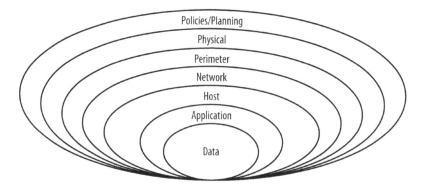

*Figure 9-2. The defense-in-depth onion*

One or more safeguards are employed at each layer, as explained in Table 9-2, requiring an attacker to compromise multiple systems in order to cause harm.

*Table 9-2. Protections in place for various layers*

| Layer | Protections |
| --- | --- |
| Policies/planning | Information security management systems |
| Physical | Physical security offered by your cloud vendor |
| | Tamper-resistant hardware security modules |
| Perimeter | Distributed denial-of-service attack mitigation |
| | Content Delivery Networks |
| | Reverse proxies |
| | Firewalls |
| | Load balancers |
| Network | VLANs |
| | Firewalls |
| | Nonroutable subnets |
| | VPNs |
| Host | Hypervisors |
| | iptables or nftables |
| | Operating system hardening |
| Application | Application architecture |
| | Runtime environment |
| | Secure communication over SSL/TLS |
| Data | Encryption |

Defense in depth can be overused as a security technique. Each layer of security introduces complexity and latency, while requiring that someone manage it. The more people are involved, even in administration, the more attack vectors you create, and the more you distract your people from possibly more-important tasks. Employ multiple layers, but avoid duplication and use common sense.

## Information Classification

Security is all about protecting sensitive information like credit cards and other personally identifiable information. Information security management systems like PCI DSS, ISO 27001, and FedRAMP exist solely to safeguard sensitive information and call for the development of an information classification system. An information classification system defines the levels of sensitivity, along with specific controls to ensure its safekeeping. Table 9-3 describes an example of a very basic system.

*Table 9-3. Information classification system*

| Level | Description | Examples | Encrypted in motion | Encrypted at rest | Tokenize | Hash |
|---|---|---|---|---|---|---|
| Public | Information publicly available | Product images, product description, and ratings and reviews | No | No | No | No |
| Protected | Disclosure unlikely to cause issues | A list of all active promotions | No | No | No | No |
| Restricted | Disclosure could cause issues but not necessarily | Logfiles, source code | Yes | Yes | No | No |
| Confidential | Disclosure could lead to lawsuits and possible legal sanctions | Name, address, purchasing history | Yes (using hardware security module) | Yes (using hardware security module) | No | No |
| Extremely confidential | Disclosure could lead to lawsuits and possible legal sanctions | Password, credit card number | Yes (using hardware security module) | Yes (using hardware security module) | Yes (if possible) | Yes (if possible) |

On top of this, you'll want to assign policies determining information access, retention, destruction, and the like. These controls may vary by country, because of variations in laws.

Once you've developed an information classification system and assigned policies to each level, you'll want to do a complete inventory of your systems for the purpose of identifying all data. Data can take the form of normalized data in a relational database, denormalized data in a NoSQL database, files on a filesystem, source code, and anything else that can be stored and transmitted. Each type of data must be assigned a classification.

A general best practice is to limit the amount of information that's collected and retained. Information that you don't collect or retain can't be stolen from you.

# Isolation

*Isolation* can refer to carving up a single horizontal resource (e.g., a physical server, a storage device, a network) or limiting communication between vertical tiers (e.g., web server to application server, application server to database). The goal is to limit the amount of communication between segments, whether horizontal or vertical, so that a vulnerability in one segment cannot lead to the whole system being compromised. It's a containment approach, in much the same way that buildings are built with firewalls to ensure that fires don't engulf the entire building.

The isolation mechanisms vary based on what's being isolated. Virtual servers are isolated from each other through the use of a hypervisor. Storage devices are split into multiple volumes. Networks are segmented using technology like virtual LANs (VLANs) and isolated using firewalls. All of these technologies are well established and offer the ability to provide complete isolation. The key to employing these technologies is to implement isolation at the lowest layer possible.

For example, the Open Systems Interconnection (OSI) model standardizes the various levels involved with network communication so that products from different vendors are interoperable. Switches, which operate at layer 2, are responsible for routing Ethernet frames. To logically segment Ethernet networks, you can tag each frame with a VLAN ID. If an Ethernet frame has a VLAN ID, the switch will route it only within the boundaries of the defined VLAN, as shown in Figure 9-3.

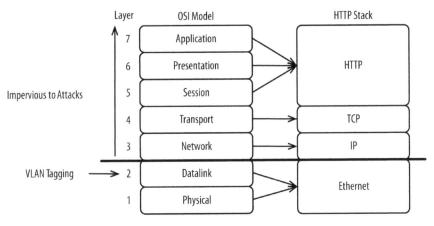

*Figure 9-3. OSI model mapped back to HTTP stack*

The advantage of this level of segmentation is that you're entirely protected against attacks in layer 3 and above. This technique can be applied to separate all traffic between your application servers and databases. This principle reduces attack vectors while providing strong isolation. The lower in any stack—whether network, storage, or a hypervisor—the stronger the protection.

Isolation is a key component of a *defense in depth* strategy.

## Identification, Authentication, and Authorization

*Identification*, *authentication*, and *authorization* are focused on controlling access to systems and data. Users can be individual humans or other systems, but the rules are mostly the same. Every user must properly identify itself (through a username, public key, or alternate means), properly authenticate itself (through a password, private key, or other means), and have designated access to the data. All three elements (identification, authentication, and authorization) must be validated before access may be granted to a system or data.

Human users should always be mapped 1:1 with accounts, as it increases accountability. With each human user having an account, you can hold individuals accountable for the actions performed by them. Accounts that multiple people hold access to are notorious enablers of malicious behavior, because actions performed by that account are hard to trace back to individuals. There's no accountability.

Users of a system, whether internal or external, should always start out with access to nothing. This is the concept of *least privileged access*. Only after a user's role is established should a user be assigned roles and rights per your information classification system. When an employee leaves the company or changes roles, the system should automatically update the user's role in the system and revoke any granted rights.

Some cloud vendors offer robust *identity and access management* (IAM) systems that are fully integrated across their suite of services. These systems are typically delivered as SaaS and offer a uniform approach to manage access to all systems and data. The advantage these systems have is that they're fully and deeply integrated with all of the systems offered by a cloud. Without a central IAM system, you'd have to build one on your own, likely host it, and integrate it with all of the systems you use. Third-party systems invariably support different protocols, different versions of each protocol, and offer limited ability to support fine-grained access. By using a cloud vendor's Software-as-a-Service solution, you get a robust solution that's ready to be immediately used.

It's important to use an IAM system that supports *identity federation*, which is delegating authentication to a third party such as a corporate directory using a protocol like OAuth, SAML, or OpenID. Your source system, like a human resources database, can serve as the master and be referenced in real time to ensure that the user still exists. You wouldn't want to get into a situation where an employee was terminated, but their account in the cloud vendor's IAM system was still active. Identity federation solves this problem.

Finally, *multifactor authentication* is an absolute must for any human user who is transacting with your servers or your cloud vendor's administration console. An attacker could use a range of techniques to get an administrator's password, including brute-force attacks and social engineering. Once logged in, an attacker could do anything, including deleting the entire production environment. Multifactor authentication makes it impossible to log in by providing only a password. On top of a password, the second factor can be an authentication code from a physical device, like a smartphone or a standalone key fob. Two authentication factors, including what you know (password) and what you have (your smartphone), substantially strengthen the security of your account.

## Audit Logging

Complementary to identification, authentication, and authorization is *audit logging*. All of the common information security management systems require extensive logging of every administrative action, including calls into a cloud vendor's API, all actions performed by administrators, errors, login attempts, access to logs, and the results of various health checks. Every logged event should be tagged with the following:

- The user who performed the event
- Data center where the event was performed
- ID, hostname, and/or IP of the server that performed the event
- A timestamp marking when the event was performed
- Process ID

Logs should be stored encrypted in one or more locations that are accessible to only a select few administrators. Consider writing them directly to your cloud vendor's shared storage. Servers are ephemeral. When a server is killed, you don't want valuable logs to disappear with it.

Logging not only acts as a deterrent to bad behavior but also ensures that there is traceability in the event of a breach. Provided that the logs aren't tampered with, you should be able to reconstruct exactly what happened in the event of a failure, in much the same way that airplanes' black box recorders record what happened during a crash. Being able to reconstruct what happened is important for legal reasons but also as a way to learn from failures to help ensure they don't happen again.

Cloud vendors offer extensive built-in logging capabilities, coupled with secure, inexpensive storage for logs.

# Security Principles for eCommerce

Among all workloads, ecommerce is unique in that it's both highly visible and handles highly sensitive data. It's that combination that leads it to have unique requirements for security. Traditional cloud workloads tend to be neither. If a climate scientist isn't temporarily able to run a weather simulation, it's not going to make headlines or lead to a lawsuit over a breach.

The visibility of ecommerce is increasing as it's moving from a peripheral channel to the core of entire organizations. As we've discussed, this shift is called *omnichannel retailing*. An outage, regardless of its cause, is likely to knock all channels offline and prevent an organization from generating any revenue. Outages like this are prominently featured in the news and are almost always discussed on earnings calls. Executives are routinely fired because of outages, but the odds of a firing increase if the outage can be traced to a preventable security-related issue. Security-related incidents reflect poorly on the organization suffering the incident because it shows a lack of competency. It makes both senior management and investors question whether an organization is competent in the rest of the business.

While outages are bad, lost data is often much worse because of consequences including lost revenue, restitution to victims, fines from credit card issuers, loss of shareholder equity, bad press, and legal action including civil lawsuits initiated by wronged consumers. An outage may get you fired, but a major security breach will *definitely* get you fired. You may also be personally subject to criminal and civil penalties. Leaked data that can get you in trouble includes all of the standard data like credit cards, names, addresses, and the like, but it also extends to seemingly innocuous data, like purchase histories, shipping tracking numbers, wish lists, and so on. Disclosure of *any* personally identifiable information will get you in trouble.

Disclosing personally identifiable information will lead to not only commercial penalties and civil action, but also possibly criminal actions by various legal jurisdictions. Many countries impose both civil and criminal penalties on not only those who steal personally identifiable information, but also those who allow it to be stolen, in the case of gross negligence. For example, Mexico's law states that ecommerce vendors can be punished with up to six years' imprisonment if data on Mexican citizens is stolen. Many countries are even more punitive and may even confiscate profit earned while its citizens' data was at risk. Many countries, such as Germany, severely restrict the movement of data on their citizens outside their borders in order to limit the risk of disclosures.

Vulnerabilities that lead to the disclosure of personally identifiable information tend to be application level. SQL injection (getting a database to execute arbitrary SQL), cross-site scripting (getting a web browser to execute arbitrary script like JavaScript), and cross-site request forgery (executing URLs from within the context of a customer's session) are preferred means for stealing sensitive data. Applications tend to be large, having many pages and many possible attack vectors, while the barriers to entry for an attacker are low. Attackers don't have to install sophisticated malware or anything very complicated—they simply have to view the source code for your HTML page and play with HTTP GET and POST parameters. In following with the defense-in-depth principle, your best approach is to layer:

*Education*
    Educate your developers to the dangers of these vulnerabilities.

*Development of best practices*
    Set expectations for high security up front; have all code peer reviewed.

*White-box testing*
> Scan your source code for vulnerabilities.

*Black-box testing*
> Scan your running application, including both your frontends and your backends, for vulnerabilities.

*Web application firewall*
> Use a web application firewall to automatically guard against any of these vulnerabilities should your other defenses fail. Web application firewalls are capable of inspecting the HTTP requests and responses.

If you're especially cautious, you can even run a database firewall. Like a web application firewall, a database firewall sits between your application servers and database and inspects the SQL. A query such as *select \* from credit_card* originating from your application server should *always* be blocked. These firewalls are capable of customizable blacklist and whitelist rulesets.

Security is a function of both your application and the platform on which it is deployed. It's a shared responsibility.

# Security Principles for the Cloud

The cloud is a new way of delivering computing power, but it's not that fundamentally different. All of the traditional security principles still apply. Some are easier; some are harder. What matters is that you have a good partnership with your cloud vendor. They provide a solid foundation and tools that you can use, but you have to take responsibility for the upper stack. Table 9-4 shows a breakdown of each party's responsibility.

*Table 9-4. Cloud vendor's responsibilities versus your responsibilities*

| Cloud vendor responsibilities | Your responsibilities |
| --- | --- |
| Facilities | N/A |
| Power | N/A |
| Physical security of hardware | N/A |
| Network infrastructure | N/A |
| Internet connectivity | N/A |
| Patching hypervisor and below | Patching operating system and above |
| Monitoring | Monitoring |
| Firewalls | Configuring customized firewall rules |
| Virtualization | Building and installing your own image |
| API for provisioning/monitoring | Using the APIs to provision |
| Identity and access management framework | Using the provided identity and access management framework |

| Cloud vendor responsibilities | Your responsibilities |
| --- | --- |
| Protection against cloud-wide distributed denial-of-service attacks | Protecting against tenant-specific distributed denial-of-service attacks |
| N/A | Building and deploying your application(s) |
| N/A | Securing data in transit |
| N/A | Securing data at rest |

Security is a shared responsibility that requires extensive cooperation. An example of the cooperation required is when you perform penetration testing. Unless you tell your vendor ahead of time, a penetration test is indistinguishable from a real attack. You have to tell your cloud vendor ahead of time that you're going to be doing penetration testing and that the activity seen between specific time periods is OK. If you don't work with your cloud vendor, they'll just block everything and, best case, your penetration won't work because security is so tight by default.

## Reducing Attack Vectors

Key to reducing your risk is to minimize your attack surface. If every one of your servers were on the Internet, obviously that would create a large surface for attacks. Ideally, you'll expose only a single IP address to the Internet, with all traffic forced through multiple firewalls and at least one layer of load balancing.

Many cloud vendors offer what amounts to a private subnet within a public cloud, whereby you can set up private networks that aren't routable from the public Internet. Hosts are assigned private IP addresses, with you having full control over IP address ranges, routing tables, network gateways, and subnets. This is how large corporate networks are securely sliced up today. Only the cloud vendor's hardened load balancer should be responding to requests from the Internet. To handle requests from your application to resources on the Internet, you can set up an intermediary server that's routable from the Internet but doesn't respond to requests originating from the Internet. Network address translation (NAT) can be used to connect from your application server instances in a secure subnet to get to the intermediary that's exposed to the Internet. The intermediary is often called a *bastion host*.

Keep your backend off the Internet. This is applicable outside the technology domain as well.

In addition to private clouds within public clouds, firewalls are another great method of securing environments. Cloud vendors make it easy to configure firewall rules that prohibit traffic between tiers, except for specific protocols over specific ports. For example, you can have a firewall between your load balancer and application server tiers that permits only HTTP traffic over port 80 from passing between the two ports. Everything else will be denied by default (see Figure 9-4).

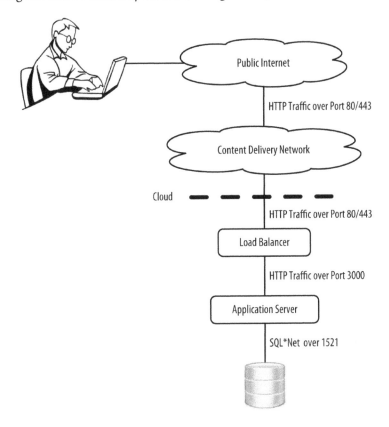

*Figure 9-4. Restricting traffic by port and type*

By having a default deny policy and accepting only specific traffic over a specific port, you greatly limit the number of attack vectors by keeping a low profile online. You can even configure firewalls and load balancers to accept traffic from a specific IP range, perhaps limiting certain traffic to and from the tier above/below and from your corporate network. For example, you can require that any inbound SSH connections be established from an IP address belonging to your company. This is a key principle of defense in depth, whereby an attacker would have to penetrate multiple layers in order to access your sensitive data.

Once within your private subnet, you have to minimize the attack surface area of each individual server. To do this, start by disabling all unnecessary services, packages, applications, methods of user authentication, and anything else that you won't be using. Then, using a host-based firewall like iptables or nftables, block all inbound and outbound access, opening ports on only an exception basis. You should have SSH (restricted to the IP range belonging to your corporate network) and HTTP (restricted to the tier above it) open only on servers that host application servers. Use a configuration management approach per Chapter 5 in order to consistently apply your security policies. Your default deny policy is no good if it's not actually implemented when a new server is built.

Going a layer lower, hypervisors themselves can serve as an attack vector. When virtualization first started becoming mainstream, there were security issues with hypervisors. But today's hypervisors are much more mature and secure than they used to be and are now deemed OK to use by all of the major information security management systems. Cloud vendors use highly customized hypervisors, offering additional security mechanisms above the base hypervisor implementation, like Xen. For example, firewalls are often built-in between the physical server's interface and guest server's virtual interface to provide an extra layer of security on top of what the hypervisor itself offers. You can even configure your guest server to be in *promiscuous mode*, whereby your NIC forwards all packets routed through the NIC to one of the guests, and you won't see any other guest's traffic. Multiple layers of protection are in place to ensure this never happens. Separation of this sort occurs with all resources, including memory and storage.

Cloud vendors help to ensure that their hypervisors remain secure by frequently and transparently patching them and doing frequent penetration testing. If a cloud vendor's hypervisor is found to have a security issue, that vendor's entire business model is destroyed. They're highly incentivized to get this right.

If you're especially concerned about hypervisor security, you can always get dedicated servers instead of shared servers. This feature, offered by some cloud vendors, allows you to deploy one virtual server to an entire physical server.

Instead of Figure 9-5, you can have one physical server and one vServer, as shown in Figure 9-6.

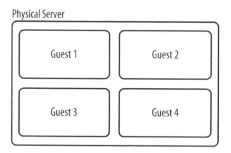

*Figure 9-5. One physical server, four vServers*

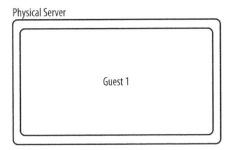

Physical Server

Guest 1

*Figure 9-6. One physical server, one vServer*

The price difference between the two models is often nominal, and you can use the same APIs you would normally use.

## Protecting Data in Motion

Data can be in one of two states: in motion or at rest. Data that's *in motion* is transient by nature. Think of HTTP requests, queries to a database, and the TCP packets that comprise those higher-order protocols. Data that's *at rest* has been committed to a persistent storage medium, usually backed by a physical device of some sort. Any data in motion may be intercepted. To safeguard the data, you can encrypt it or use a connection that's already secure.

Encryption is the most widely used method of protecting data in transit. Encryption typically takes the form of Secure Sockets Layer (SSL) or its successor, Transport Layer Security (TLS). SSL and TLS can be used to encrypt just about any data in motion, from HTTP [HTTP + (SSL or TLS) = HTTPS], to VPN traffic. Both SSL and TLS are well used and well supported by both clients and applications, making it the predominant approach to securing data in motion.

 Extensive use of SSL and TLS taxes CPU and reduces performance. By moving encryption and decryption to hardware, you can entirely eliminate the CPU overhead and almost eliminate the performance overhead. You can transparently offload encryption and decryption to modern x86 processors or specialized hardware accelerators.

SSL and TLS work great for the following:

- Customers' clients (web browsers, smartphones) <-> load-balancing tier
- Load-balancing tier <-> application tier
- Administrative console <-> cloud

- Application tier <-> SaaS (like a payment gateway)
- Application tier <-> your legacy applications
- Any communication within a cloud
- Any communication between clouds

SSL and TLS work at the application layer, meaning that applications must be configured to use it. This generally isn't a problem for clients that work with HTTP, as is common in today's architectures. IPsec, on the other hand, will transparently work for all IP-based traffic, as it works a few layers lower than SSL and TLS by encapsulating TCP packets. You can use this for VPNs to connect to clients that don't support SSL or TLS, such as legacy retail applications and the like. IPsec is commonly used for VPNs back to corporate data centers because of its flexibility.

SSL, TLS, and IPsec all require that you terminate encryption. For example, you can terminate SSL or TLS within a Content Delivery Network, load balancer, or application server, as shown in Figure 9-7.

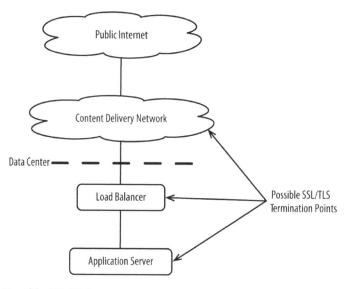

*Figure 9-7. Possible SSL/TLS termination points*

If you're using a web server, you can terminate there, too. Each intermediary you pass encrypted traffic through may have to decrypt and then re-encrypt the traffic in order to view or modify the request. For example, if you terminate at your application tier and you have a web application firewall, you'll need to decrypt and then re-encrypt all HTTP requests and responses so the web application firewall can actually see and potentially block application-level vulnerabilities.

Sometimes, it may be unnecessary or impossible to encrypt connections. We'll talk about this in Chapter 11, but many cloud vendors offer colo vendors the ability to run dedicated fiber lines into their data centers. These private WANs are frequently used to connect databases hosted in a colo to application servers hosted in a cloud. These connections are dedicated and considered secure.

Once in a database, data transitions from being *in motion* to *at rest*.

## Protecting Data at Rest

Data at rest is data that's written to a persistent storage device, like a disk, whereas data in motion is typically traveling over a network between two hosts. Data at rest includes everything from the data managed by relational and NoSQL databases to logfiles to product images. Like data in motion, some is worth safeguarding, and some is not. Let's explore.

To begin, you must first index and categorize all data that your system stores, applying different levels of security to each. This is a standard part of all information security management systems, as we discussed earlier in this chapter. If you can, reduce the amount of sensitive data that's stored. You can:

- Not store it
- Reduce the length of time it needs to be stored
- Tokenize it
- Hash it
- Anonymize it
- Stripe it across multiple places

The less data you have, the less risk you have of it being stolen. Tokenization, for example, is substituting sensitive data in your system with a token. That way, even if your database were to be compromised, an attacker wouldn't gain access to the sensitive data. Tokenization can be done at the edge by your CDN vendor or in your application. When you tokenize at the edge, only your CDN vendor and your payment gateway have access to the sensitive data.

Sensitive data that's left over needs to be protected. Encryption is the typical means by which data at rest is safeguarded. You can apply a secure off-the-shelf algorithm to provide security, by encrypting files or entire filesystems. Encryption is a core feature of any storage system, including those offered by cloud vendors. To provide an additional level of security, you can encrypt your data twice—once before you store it and then again as you store it. The filesystem it's being written to itself may be encrypted. Layering encryption is good, but just don't overdo it. Encryption does add overhead, but it can be minimized by offloading encryption and decryption to modern x86 processors or specialized hardware accelerators.

Anytime you use encryption, you have to feed a key into your algorithm when you encode and decode. Your key is like a password, which must be kept safe, as anyone with access to an encryption key can decrypt data encrypted using that key. Hardware security modules (HSMs) are the preferred means for generating and safeguarding keys. HSMs contain hardware-based cryptoprocessors that excel at generating truly random numbers, which are important for secure key generation. These standalone physical devices can be directly attached to physical servers or attached over a network, and contain advanced hardware and software security features to prevent tampering. For example, HSMs can be configured to zero out all keys if the device detects tampering.

Some cloud vendors now offer dedicated HSMs that can be used within a cloud, though only the cloud vendor is able to physically install them. You can administer your HSMs remotely, with factors such as multifactor authentication providing additional security. If you want to use or manage your own HSMs, you can set them up in a data center you control, perhaps using a direct connection between your cloud vendor and a colo. This will be discussed further in Chapter 11.

Databases, whether relational or NoSQL, are typically where sensitive data is stored and retrieved. You have three options for hosting your databases:

- Use your cloud vendor's Database-as-a-Service offering
- Set up a database in the cloud on infrastructure you provision
- Host your database on premises in a data center that you control, using a direct connection between your cloud vendor and a colo (discussed further in Chapter 11)

All three approaches are perfectly capable of keeping your data secure, both in motion to the database and for data at rest once in a database. You can even encrypt data before you put it into the database, as an additional layer of security. Again, possession in no way implies security. What matters is having a strong information security management system, categorizing data appropriately, and employing appropriate controls.

# Summary

The cloud isn't inherently more or less secure than traditional on-premise solutions. Physical possession in no way implies security and can in fact make it more difficult to be secure by increasing the scope of your work. Control is what's needed to be truly secure. Cloud vendors do a great job of taking care of lower-level security and giving you the tools you need to focus on making your own systems secure. Let your cloud vendors focus on securing the platform or infrastructure and below.

# CHAPTER 10

# Deploying Across Multiple Data Centers (Multimaster)

The focus of this chapter is taking a single ecommerce platform and running it out of two or more physical data centers that are geographically separated from each other. While the assumption is that these data centers are within a cloud, most of the principles discussed are applicable to traditional hosting arrangements. We'll start by discussing the fundamental problem of running eCommerce from multiple data centers, the architecture principles underpinning distributed computing, how to assign customers to individual data centers, and finally the various approaches to operating from multiple data centers.

Many ecommerce vendors already operate out of two data centers in some capacity to ensure the highest possible availability. This trend will only accelerate over the coming years as ecommerce platforms are becoming increasingly important to business. In today's omnichannel world, an outage increasingly has the effect of shutting down every single channel you have for generating revenue. It used to be that a website failure would, of course, be unpleasant but it was isolated to that channel. Now, many point-of-sale systems, kiosks, and mobile applications, all use the same underlying platform. Outages today tend to be platform-wide and thus affect all channels.

 Next to a security breach, an extended outage or repeated outages are the surest way to become unemployed.

Deploying the same platform across two or more data centers in an active/passive or multimaster configuration helps to ensure availability by providing resiliency against natural disasters (e.g., hurricanes, typhoons, fires, floods), human errors (e.g., cable cuts, misconfigurations), upstream outages (e.g., loss of power, loss of Internet connectivity), and software problems (e.g., bugs, upgrade challenges). It's highly unlikely, for example, that any two data centers in the world are likely to be affected by the same fire or cable cut. There's *supposed* to be redundancy within each data center, and generally it works very well. But would you trust your job to your cloud vendor and the safeguards that vendor has employed in each data center? As we've repeatedly seen, the only way to ensure availability is to use multiple data centers, preferably as far apart as possible.

Historically, ecommerce platforms have been designed for the best possible availability, usually just within a single data center. This focus on availability has precedence: retail point-of-sale systems. Most point-of-sale systems have two or more unique methods of connecting back to the home office to perform critical functions such as charging credit cards and issuing returns. Dial-up is still commonly used as a backup. If the primary and backup fail, many retailers will continue to accept orders under $25 or $50 and then run the credit card authorizations through later, when the connection can be reestablished. While it's possible a few charges aren't successfully authorized, the loss is likely to be lower than the cost of not being open for business.

Many ecommerce systems function the same way: if the payment gateway, inventory management system, or some other system is down, the system can still collect orders but wait to actually charge credit cards, decrement inventory, and so forth. An advantage ecommerce transactions have is that any problems discovered can be corrected before the goods are shipped. In a physical retail store, customers walk out with the products. If you later discover that a credit card authorization was unsuccessful, you can't get the products back.

While the need for availability is increasing, cloud and its prerequisites make it even easier and more affordable to operate from multiple data centers. Auto-scaling (Chapter 4), installing software on newly provisioned hardware (Chapter 5), solid architecture (Chapter 8), and Global Server Load Balancing (this chapter) are all fundamental to operating out of multiple data centers.

The cloud itself and the elasticity it brings make operating from multiple data centers incredibly inexpensive. Prior to cloud computing, each data center you operated from had to have enough hardware to be able to support 100% of production traffic in case one of the data centers had an outage. All of this hardware typically sits idle for all but a few minutes of the year. Building up an entire second (or third) replica is enormously expensive—both in terms of up-front capital outlay and ongoing maintenance. The introduction of the cloud completely changes this. You can have a *shell* infrastructure in place and rapidly scale it up in the event of a failure. All of this depends on how well you install software on newly provisioned hardware, how good your architecture is, whether you've employed Global Server Load Balancing, and how well you can auto-scale. Without meeting these prerequisites adequately, you shouldn't even attempt this. Like the cloud itself, the adoption of a multimaster archi-tecture only exacerbates technical and nontechnical deficiencies.

# The Central Problem of Operating from Multiple Data Centers

The central problem with operating from multiple data centers that's fairly unique to ecommerce is that you can have multiple customers logging in, using the same account (e.g., username/password combination) from different data centers. Each account has its own customer profile, shopping cart, and other data. This data is stored in a database of some sort, with all of that data needing to be replicated across the various data centers a platform is being served from. None of the core data in ecommerce, such as customer profiles and shopping carts, can be lost.

The problem that multiple concurrent logins creates is that if two customers update the same data at the same time from two different locations, one customer's action is going to succeed and the other is going to fail, possibly corrupting data along the way. Because of latency, a database in one data center doesn't know in real time what's going on in a database in another data center. Unless you block concurrent logins, there will always be the problem of multiple updates from different data centers (see Figure 10-1).

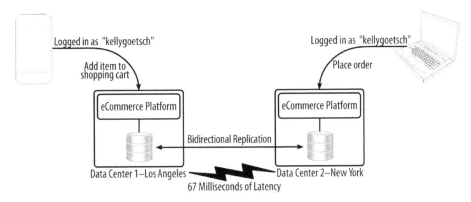

*Figure 10-1. The central problem of multimaster*

It's surprisingly common to have multiple concurrent logins for the same account in different data centers. It can happen when customers share their logins within fami-lies, with friends, and increasingly, with social media. Loyal customers get special dis-counts, so there's a strong incentive to share login credentials to secure a better deal or simply out of convenience. This issue can also happen when contact center agents are modifying an order the same time a customer is. Imagine a scenario where a cus-tomer calls in to a contact center to update an order but actively continues to try to fix the problem while on the phone. These scenarios are common. The cost of a failure is generally corrupted data.

This problem is only increasing as:

- Customers transact across more channels from more devices.
- ecommerce vendors target segments or specific customers for promotions, thus increasing the incentive to share accounts.
- Social media continues to enable customers to share accounts.

The way to reduce (but not eliminate) the likelihood of this scenario happening is to use accurate proximity-based Global Server Load Balancing, which ensures that customers in the same city, state, collection of states, country, or continent all hit the same data center. So if a customer is in one room on an iPad shopping and his daughter is in the other on a laptop, the two should at least hit the same data center and transact against the same database. We will discuss this shortly.

## Architecture Principles

While there are methods to reduce the likelihood of collisions from occurring, the problem needs to be comprehensively addressed. You'll corrupt your data and upset customers if you do nothing or if you implement a poor solution.

The principle to adhere to is to ensure that all customers logged in to the same account are updating the same database (or other system of record) within a single logical database.

You can have two or more active databases with full bidirectional replication, but all writes for a given account must hit the same logical database within the same data center.

Two factors will largely determine the approach you choose:

*Recovery time objective (RTO)*
How quickly must you recover from the failure of a data center? Values range from zero to many hours, depending on the approach you choose. If you deploy out of only one data center, this value could be *weeks*. Active/passive is typically at least an hour. Forms of active/active usually offer zero downtime, even in the event of an entire data center outage. The lower the RTO, the more work and the greater the expense.

*Ability to execute*

How good are you and your organization at doing difficult things? This is all very complicated, especially with the cloud thrown in the mix. Implementation requires considerable technical expertise, time, full organizational support, and plenty of money. If you're struggling with keeping the platform available from one data center that you manage, deploying it across two or more data centers in a cloud isn't something you should even consider.

Recovery point objective (RPO) defines how much data can be lost and is usually a staple of business continuity planning. However, nobody involved with ecommerce is OK with anything less than zero for core data such as customer profiles and shopping carts. Data loss is simply not acceptable for certain classes of data. The principles and approaches in this chapter are all oriented around this assumption.

## Principles Governing Distributed Computing

There's an enormous amount of academic and industry literature on the computer science behind distributed computing. An in-depth discussion of these principles is not in the scope of this book, but a brief overview of the principles and the trade-offs involved in distributed computing are in order before continuing.

Consistency models govern the conditions under which a write in a distributed database will be visible to other readers.[1] A distributed database could be a single database instance comprised of multiple nodes or multiple database instances in different data centers. Databases tend to follow one consistency model, or a variation of that model. Consistency models apply to all distributed computing problems in computer science, from filesystems to memory.

Strong consistency, known as *ACID*, stands for the following:[2]

*Atomicity*

The whole transaction either succeeds or fails.

*Consistency*

A transaction is committed without violating any integrity constraints (e.g., data type, whether column is nullable, foreign-key constraints).

*Isolation*

Each transaction is executed in its own private sandbox and not visible to any other transaction until it is committed.

---

1 Wikipedia, "Consistency Model," (2014), *http://en.wikipedia.org/wiki/Consistency_model*.

2 Wikipedia, "ACID," (2014), *http://en.wikipedia.org/wiki/ACID*.

*Durability*

A committed transaction will not be lost.

The assumption would be that *all* transactions should be ACID compliant, but that's often unnecessary. For example, product-related data (e.g., description, attributes, and search engine optimization–related metadata) can probably be written on one node in one database and propagated across other nodes and databases asynchronously. If readers see inconsistent data for a few seconds, it's probably not a big deal. Very little data *needs* to be strongly consistent. Customers won't tolerate not seeing customer profile and order-related changes reflected immediately. Core customer data should always be stored in an ACID-compliant database. By forcing all customers logged in to the same account to use the same database, you ensure strong consistency for a specific customer's data across database instances.

Weak consistency, known as *BASE*, eschews the tight confines of ACID:[3]

**Basic Availability**

The system is generally available for updates.

*Soft-state*

Data is not durable—it may reside in memory and could be lost in the event of a failure.

*Eventual consistency*

A reader may not see the most up-to-date copy of data, as replication happens asynchronously.

BASE is becoming increasingly common as writes are much faster and systems are much more scalable, with the trade-off in consistency that is *good enough* for many types of data. All of the popular social media platforms are mostly BASE. Again, only a relatively small subset needs full ACID compliance.

There's a continuum between ACID and BASE. You have to pick what works best for you and each type of data you need to store. Often databases themselves allow you to specify the desired consistency model on a fairly granular basis. Clearly, BASE is probably *good enough* for writing an audit log, whereas ACID is required for orders. But what about things like inventory and prices? That's a bit of a grey area. Careful consideration and then implementation is required. Table 10-1 provides a quick summary of the two approaches to consistency.

---

3 Wikipedia, "Eventual Consistency," (2014), *http://en.wikipedia.org/wiki/Eventual_consistency*.

Table 10-1. ACID/strong consistency vs. BASE/weak consistency

| | ACID/strong consistency | BASE/weak consistency |
|---|---|---|
| Defining adjectives | Synchronous, smart, slow | Asynchronous, dumb, fast |
| Design priorities | Data validity | Availability/Scalability/Performance |
| Examples | ecommerce orders, online banking | Caching, DNS |
| Database implementations | Traditional relational databases | Object-based key-value stores/NoSQL |
| Consistency | Immediate | Eventual |

No discussion of consistency models is complete without a brief discussion of Eric Brewer's CAP theorem, which states any distributed system can guarantee two of the following three:[4]

*Consistency*
> No data conflicts

*Availability*
> No single point of failure

*Partition tolerance*
> System maintains availability and consistency if a network problem isolates part of the system

Distributed systems, especially with cloud computing, cannot guarantee partition tolerance because connections between databases are inherently unreliable. Therefore, you have to make a trade-off between consistency (favors ACID) and availability (favors BASE). You can't have both.

For more information on this topic, read *Cloud Architecture Patterns* by Bill Wilder (O'Reilly).

### Avoiding conflicts

Bidirectional database replication tools all have the ability to detect and resolve conflicts. Conflict detection and resolution is an integral part of these offerings. If two customers are updating the same order at the same time from two data centers 100 milliseconds apart, and they both update the same record at the same time within that 100-millisecond window, there will be a collision. Likewise, if two customers are updating the same *object* (such as a customer profile or an order), there will also be a collision. The following examples illustrate this potential issue.

Customer 1, account "kellygoetsch," data center A:

```
update order set submitted = 1 where order_id='12345';
```

---

4 Dr. Eric A. Brewer, "NoSQL: Past, Present, Future," (8 November 2012), *http://bit.ly/1gAdvwO*.

(100 milliseconds of latency)

Customer 2, account "kellygoetsch," data center B:

```
insert into order_lines (order_id, sku_id, quantity)
values ('12345', '54321', 1);
```

In this example, two customers are performing opposing actions: one is submitting an order (executing final pricing, submitting it to a backend system), while the other is adding another item to the order. This obviously will lead to problems. You can't add an item to the order if the order is submitted but the other customer doesn't know it's been submitted yet because of that 100 milliseconds of latency. This example highlights the central problem with conflict detection and resolution. Yes, it often *can* technically work, but the results may not be as you expected. Would this customer's order ship with SKU 54321 included? Would her credit card be charged? Did this customer want that item to be added to the cart, or was it her child who was playing on an iPad in the other room? Who knows. That's the problem.

A more technical issue is that most ecommerce platforms write to the database through an object-relational mapping (ORM) system. These systems allow your code to interact with actual objects represented in code, as opposed to SQL. For example, you can call `order.setProperty("submitted", true)` as opposed to manually constructing the `update order set submitted = 1 where order_id=12345`; SQL by hand. These systems produce an enormous number of SQL statements, as they're built for maximum flexibility and portability, as opposed to SQL efficiency. With a single action (e.g., add to cart) producing potentially dozens of individual SQL statements, you can run into potential inconsistencies as some of the updates and inserts succeed, while others fail. It's hard, if not impossible, to demarcate actions based on database transaction. SQL statements tend to flow from applications down to the database in messy, overlapping, overly granular transactions, or with no transactions at all. It's exceedingly difficult to demarcate an action (e.g., adding an item to a cart) with clear database transaction boundaries.

Even if you did manage to get conflict resolution and detection working, you would deal with the issue of cache staleness. Platforms liberally cache data at all layers. How do you refresh those higher-level, object-level caches when a change is applied through database replication? Caches are usually set to update only if the change is made through the ORM layer. But when the change is applied directly to the database, it's tough to tell the platform how to update its caches.

If you don't use a traditional relational database, you still have many of these same problems but just in a different form. When you're dealing with objects or key-value pairs, you end up overwriting more data because these systems aren't as granular as a proper relational database with normalized data. You'll just overwrite the whole order as opposed to a property of the order, but that's just as bad because of all the inter-dependencies between objects.

The only way to ensure consistency is to make sure that all customers logged in to the same account are updating the same database or other system of record. That still has challenges, but it's at least the status quo, and those issues can be dealt with.

## Selecting a Data Center

Prior to cloud computing, the fixed cost to operate from a data center was very high. You had to physically build the data center or lease some space in an existing data center. Then you had to statically build out your environment, such that it could handle 100% of the production load in the event it was the sole data center or that another data center went offline. The cloud makes it exceedingly easy to run from multiple data centers by eliminating the overhead of operating from a new data center and by allowing you to elastically scale up. No longer do you have to scale up an environment only to have it sit entirely idle. From an API standpoint, the data center is often just one more variable.

The optimal number of data centers to operate from is two or three. Anything more than that is fairly wasteful. Anything less than that, and you don't have enough redundancy to guard against outages. Many cite wanting to reduce latency as a reason for building out so many data centers. As we discussed in Chapter 7, the server-side response time and latency are a small fraction of the total time it takes for a page to display. Customers routinely access ecommerce platforms hosted on different continents. Just because the cloud offers the ability to easily use many data centers doesn't mean you should.

Cloud vendors have many data centers around the world, but they can be segmented by the concept of a *fault domain*. Each vendor has its own name for this concept, but what it amounts to is that there are few to no dependencies or connections between data centers in different fault domains. This isolation should stop issues from propagating across different domains, thus ensuring the highest level of availability. For example, software upgrades tend to happen based on fault domains. You should always pick data centers that are geographically separated (to avoid the same natural disaster, power outage, or fire) but that also are in different fault domains. Again, all you need are two (or maybe three) data centers, but they must be properly chosen.

Cloud-wide outages are exceptionally rare but do occur, as discussed in Chapter 3. To protect yourself against a cloud-wide outage, you can deploy to multiple cloud vendors. It's counterintuitive, but that may actually reduce your uptime, as two vendors creates at least double the complexity. Complexity and misconfiguration arising from complexity is the number one cause of outages. When coupled with the extremely high availability, running across two data centers may not give you the extra boost in availability you'd expect.

# Initializing Each Data Center

The use of the cloud for ecommerce differs substantially from traditional static deployments because of the elasticity that the cloud provides. You no longer need to scale up each of your data centers to handle 100% of your production load. You can now scale up and down freely to meet real-time demands. The problem with that approach is that in the event of a sudden failure, the surviving environment(s) is unlikely to have enough capacity pre-provisioned to handle the sudden rush of traffic. At this point, your auto-scaling system should kick in (see Chapter 4) to start provisioning more hardware. Once the hardware is provisioned, each server must have software installed on it per Chapter 5. Provisioning hardware and then building each server takes time—potentially tens of minutes.

You must set up each cloud data center ahead of time with a skeletal structure that you can then scale out. It's not practical to build up a whole new data center on the fly in response to an outage. But it is practical to take something that's in a data center and scale it out very quickly. Each data center should contain at least two instances (for redundancy) of everything you need for your environment to function—from a cache grid, to application servers, to a service bus. Think of this environment as being the size of a development environment but configured for production. This can all be on dedicated hardware, as opposed to the hourly fees normally charged. Dedicated hardware is often substantially cheaper than per-hour pricing, but using dedicated hardware requires up-front payment for a fixed term, usually a year. Again, this should be a fairly small footprint, consisting of only a handful of servers. The cost shouldn't be much.

If you're deploying your own relational database, it needs to be built out ahead of time. It's hard to add database nodes for relational databases in real time, as entire database restarts and other configuration changes are often required. A database node for a relational database isn't like an application server or web server, where you can just add another one and register it with the load balancer. Databases offered by cloud vendors are more elastic, but of course there are downsides to using shared resources. Your database utilization should be fairly light if you have the right architecture in place. The vast majority of page views are from anonymous customers (or search engine bots) for static cacheable pages, such as home pages and category detail pages. You can offload most reads to slave databases. Full use of a cache grid helps. Your core database for transactional data (e.g., orders, customer profiles) ends up being fairly small, usually no more than a few nodes using no more than a few terabytes of storage.

# Removing Singletons

Every platform, it seems, has software that may be deployed on exactly one server per environment. Common examples include coordination servers, messaging servers, lock brokers, administrative user interfaces, and servers that execute batch jobs. These instances, known as *singletons*, are a classic example of Pareto's principle, whereby you spend 80% of your time on 20% of your servers. The 20% tends to be singletons.

Problems with singletons include the following:

- They may be a single point of failure. You'll have to spend extensive time and effort to ensure the highest possible availability.

- Each server must generally point to the singleton, either with a unique name, URL, IP address, or domain name. It takes a lot of work to update dozens, if not hundreds, of individual servers every time the name or location of the singleton changes.

- Some singletons must be unique to an environment, while others must be unique to a database. If a singleton must be unique to an environment, at least half of the requests to that singleton must be made cross–data center. If a singleton is unique to a database, you'll potentially have to deal with database replication conflicts as each singleton updates its own database and the data is unidirectionally replicated between the two.

- With active/active, you'll have to activate the singleton in the newly active data center following a failover.

- As your environment grows, your singleton may run into limits as to how far it can be vertically scaled. In a normal environment that you control, you can throw a lot of hardware at problems like this. In a cloud, you're limited to the maximum amount of hardware the vendor offers you for a single server.

- You must create a deployment unit (Chapter 5) for that singleton.

It's best to architect your solution to avoid singletons entirely, or if they must exist, allow any instance to assume that responsibility. For example, rather than have a dedicated server that is responsible for periodically rebuilding a search index, each server that responds to queries could build a small part of the index on the side. Or, have your nodes nominate one node to perform that task periodically. Architecture that doesn't rely on singletons tends to be better by almost every measure.

## Never Replicate Configuration

Avoid the temptation to replicate configuration, whether it happens to be in a database or a filesystem. It makes logical sense to replicate everything, but keep in mind that most outages are caused by the introduction of bad configuration. If you replicate configuration, you just replicate the problem. This is exactly the reason you don't deploy code to two or more data centers simultaneously. Wait to see how it works out and then deploy it elsewhere. The same applies for configuration.

# Assigning Customers to Data Centers

## DNS

### DNS primer

As we briefly discussed in Chapter 2, DNS exists so customers don't have to remember IP addresses. Instead, they can remember short names like *website.com*, which are paired up with IP addresses. Each data center you operate from is typically exposed to the world as a single IP address.

At the heart of the system is a record. A standard record looks something like Figure 10-2.

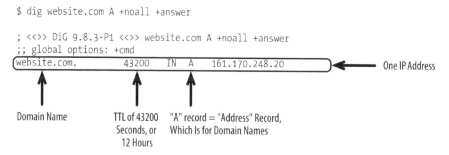

*Figure 10-2. Sample "A" record*

Each domain name has an *authoritative* DNS server, which is the sole source of truth for that domain name. Your client (e.g., web browser, mobile device) will probably have its own cache of DNS records. Your client's operating system likely has its own cache. Your ISP most likely has DNS servers, which also cache records. DNS servers recursively cascade the resolution request up to the authoritative DNS server, with each intermediary caching the record along the way. Each record has a time to live (TTL), designating how long a record can be cached by any intermediary between the client and authoritative server. TTL values range anywhere from zero seconds to several days, with records typically expiring after five minutes. DNS is an *eventually consistent* system, whereby records may be stale for a period not to exceed the TTL.

DNS does support multiple A records, meaning you can have *website.com* resolve to two or more unique IP addresses, with each IP address representing a data center. Results are ordered, so that the first IP address returned is supposed to be the first IP address the client connects to.

Every website on the Internet needs an authoritative DNS server. You can self-host DNS or outsource to a DNS Software-as-a-Service vendor. Software-as-a-Service vendors include standalone vendors, your cloud vendor, or your CDN vendor. All typically offer some form of DNS. Definitely use a third-party vendor for DNS. The risk of outages are too high to self-host DNS.

DNS, while an incredibly resilient and innovative system, has shortcomings:

- Inability to load balance with any real intelligence. You're limited to round-robin or basic algorithms of that nature.
- Inability to determine whether the IP addresses you've put in your record actually work. That determination is left to clients, which don't do it at all or do it poorly.
- Intermediaries between the authoritative DNS server and client can change the order of the IP addresses in an attempt to load balance. This is very bad for active/passive.
- Intermediaries extending to the client itself can ignore the TTLs you specify in an attempt to reduce DNS queries.

Global Server Load Balancing (GSLB), which we'll discuss shortly, seeks to address many of the deficiencies in plain DNS.

### Assigning customers to a single data center

Until fairly recently, most large ecommerce platforms were served out of only one data center, with a single virtual IP address (VIP) exposed for that one data center. With one data center, you can just use plain DNS to tie your friendly domain name (website.com) to the IP address (161.170.248.20). You could set TTL of a few hours and, provided you had a reliable DNS vendor, never think about DNS again.

Your DNS record would look something like that shown in Figure 10-3.

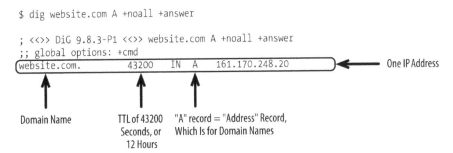

*Figure 10-3. Sample record with one IP address returned*

### Active/passive data center assignment

With the addition of passive data centers in an active/passive configuration, you have to lower your TTL so changes can take effect quickly. If you have a 12-hour TTL, it could be up to 12 hours for any DNS changes to take effect. A TTL of a few minutes works well. Anything shorter than that, and you force your clients to unnecessarily query DNS servers, which harms performance. Following the proper TTL, you then have to be able to publish updates to your DNS record quickly in the event you need to failover from your primary data center to your standby data center.

Your DNS record would look something like Figure 10-4.

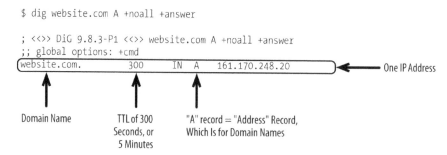

*Figure 10-4. Sample record with one IP address returned*

As previously mentioned, DNS does support multiple A records, meaning you can have *website.com* resolve to two or more unique IP addresses, with each IP address representing a data center. Results are ordered, so that the first IP address returned is supposed to be the first IP address the client connects to. The three problems with that approach for active/passive are as follows:

- You can't guarantee that the order of IP addresses won't be changed by an intermediary.

- You can't guarantee that the clients will always connect to the first IP address listed.

- Short outages may occur, as there are hiccups in Internet connectivity and the like. You don't want clients connecting to your passive data center until you flip the switch by publishing an updated A record.

 Any IP address in your A record can be connected to at any time by any client. There are no guarantees.

Instead, it's best to use proper GSLB with in-depth health checking, or use standard DNS but have only one IP address listed in your A record. GSLB will be discussed shortly.

### Active/active data center assignment

When two or more data centers are actually receiving traffic from customers, each customer must be presented with an accurate ordered list of IP addresses that the client should try connecting to. DNS does support having multiple A records, but this feature should be used only when it is acceptable for a client to connect to any IP address returned. Clients are supposed to connect in the order the IP addresses are returned, but it's entirely possible that an intermediary changed the order of the IP addresses or that a client disregards the order of the addresses that are returned. TTLs tend to be fairly low too, as you want to be able to quickly push changes in the event of a failure.

Your DNS record would look something like Figure 10-5.

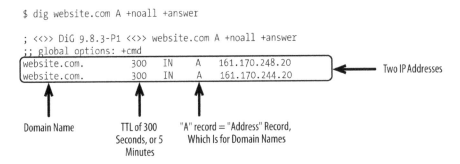

*Figure 10-5. Sample record with two IP addresses returned*

Again, clients can connect to any IP address listed, so make sure you return IP addresses that can actively handle traffic.

## Global Server Load Balancing

### Global Server Load Balancing primer

GSLB amounts to very intelligent DNS that can pick the optimal data center for a given customer. Factors it uses can include the following:

- Availability of a data center (both whether IP responds to pings as well as more in-depth health checking)
- Geographic location of the client
- Roundtrip latency between the client and each data center
- Real-time capacity of each data center
- A number of load-balancing algorithms

The most substantial difference from standard DNS is that it allows you to do much more advanced health checking of a data center, with the ability to automatically drop a data center in real time if it becomes unhealthy. With standard DNS, the only health checking involved is entirely performed on the client side. If a client cannot connect to the IP address returned in the A record, it continues on to the next one in the list. Each client performs this checking slightly differently or sometimes not at all. Worse yet, there are numerous ways an IP address could respond to a ping but not be healthy. Clients don't know the difference between HTTP 200, 404, and 500 responses, for example. GSLB assumes those health-checking responsibilities from the client and can perform a much more thorough interrogation as to the health of a data center. We'll talk about that in "Global Server Load Balancing health checking", but broadly you should apply the health-checking approach from Chapter 5 to an entire data center and configure your GSLB service to probe that page to test the health of a data center. If you're running your platform from two or more data centers, the benefit is that failover happens automatically, without any interaction. Pushing DNS records manually takes time.

In addition to health checking, a GSLB's ability to pinpoint the location of a customer can be incredibly beneficial. Uses include the following:

- Directing customers to the closest data center best able to service their requests. This improves performance and increases conversion rates.

- Making the concurrent login problem discussed earlier in this chapter much less likely to occur. With two data centers and no geolocation, any two customers sharing the same account have a 50% chance of hitting the same data center. With proper geolocation offered by GSLB, you reduce the problem substantially. People in the same household, city, state, or region, are far more likely to be sharing logins, and with proper geolocation are far more likely to hit the same data center.

- You can personalize the experience for customers. For example, you may want to show your Wisconsin customers winter gloves and your Florida customers swimming suits in January.

- You may need to restrict certain functionality based on the physical location of a customer. For example, a promotion may be legal in one state but illegal in another. Rather than show customers a contest that they cannot participate in, it's best to simply remove it for those where it is illegal.

- You can roll out functionality slowly. Say you're cutting over to a new platform. You can do it on a city-by-city basis as you pilot it. This is how consumer packaged-goods companies test out new products.

GSLB can be offered like DNS—self-hosted or as a service. When hosted in-house, it's often through the use of hardware appliances. These appliances likely cannot be used in a cloud. Like DNS, it's best to choose a GSLB Software-as-a-Service vendor rather than trying to do it in-house.

CDNs that offer GSLB are best because they can respond to customers' requests from the edge rather than from a centralized server. That leads to improved performance, as every customer will be making a request to the authoritative DNS server at the beginning of the session. With traditional DNS, there's far more caching involved because the same record can be used for every customer. GSLB returns a unique record for each customer.

CDNs that serve as a reverse proxy also have a substantial advantage over standard DNS for the full active/active approach, whereby a small fraction of customers are forcibly moved from one data center to another. Rather than try to force you to switch IP addresses for a given domain name, you can instead instruct your CDN to proxy the requests at the edge, as shown in Figure 10-6.

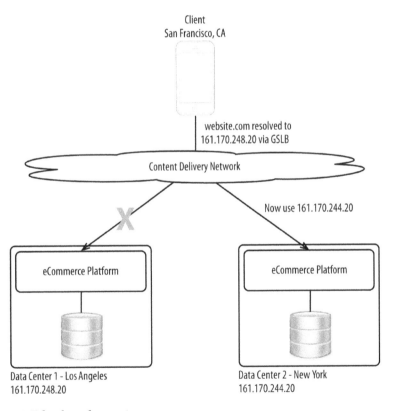

*Figure 10-6. Edge-based proxying*

Even though a client may still map *website.com* back to the wrong IP address, your CDN will simply ignore it and redirect the request to the right data center. The CDN can be told of this change through an HTTP response header, cookie, or similar.

Traditional appliance-based GSLB solutions offer this through proxying. A request may hit the wrong data center, but the appliances can cooperate to proxy the request over to the right data center. The downside is you'll always be proxied through an intermediary data center, perhaps traveling thousands of miles out of the way with each request.

### Global Server Load Balancing health checking

Just as we discussed health checks for individual *deployment units* (Chapter 5) within a data center, you'll need to health check an entire data center in a way that makes sense for your platform.

For a single application server, representative tests include these:

- Querying the cache grid for a product
- Adding a product to the shopping cart
- Writing a new order to a database and then deleting it
- Querying the service bus for inventory availability
- Executing a query against the search engine

If all of the tests came back OK, the response would be the string PASS. Otherwise, the response would come back FAIL. You can configure load balancers to poll for an HTTP 200 response code and PASS in the response. A simple TCP ping isn't good enough.

The same concept holds true for assessing the health of an entire data center (see Figure 10-7). Responding to a simple TCP ping tells you nothing about its health. It's best to build a small standalone web application to poll the dynamic health-check pages of each stack and any other monitoring points. If, say, 75% of the tests come back as a PASS, then report PASS. Have your GSLB query for this page and make it highly available.

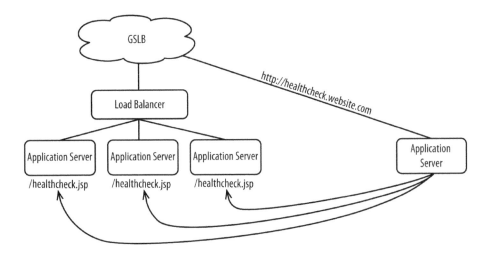

*Figure 10-7. Health checking a data center*

Whereas in the past you had to check the capacity of each data center, you no longer need to do that because you can scale each data center out as required. In other words, the capacity of each data center will be dictated by the amount of traffic GSLB gives it as opposed to how much capacity the data center reports back to GSLB.

# Approaches to Operating from Multiple Data Centers

Pragmatism should be your guiding force as you operate from two or more data centers and, more generally, as you adopt cloud computing. It's important to do your research and then do what works well for you. The approaches outlined here are simply starting points, meant to be customized and extended to suit your exact needs. Broad approaches are described in the following sections.

## Active/Passive

This approach is fairly traditional, whereby only one application tier and database tier in a data center are active at a time (see Figure 10-8). One data center is active, and the other is passive. Replication is often limited to just the database and is unidirectional. A data center failure is unlikely to result in any data being lost (called recovery point objective) but is very likely to result in lengthy downtime (called recovery time objective).

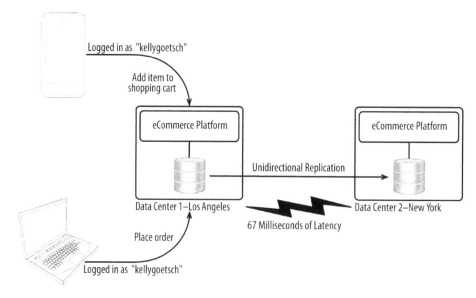

*Figure 10-8. Active/passive deployment architecture*

Lengthy downtime is expected because switching over to the passive data center entails the following:

- Provisioning hardware (Chapter 4)
- Installing software on the newly provisioned hardware (Chapter 4)
- Initializing your database
- Reversing the database synchronization so you have a backup for your newly active database
- Pointing your Global Server Load Balancer to your new data center

This all takes time, with the system down while these activities take place. Unless you invest a lot of time in automating this, it will probably have to be done manually.

With a traditional hosting model, the passive data center would be fully built out with dedicated hardware. This reduces your downtime but at the cost of having double the hardware you would otherwise need sitting completely idle for the vast majority of the year. It's enormously wasteful, but the waste may be outweighed by the reduction in the length of outages.

Active/passive is easiest to use when you want to make as few changes as possible to your applications and your deployment architectures. Since replication happens at the database only and tools exist to do that, you don't have to change any of your other software if you don't want to. That saves a lot of time and money, especially if you're working with software that is difficult to change. You may not even be able to change some software, making this the only viable approach.

## Active/Active Application Tiers, Active/Passive Database Tiers

With this approach, shown in Figure 10-9, you have two or more data centers fully built up and operating independently, with only the database being active/passive. This approach is a great middle ground that avoids most of the headaches of full multimaster (where both your application and database tiers are fully active) but comes with the limitation that your data centers can't be too far apart.

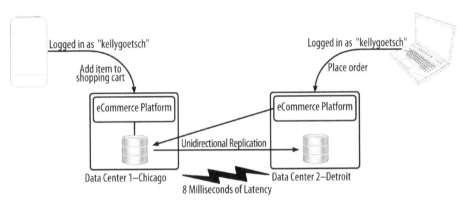

*Figure 10-9. Active/passive application tiers, active/passive database tiers deployment architecture*

Because half of your application tiers will be writing to a database residing in a different data center, the success of this approach depends very much on how often you write to your database, whether those writes are synchronous, and how much latency there is between your application tiers and database. If you're writing to the database five times for every page view and you have 20 milliseconds of latency, you're looking at overhead of 100 milliseconds in pure latency on top of however long it takes for your database to generate the response. The key is picking data centers that are close enough together to minimize the impact of latency, but far enough apart to not be affected by the same natural disasters, human errors, and upstream outages. For example, round-trip latency between Chicago and Detroit is only 8 milliseconds. You could make 12 round-trips between the two and add only 96 milliseconds of latency. By choosing data centers there, you get some good physical separation yet incur very little latency.

If you have an issue with a data center or your software deployed in that data center, you can just stop directing traffic to it and failover to the other data center. You can switch your customers over to the surviving data center within seconds, either through the automated health checking–based approach we discussed earlier in this chapter or by manually making the change.

The real advantage is that you shouldn't have to change your applications all that much. The changes are mostly at the database level. You may have to optimize your code to reduce the number of calls to your database, but that's about it.

## Active/Active Application Tiers, Mostly Active/Active Database Tiers

As discussed earlier in this chapter, the central problem with multimaster is having multiple logins to the same account. When that happens, you can run into data conflicts as the same data is updated from two different databases. The two approaches mentioned don't have this issue because there's only one live database. Even though there may be multiple physical data centers, all writes occur to the same ACID-compliant database. This approach is the first in which each data center has its own active database.

Each data center in this approach, shown in Figure 10-10, has its own application and database stack. By default, customers write to the local database in the data center they've been assigned to. But when the application detects that a customer already has a concurrent login in another data center, the customer will write cross-WAN to the data center having the active session. By doing this, you have full active/active except for the very small percentage of customers with multiple concurrent logins.

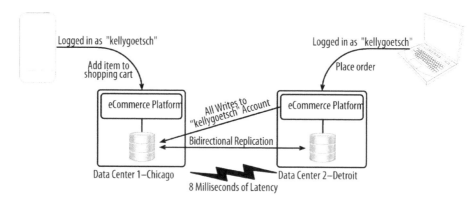

*Figure 10-10. Active/passive application tiers, mostly active/active database tiers deployment architecture*

To implement this approach, you need to change your login process to tag each account with the data center the account is signed in from and the time that a login was last performed. All logins then need to check those two values to see whether someone else is already signed in using those credentials in a different data center. If during the login process you find that somebody else is already logged in to that account from a different data center, you point that customer to the database in the data center where there's already an active login. All reads can still happen from the local database.

Since this is the first approach that uses two or more live databases, all primary keys (or other persistent identifiers) must be prefixed with a unique identifier. For example, a data center in New York could have all of the primary keys generated there prefixed with *ny*. This allows primary keys to remain unique across all data centers.

A complicating factor is how you assign databases to individual customers. The key is to configure your application server to have multiple connection pools, each representing a unique database. If you have a data source for your orders, you would define a data source with an identifier of Order_DS_Local and another one with an identifier of Order_DS_Remote. Then in your application tier, you change data source resolution from a global scoped variable to a session scoped variable. Pseudocode would look something like this:

```
public boolean handleLogin(HttpServletRequest request,
                           HttpServletResponse response)
{
        if (!super.handleLogin(request, response)) // loads Account into session
        {
                return false;
        }

        Account account = (Account)request.getSession()
        .getAttribute("CurrentAccount"); // returns "Chicago"
        String thisDataCenterName = Constants.CURRENT_DATA_CENTER_NAME;


        // if account.getCurrentDataCenter() = "Chicago"
        if (account.getCurrentDataCenter().equals(thisDataCenter))
        {
                request.getSession().setAttribute("Order_Data_Source",
                        Constants.LOCAL_ORDER_DATA_SOURCE);
            // sets to "Order_DS_Local"
        }
        else // if account.getCurrentDataCenter() = "Detroit"
        {
                request.getSession().setAttribute("Order_Data_Source",
                        Constants.REMOTE_ORDER_DATA_SOURCE);
            // sets to "Order_DS_Remote"
        }

        return true;
}
```

Your implementation will be substantially different, but the logic should be fairly similar.

# Full Active/Active

This approach (Figure 10-11), like the previous approach, has data centers that operate autonomously, with each data center equipped with its own application and database tiers. Rather than writing cross-WAN for the handful of customers with active logins in another data center, this approach requires those customers be forcibly moved to the data center having the active login. This allows all customers to always be served from a local database, with no communication occurring cross-WAN.

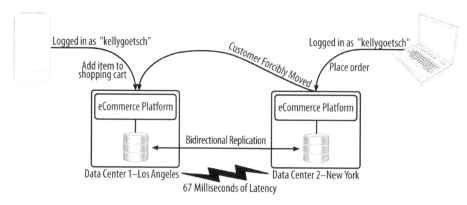

*Figure 10-11. Full active/active deployment architecture*

The implementation of this approach starts out being the same as the prior one. You need to tag each account with the data center the account signed in from and the time that a login was last performed. You then need to write a bit of code to determine whether the customer is signed in somewhere else. This is all the same as the prior approach. The difference is that a customer found to be in the "wrong" data center is forcibly moved to the data center that has an active session for the account. Following the redirection, all HTTP requests and HTTP sessions belonging to that account are served from the same data center, application tier, and database. Anonymous customers never need to be redirected because they don't have a home data center.

The problem with this approach is that it's very difficult to *unstick* a customer from a data center. IP addresses (with data centers each represented by a single domain name and each IP address mapping back to a single data center) are cached through various intermediaries. For example, many web browsers cache IP address/domain name combinations longer than called for by the DNS record (time to live). You can't just force a client to reliably re-resolve a domain name and have that change take effect immediately. We'll discuss this in greater detail shortly, but at a high level you have to intercept the HTTP requests at the edge by using a Content Delivery Network and have proxying done there. There may be some ways to force clients to re-resolve the IP address, but that would be even more challenging to do than the CDN/proxying approach. With full active/active, this may not even be possible to do, but this approach offers substantial benefits above the previous. Again, we'll discuss this in more detail shortly.

## Stateless Frontends, Stateful Backends

This approach will be discussed extensively in Chapter 11, but it amounts to separating your frontend from your backend as part of an architecture for omnichannel (see Figure 10-12).

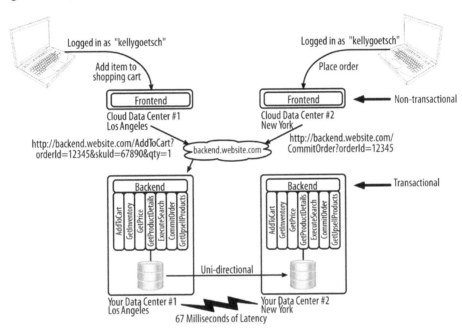

*Figure 10-12. Stateless frontends, stateful backends deployment architecture*

In this scenario, your backend is used only for transactional actions, like placing an order or finding out which products to pitch to a customer. You interact with it through basic HTTP requests, like this:

```
http://backend.website.com/CommitOrder?orderId=12345
```

Your responses are JSON, XML, or some other generic format that your frontend can parse and display back to the customer:

```
{
    "success": true,
    "message": "Your order has been successfully placed.", ...
}
```

Your backend is deployed to data centers that you control, leveraging the hardware and software you want. This requires statically provisioning hardware and scaling for the peak, but the difference is that your backend is now handling a much smaller amount of traffic because your frontend is serving much of it. Refer to the traffic funnel: most of your traffic is for anonymously browsed pages that don't require any interaction with your backend. Your frontend is deployed in a cloud, where it can be elastically scaled.

A key advantage of this approach is that you can throw many frontends on the platform and maintain a consistent customer experience across all the channels and devices. The frontends become dumb presentation layers. They're more or less disposable. Almost all native iPhone and Android applications work like this today, with the trend increasing as more channels and device types must continue to be supported. This architecture is a significant departure from the past, where frontends were tangled up with the backends, to the point where you couldn't separate the two. Many ecommerce platforms still ship the backend (e.g., classes, libraries) in the same package (e.g., an EAR file) as the frontend (e.g., JSP, ASP, HTML, CSS, or JavaScript). Rendering HTML is what consumes most of the CPU cycles. If you skip the user interface, you can get far more throughput than you otherwise would be able to if the two were combined.

The other advantage of this approach is that you can now deploy your backends active/passive across two data centers. So long as your frontends all point back to the same backend, you won't run into any of the problems mentioned in this chapter because every update to a given customer's data ultimately terminates in the same database.

Again, we'll discuss this approach further in Chapter 11.

# Review of Approaches

As we've discussed, there are numerous approaches to operating from multiple data centers. Table 10-2 quickly summarizes each approach.

*Table 10-2. Approaches to operating from multiple data centers*

| Approach | Number of active databases | Recovery point objective | Recovery time objective | Max distance between data centers | Changes to application | Database replication | Competency required for implementation |
|---|---|---|---|---|---|---|---|
| Active/passive | 1 | Zero | 1 hour+ | Unlimited | None | Unidirectional | Low |
| Active/active application tiers, active/passive database tiers | 1 | Zero | 5 minutes | <25 ms | Minor | Unidirectional | Low |
| Active/active application tiers, mostly active/active database tiers | 2+ | Zero | Zero | <25 ms | Moderate | Bidirectional | Moderate |
| Full active/active | 2+ | Zero | Zero | Unlimited | High | Bidirectional | High |
| Stateless frontends, stateful backends | 1+ | Zero | Zero | <100 ms | High | Unidirectional or bidirectional | High |

As discussed earlier, pragmatism should be your guiding force as you select the approach that works for you and then customize it to meet your needs.

# Summary

While all forms of operating from multiple data centers take work, it's something that the industry is rapidly adopting because of the increasing importance of ecommerce. Outages simply cannot happen in today's world.

Operating from multiple data centers is also a prerequisite for a hybrid model of cloud computing, which we'll discuss in the next chapter.

# CHAPTER 11

# Hybrid Cloud

Though ecommerce applications have traditionally been viewed as monolithic with the frontends (e.g., HTML, CSS, JavaScript) being inseparably combined with backends (e.g., one or more applications containing business logic connected to a persistence layer), it doesn't have to be this way. In today's omnichannel world, the approach of having the two inseparably combined no longer makes sense technically or strategically. "Backend" in this chapter can refer to a single monolithic application or a collection of finegrained microservices that are indivdually designed, developed, deployed and managed, or any point on the spectrum between monoliths and microservices.

If you split your frontend from your backend, most page views can be served from your frontend without the backend ever being touched. Only when you transact—add to cart, check out, update profile, and so forth—do you actually have to touch your backend. In this model, your backend substantially shrinks and remains under your firm control while your frontend can elastically soak up most of the page views in a public cloud. DNS ultimately resolves to your frontend, with your frontend then calling your backend when necessary, as shown in Figure 11-1.

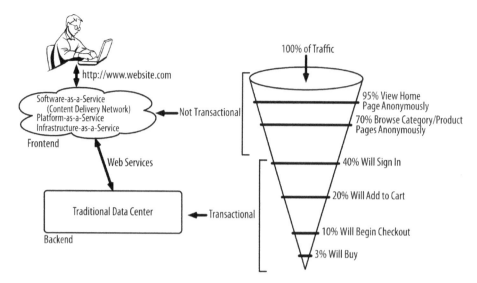

*Figure 11-1. Nontransactional frontend served from a cloud, transactional backend served from a traditional data center*

This is exactly how most other channels work today, with the exception of the Web. Thick client applications like those found on kiosks or smartphones already interact with your backend in this way. It's time for the Web to catch up to this model.

In addition to strategic reasons, there are practical reasons the two should be split. The hosting needs for a frontend are different from what a backend needs. Your backend needs the following:

- One or more highly available and fully backed-up datastores
- Terabytes of highly available and fully backed-up storage
- High-quality, reliable hardware
- Multiple firewalls
- Integration with other backend systems (ERP, CRM, data warehouse, etc)
- Highest possible availability
- Highest possible security for data at rest

While clouds *can* offer this, many will find it easier and safer to keep this in-house. Your frontend needs the following:

- Rapid elasticity
- A lot of bandwidth
- Highest possible security for data in motion
- To be inexpensive

These attributes make cloud a natural fit for frontends. Before we explore the various flavors of how to split frontends from backends, let's explore how this architecture is a natural by-product of an architecture for omnichannel.

# Hybrid Cloud as a By-product of Architecture for Omnichannel

Traditionally, ecommerce applications have been written and deployed in a single package containing the following:

- HTML/CSS/JavaScript
- Server-side scripting code like JSP and ASP
- Server-side code like Java or C#

This package was typically deployed to an application server as a single archive, like a WAR or EAR file. To get to the compiled server-side code, you had to first go through your server-side scripting code. Developers worked on both frontend and backend code. When the Web was the only channel, this worked just fine (see Figure 11-2).

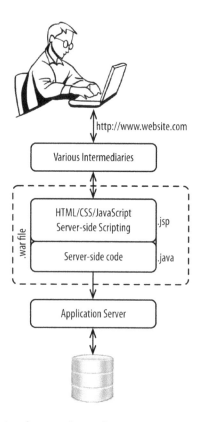

*Figure 11-2. Code packaging for one channel*

Then multichannel came of age in the mid-2000s as mobile began to take off. No substantial architecture changes were made to support mobile and the new channels that followed it. Additional channels were built alongside the existing stack supporting the web browser–based HTML user interface, with integration gluing everything together. Each channel operated in a silo, unaware of what was going on in another channel unless there was full bidirectional integration between each channel, as shown in Figure 11-3.

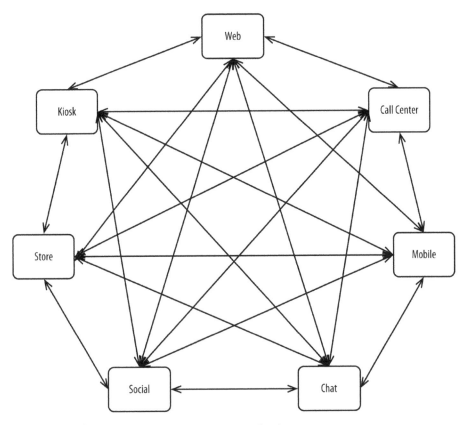

*Figure 11-3. What multichannel ecommerce evolved into*

Even with full bidirectional integration, the customer experience was still poor because integrating heterogeneous systems is inherently error prone and updates are always asynchronous. As we've discussed in previous chapters, the solution to this problem is to build a single *omnichannel* platform whereby core functionality (inventory, pricing, promotions, product, etc) is each exposed as a service, with any user interface able to consume those services (see Figure 11-4). These pieces of functionality may be exposed as traditional SOA-flavored services (single monolithic application exposing multiple SOAP or REST endpoints) or as microservices (small single-purpose applications that are individually designed, developed, deployed and managed).

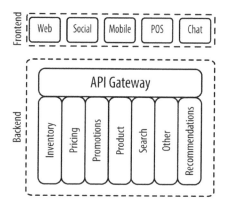

*Figure 11-4. Omnichannel-friendly architecture*

This architecture entirely eliminates the need to perform any integration, because the various channel-specific user interfaces now hit the same backend monolithic application or collection of microservices. The backend is now *the* system of record, as opposed to something off to the side.

 Both omnichannel retailing *and* hybrid clouds require the frontend to be split from the backend. The split is a natural outcome of an omnichannel-based architecture.

Once you break the frontend from the backend, you can deploy each tier and possibly each backend microservice separately, with all interaction taking place through a clearly defined API, as depicted in Figure 11-5.

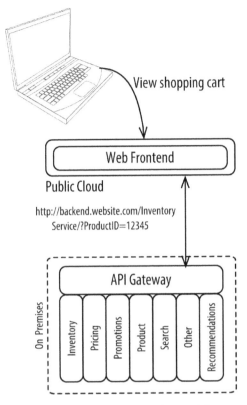

*Figure 11-5. Frontend in a cloud, backend in a traditional data center*

These APIs can be reused across any channel and frontend, with all clients transacting against the same backend services. Customers love the seamless interaction across channels for the following reasons:

- Pricing, promotions, inventory, product assortment, and all other data is the same across all channels.
- Customers don't have to create profiles unique to each channel.
- Customers can update the same shopping cart across multiple channels. For example, a customer can begin an order on a mobile device and finish it on a desktop at work.
- Customers can have contact center agents or employees in a physical store help to complete an order started online.

Multichannel inherently leads to fragmentation, which upsets customers. Omnichannel, on the other hand, allows for seamless customer engagements across channels.

Before we can discuss the different approaches to a hybrid cloud and how it intersects with omnichannel retailing, we have to discuss how to best connect your backend to your frontend in a cloud.

# Connecting to the Cloud

When your frontend is physically distant from your backend, you need to bridge them together with a connection. Every HTTP request to your frontend may result in between zero and potentially dozens of requests to your backend services. Requests are typically HTTP, but may be any protocol. The connection discussed in this chapter is a vitally important link between the two halves of your platform, so it must at least be highly available and offer enough bandwidth. Beyond that, the connection can optionally offer security and low latency.

Despite this seeming like an important attribute, security doesn't matter all that much. The *contents* of each HTTP request or other communication protocol must be secured (e.g., SSL/TLS in the case of HTTP), but the communication can flow over the Internet. For example, VPNs secure the payload but operate over the Internet. Securing the payload should be your focus, as your assumption should be that your connection is always compromised.

Latency is also a less important attribute, though it depends on your architecture. The more calls you make from your frontends to your backends and the more those calls are synchronous, the more you'll need low latency. Some applications will require that your frontend be almost colocated with your backend because of the number of lookups that are made to backend systems. To improve performance, strongly consider using a WAN accelerator.

If you serve your backend out of two or more data centers, strongly consider pointing your frontends to your backends through a Global Server Load Balancer with latency-based routing. This will ensure that each frontend is connecting to an available backend that offers the lowest possible latency.

When selecting a vendor, the breadth and depth of connectivity options a prospective cloud vendor offers should be heavily weighted. Let's explore the three broad approaches to connecting your backends to your frontends in a cloud.

## Public Internet

The first approach is to use the public Internet. You can expose your backend to the Internet through a domain like *backend.website.com*. This is exactly what's done today for every channel but the Web. Data can then be transferred between the frontend and backend over HTTPS, exactly as it is between your customer and the cloud. In other words, data in flight between your frontend and backend is no more unsecure than it is between your customer and the cloud.

With this approach, HTTP GET (e.g., *https://backend.website.com/AddToCart? orderId=12345&skuId=67890&qty=1*) is unsecure because even though the contents of the HTTP request are secure, the URL is visible to the world. To avoid this issue, you'd have to HTTP POST the data to *https://backend.website.com/AddToCart*:

```
{
    "orderId": "12345",
    "skuId": "67890",
    "qty": 1, ...
}
```

In addition to HTTPS, you'll want to use an additional security mechanism to ensure that nobody but your frontend is able to transact with your backend. Otherwise, anybody on the Internet would be able to arbitrarily execute commands against your backend. Certificate-based mutual authentication is a great way of doing this, though there are others. The requirement should be that only authenticated clients are able to issue HTTP requests to your backend.

You could configure your backend load balancer to accept only traffic from a range of IP addresses belonging to your cloud vendor, but with ecommerce so elastic, you'll never be able to configure your backend load balancer to whitelist every IP address. It also wouldn't take much for a hacker to provision a server from a public cloud and issue HTTP requests from there to bypass your range filter.

## VPN

In addition to HTTPS, you can add another layer of security over communication between your frontend and backend by making use of an IPsec-based VPN. Traffic is still going over the Internet, but now you have two layers of security: SSL/TLS for HTTPS, and IPsec. Cloud vendors offer these VPNs as an integrated part of their offering.

As always, you should avoid using HTTP GET to move sensitive data back and forth.

## Direct Connections

Many cloud vendors offer colo vendors the ability to run dedicated fiber lines into their data centers. This allows colo vendors to build data centers in the same metro area as the cloud vendors and offer what amounts to private LAN connections into a cloud. With the data centers physically close, you get millisecond-level latency and multigigabit per second throughput. These connections are dedicated and do not touch the Internet, thus adding another layer of security.

# Approaches to Hybrid Cloud

## Caching Entire Pages

A great first step in adopting cloud computing is to move static pages out to a cloud in much the same way that CDNs serve static pages and static content (e.g., images, JavaScript, and CSS; see Figure 11-6).

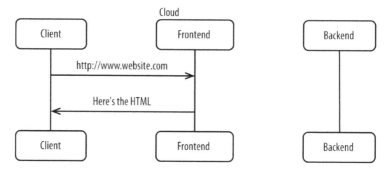

*Figure 11-6. Serving static pages from your frontend in the cloud*

Of course, anything dynamic or not yet cached must be served directly from the origin, as Figure 11-7 shows.

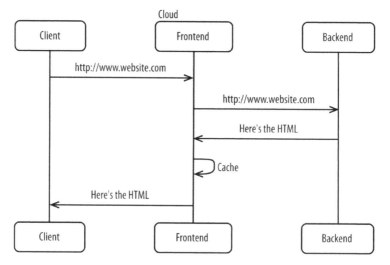

*Figure 11-7. Serving static pages from your frontend in the cloud, going back to backend as required*

HTTP responses, whether the response type is HTML, XML, JSON, or some other format, work in much the same way, except that the content can vary based on several factors:

- Whether the customer is logged in
- Web browser/user agent
- Physical location (often accurate to zip + 4 within the US or post code outside the US)
- Internet connection speed
- Locale
- Operating system

Provided you can identify the variables that affect HTTP responses and vary the HTTP responses accordingly, this approach works very well for offloading most of your HTTP requests. Caching of this nature is commonly employed, especially in advance of large bursts of traffic, like before a holiday or during a special event like the Superbowl.

Use this approach to optimize any existing ecommerce website, whether or not it's adhering to the omnichannel architectural principles. It's quick and easy to do and works best for pages that don't change all that much. Home pages, category landing pages, and product detail pages work best for this.

To do this, you need software that does the following:

- Sits between the client and your endpoint (typically an application server). Proxies and load balancers commonly meet this need.
- Can examine each HTTP request. In the OSI stack, this refers to layer 7. For example, the software should be able to look at the user agent HTTP request header.
- Can accept blacklist rules for what not to cache. For example, you should be able to define a rule that says anything under /checkout should be immediately passed back to the origin.
- Can understand the variables that affect the response. For example, you may vary your response based on whether the customer is logged in, what the user agent is, and physical location. Each of those attributes would come together to form a unique key. If a cached copy of, say, XML corresponding to that key exists, it should be returned. If not, the request should be passed back to the origin, with the response the origin generates being cached.

- Can store and retrieve gigabytes worth of cached data quickly and effectively.
- Can quickly flush caches following updates to the underlying data.

The key is identifying the variables that cause the output of each URL to vary its response. Once you've identified those, you can cache the vast majority of HTTP requests.

Intermediaries of all types are capable of doing this. Load balancers and proxies are common examples, but even many web servers are capable of this. This functionality is built into CDNs that are capable of serving as reverse proxies, but you can also deploy software of your choosing to public IaaS clouds.

It's generally best to rely on CDNs to provide this functionality, as they have the advantage of pushing your cached pages out to each of their dozens or even hundreds of data centers around the world. Customers are unlikely to be more than a few milliseconds away from an endpoint, meaning most HTTP requests can be served with virtually no latency and no waiting for the response to be generated. In addition to performance, CDNs expose this functionality as SaaS, which frees you up to focus your energy higher up the value chain.

The only case for doing this in a public Infrastructure-as-a-Service cloud is if this is your first foray into more-substantive cloud computing and you want to do this as an educational exercise. This is something that's fairly easy to do yet provides substantial benefits.

If you're not yet sold on public clouds, you can also do this in your existing data center(s). The load balancer you use today probably has this functionality. While this is an excellent approach for a fraction of your traffic, to cache more you have to look at the next approach.

## Overlaying HTML on Cached Pages

While many HTTP requests can be served directly from cache, some cannot. For example, customers viewing a product detail page often see a list of products recommended based on their browsing history or purchase history. They look like Figure 11-8.

Other products you might like

| Arrow Men's Quarter-Zip Fleece | Covington Men's Cotton Crew Neck Sweater - Striped | Outdoor Life Men's Quarter Zip Microfleece Sweatshirt | Dockers Men's Soft Touch Sweater - Windowpane |
| --- | --- | --- | --- |
| $60.00  **$19.99** | $40.00  **$12.99** | $50.00  **$19.99** | $60.00  **$19.99** |

*Figure 11-8. You Might Also Like products*

These are called *You Might Also Like* products, abbreviated YMAL for short.

When most of a given page is the same but only a small part varies, you can cache the entire page in an intermediary as per the prior approach, but then dynamically overlay the few fragments of content that actually change on the client side, as in Figure 11-9.

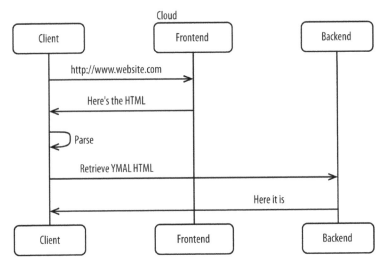

*Figure 11-9. Overlaying HTML on cached pages*

You can easily apply this technique to the following:

- Ratings and reviews
- Shopping carts
- Breadcrumbs
- "Hello, <First Name>!" banners in the header

Here's a very simple example of what the code would look like to do this:

```
<head>
    <script src="http://www.website.com/app/jquery/jquery.min.js">
    </script>
    <script>
        $.ajax({url:"http://backend.website.com/app/RetrieveYMALs?
        productId=12345&customerId=54321",
        success:function(result){
            $("#YMALs").html(result);
        }});
    </script>
</head>
<body>
    <!-- Product details... -->
    <div id="YMALs"></div>
    ... rest of web page
</body>
```

To make this work, your asynchronous HTTP request must be returned as quickly as possible. If you wait too long to make the asynchronous request, the customer will see a fully rendered page but without the overlay. In the YMAL example, the customer will see screen repainting or, worse yet, whitespace where the products are supposed to be listed. To do this, make the asynchronous call as early as you can when loading the main page to parallelize as much of the loading as possible. Put the call at the top of the header. Also, ensure the response time of the service delivering the content responds as quickly as possible. It should take just a few milliseconds to get a response to avoid the page "jumping around" as various parts of the page are painted.

You also have to design your user interface for failure. If the asynchronous request doesn't work, the customer should never know. In other words, there shouldn't be a hole where the content loaded asynchronously is supposed to be.

Finally, design your user interface for graceful fallback. If the client doesn't support JavaScript, either omit the dynamic content entirely or go back to the origin to render a dynamic version of the page. For example, most search engine bots don't support JavaScript. You'll want the entire page to be indexed.

When fully and properly implemented, this technique can substantially decrease the amount of load that hits your backend. The more you serve out of your frontend in the cloud, the less you have to serve out of your backend.

## Using Content Delivery Networks to Insert HTML

Rather than overlay your dynamic fragments on the client side as with the previous approach, you can overlay them in a CDN or an equivalent intermediary (see Figure 11-10).

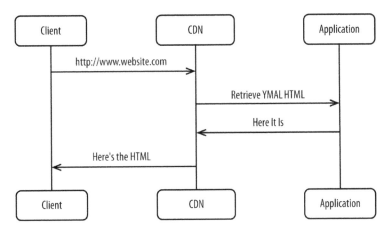

*Figure 11-10. Using CDNs to insert HTML*

By not doing anything on the client side, you don't have to worry about gracefully falling back if the client doesn't support JavaScript or any of the other issues that arise when you're trying to build a page by asynchronously loading HTML from somewhere else. The other advantage is that you don't have to forcibly split your frontend from your backend, as we'll discuss in the next approach. If you're looking to increase the number of pages you can serve from cache and don't want to rewrite your application, this is your approach.

As with the client-side overlay, the technology to implement this doesn't matter all that much. What matters is that you're able to clearly demarcate where you'd like to insert dynamic content and from what source. The most common framework is Edge Side Includes (ESI). ESI is a simple markup language that closely mimics the capabilities of server-side includes, which we'll discuss next.

Here's an example of what the code would look like to do this:

```
<body>
    <!-- Product details... -->
    <div id="YMALs">
        <esi:include
            src="http://backend.website.com/app/
            RetrieveYMALs?productId=12345&customerId=54321" />
    </div>
    ... rest of web page
</body>
```

Most of the major CDNs support ESI, as do some load balancers and reverse proxies. While it's best to use this technique with CDNs because of their ability to cache content and push it to the *edge*, you can certainly use load balancers and reverse proxies.

The code here is much easier to write because you don't have to worry about doing anything asynchronously or the problems arising from that. You just insert the dynamic fragments of your page and return the entire HTML document to the client when it's ready. Some frameworks even allow you to load each of the includes asynchronously, with the entire page not returned to the client until the last include is returned. This improves performance, especially if you have many different includes.

Again, this approach is a great middle ground that will allow you to cache much more than you otherwise would, but without having to rewrite your application.

## Overlaying HTML on the Server Side

This next approach is where the frontend for your website is independently served out of a cloud, with dynamic content from your backend woven into the page generated by your frontend. This is a fundamentally different approach than using a CDN or client to overlay fragments, because with this model you're actually serving your frontend independently of your backend, as shown in Figure 11-11.

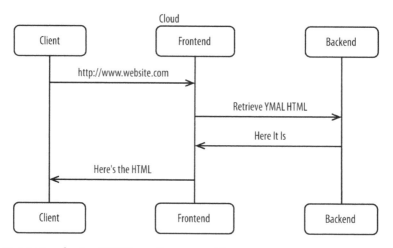

*Figure 11-11. Overlaying HTML on the server side*

With the frontend split from the backend, you're pulling in only small, dynamic fragments from your backend. Your frontend is then free to run wherever you want, as in a public cloud. Your frontend, which handles most of the traffic, can then dynamically scale up and down, pulling in dynamic fragments from your backend as required. Your backend can then be much smaller and hosted traditionally.

The capabilities to insert dynamic content into an existing page have existed since the early days of the Internet, beginning with server-side includes, which are still used today. All scripting tag libraries also have support for this, through import or include tags.

Here's an example of what the code would look like to do this:

```
<body>
    <!-- Product details... -->
    <div id="YMALs">
        <!--#include
            virtual="http://backend.website.com/app/
            RetrieveYMALs?productId=12345&customerId=54321" -->
    </div>
    ... rest of web page
</body>
```

While the technology is fairly simple, the architectural implementations are enormous. Rather than simply serving a static HTML document and then overlaying the dynamic bits, you're actually *generating* a dynamic page for each customer in the cloud and simply including the dynamic fragments that you need from your backend where appropriate. This is a great way to move much of the workload out to a dynamic cloud. In this model, the backend is solely responsible for delivering a small amount of content, and the frontend is responsible for delivering much of the actual content. It's a big difference, though the technical underpinnings have existed for decades.

## Fully Decoupled Frontends and Backends

All of the approaches documented thus far have assumed that the content that would be overlaid is HTML. But as you recall from earlier in the book, the web channel where HTML is used is rapidly being marginalized in favor of mobile and other channels. Only web browsers use HTML. Every other channel consumes some form of XML or JSON from your origin, making all of the approaches thus far irrelevant to nonweb channels.

With this approach, your frontend is out in a cloud, retrieving small fragments of dynamic content from your backend as required. The difference between this and the previous approach is that the response from the backend should be XML or JSON instead of HTML, as Figure 11-12 shows.

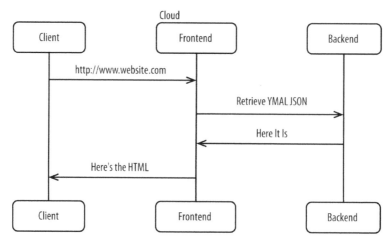

*Figure 11-12. Fully decoupled frontends and backends*

It's certainly easier to return responses in HTML, because you don't have to change your code all that much. But the problem with that is it prevents you from ever reusing your backend services across channels because none of the other channels can consume HTML. In this model, you construct your HTML pages by using data from your backend but not the presentation. It's a clean separation between presentation and business logic.

Here's an example of what the code would look like to do this:

```
<body>
<!-- Product details... -->
<div id="YMALs">
    <c:import url="http://backend.website.com/app/
        RetrieveYMALs?productId=12345&customerId=54321"
        var="ymals" />
    <h2><c:out value="${ymals.displayText}"></h2>
        <c:forEach items="${ymals.products}" var="product">
            <jsp:include page="/app/productDetailYMAL.jsp">
                <jsp:param name="product" value="${product}" />
            </jsp:include>
        </c:forEach>
</div>
... rest of web page
</body>
```

Again, this is a fundamental departure from how many web pages are constructed today, with the backend providing only structured data. What's best about this approach is that the services exposed by the backend (e.g., *http://back end.website.com/app/RetrieveYMALs*) can be reused across all channels because all you're exposing is raw data.

If you adopt a pure microservices architecture, this is really the only approach that works.

 This is the future of ecommerce architecture, regardless of where you deploy your front and backends. This approach requires substantial changes to your code and architecture, but the long-term benefits are transformational to the way you do business.

## Everything but the Database in the Cloud

The most extreme form of hybrid computing is putting *everything* out in a public cloud except the database. Your frontend is fully split from your backend to adhere to omnichannel architecture principles, but you deploy both tiers to a cloud, with your frontend-to-backend communication occurring entirely within the cloud. Only your database is outside the cloud, as Figure 11-13 shows.

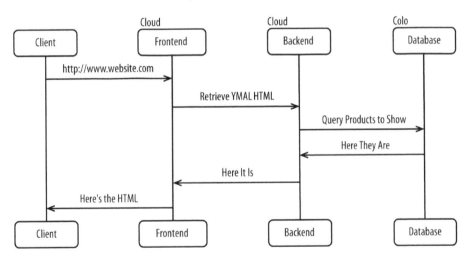

*Figure 11-13. Everything but the database in the cloud*

Because latency is so important, this approach must be used in conjunction with the direct-connection approach from "Connecting to the Cloud", whereby you host your database in a colo that has a direct physical connection to the cloud you're operating from. Pulling a single product from the database may result in dozens of SQL queries, because data may be spread out across dozens of tables. When you have potentially dozens of serial SQL statements executed per HTTP request, latency quickly kills performance. With a direct connection, you should have a millisecond or less of latency, making this no longer an issue.

Databases can be deployed in a cloud, but you may find it easier to deploy them in a colo connected to the cloud, as databases have stringent software, hardware, networking, storage, and security requirements that may not be fully offered by a database in a cloud. Monolithic applications with inseparable frontends and backends can also benefit from this approach.

We'll discuss this more in the next chapter.

# Summary

As with everything, there are benefits and trade-offs to each of the approaches listed. Clearly the trend is moving toward a design that supports full omnichannel retailing, whereby the backend is serving snippets of XML and JSON to a frontend in a cloud that builds the HTML responses. Until that goal can be fully realized, the approaches before it are great steps that provide substantial benefits.

Here's a quick summary of the approaches in Table 11-1.

*Table 11-1. Summary of hybrid approaches*

| Approach | Where fragment is included | Relative level of backend offload | Format of HTTP response from backend | Requires clean front/ backend separation | Channels applicable to | Level of changes to application |
|---|---|---|---|---|---|---|
| Caching entire pages | N/A | Low | N/A | No | All | None |
| Overlaying HTML on cached pages | Client | Medium | HTML | No | Web | Low |
| Using Content Delivery Networks to insert HTML | Content Delivery Network | High | HTML | No | Web | Medium |
| Overlaying HTML on the server side | Frontend servers | High | HTML | No | Web | High |
| Fully decoupled frontends and backends | Frontend servers | High | XML or JSON | Yes | All | High |
| Everything but database in the cloud | N/A | N/A | N/A | No | All | None |

It's best to start at the top of this table and work your way down as you build competence.

For more information on hybrid cloud-based architectures, read Bill Wilder's *Cloud Architecture Patterns* (O'Reilly).

As the move to smartphones, tablets, and other nonweb browser devices accelerates, HTML-based frontends are going to be increasingly marginalized. The value of a hybrid cloud is that your frontend, which is handling most of the traffic today, can leverage what a cloud has to offer—elasticity, unlimited ability to scale up, and cost savings. But over time, the traffic to your frontend will drop, eventually reaching a point where a majority of traffic is from devices that have thick clients. A hybrid cloud is fundamentally a transitional technology. It will be around for a while, but eventually many workloads, like ecommerce, will shift entirely to the cloud.

# CHAPTER 12

# Exclusively Using a Public Cloud

Deploying your entire ecommerce platform to a cloud, or as much as possible, is the future of ecommerce. We're rapidly moving away from an era where software is deployed in-house on dedicated hardware that you or someone else manages. Cloud computing is revolutionary to business because it commoditizes computing power in much the same way that public utilities have commoditized power and water. Tapping computing power allows you to focus on your core competency of, say, selling apparel, rather than building and maintaining infrastructure. The overall lower costs and shift from capital to operational expenditures is equally transformational.

In Chapter 3, we discussed the various service models (Infrastructure-as-a-Service, Platform-as-a-Service, and Software-as-a-Service) and deployment models (public, hybrid, and private). This chapter focuses on public deployment models, with either IaaS or PaaS being the service model. Let's review why you would want to deploy your entire platform to a cloud.

## Why Full Cloud?

### Business Reasons

Full cloud, whereby your entire platform is deployed in a cloud, is more revolutionary to your business than it is from a purely technology standpoint. The more you use a cloud, the more benefits you realize. Even using it for just preproduction will yield substantial benefits.

The first and most salient argument for a full cloud solution is that it frees you up to focus on your core competency. Building and maintaining infrastructure is incredibly distracting from your core business. You have to hire the right people, select software/hardware/hosting vendors, set up the hardware and software, keep the systems patched, deal with failures, and so on. The challenges only multiply when you build your own Platform-as-a-Service and Software-as-a-Service offerings. You should focus your limited resources on where you can add value—for example, by offering the most comprehensive ratings and reviews system. You will never gain a competitive advantage by applying a patch or tuning a Linux kernel. Let the cloud vendors handle this for you and focus on where you can add value.

The second argument for a full cloud solution is that you can drive as much traffic to the platform as you want, provided you have a full auto-scaling solution, as discussed in Chapter 4. A valid concern with traditional and hybrid platforms has always been the fear that an unanticipated spike in traffic will bring down the whole platform. If part of your environment is statically provisioned, there will always be the possibility of it being fully utilized. In the Internet age, a promotion can quickly travel around the Internet, driving potentially millions of customers to your platform. With a fully cloud-based solution, there is no such thing as not having enough capacity when you can spin up thousands of servers in minutes. In addition to preventing outages, your technical administrators no longer need to monitor and curtail what business users are doing. When outages due to overcapacity were a concern, business users were always handcuffed as to what they could do. Now they're free to do pretty much whatever they want on their own.

The third argument for a full cloud is that you can save money and potentially use the savings to fund initiatives that grow your revenue. The elasticity and metering offered by cloud computing allows you to pay for what you use as you realize value. No longer do you have to buy hundreds or even thousands of servers only to have them sit underutilized. Cloud vendors themselves add value by handling the routine setup and ongoing maintenance for you. You just pay for infrastructure, platform, and/or software, and the vendor does the rest.

While these three business-level arguments are compelling, the technical arguments for a full cloud solution are even more compelling.

## Technical Reasons

While the cloud is revolutionary to business, it is more *evolutionary* from a technology standpoint. The concept of another vendor offering infrastructure, platform, or software as a service is not new. What is new is the packaging and mainstream adoption of these principles. Again, the more cloud you use, the more value you see.

Cloud vendors offer superior availability, security, and functionality by being able to specialize on their core competency, which in their case is offering infrastructure, platform, and/or software as a service. They can hire the best people in the world and pay them exorbitantly to ensure their offerings are of the highest quality. Your business is ecommerce. You can't and shouldn't focus on any of the lower-value activities that the cloud vendors do so well. For example, some cloud vendors offer an advanced virtualization technique that's known as single-root I/O virtualization (SR-IOV). This technology allows you to bypass the hypervisor for any network-related communication. The business value is that it can substantially improve the performance of your platform. The downside has always been the cost and complexity required to implement, as implementation involves changes to numerous layers from the operating system on down. It would take weeks for you to implement this on your own, *if* you could even do it.

# Why Not Full Cloud?

Deploying your entire platform to a public cloud may not be fully realizable or even advisable, depending on your circumstances. A hybrid approach shouldn't be seen as a *lesser* solution, but as different while still providing many advantages. As with all decisions, don't let idealism influence your decision making (too much).

Here are four technical reasons you wouldn't be able to adopt a full cloud solution:

- Your software won't operate from a cloud. For example, some software cannot support virtualization or tolerate any network latency.
- You need custom hardware, and your cloud doesn't support hosting custom hardware. For example, you may use hardware-based encryption for your database.
- Your software may not be formally certified on the exact software and hardware stacks offered by your vendor. For example, some legacy software may require a legacy version of Windows or an esoteric distribution of Unix.
- Some software, like databases, have unique requirements around storage that requires a more customized solution. For example, your database may require Fibre Channel, which requires special-purpose cabling.

While there may be some valid technical reasons for not adopting a full cloud-based solution, the issues you're likely to encounter are probably of the nontechnical variety:

- Not enough organizational competence to make such a big change.
- An organization that has entrenched interests that oppose a cloud. For example, you're likely to face stiff opposition from a team that currently manages its environment. It's only natural to be threatened by changes that could put you out of a job.
- Concerns about security. While security should be *better* in a cloud, not everybody will see it that way. Not everybody understands how secure a cloud can be. It's often easier to just say "no," especially for those who don't benefit from moving to a cloud.

- Licensing of commercial products may not support a cloud. Unless you have a license that allows unlimited use of software, you'll have to license for your peak usage, which negates many of the benefits of a cloud. You'll also have to be able to demonstrate exactly how many cores your software is running on, which may be difficult when you're rapidly scaling up and down.

- Not enough capital to fund the cutover. It costs a lot to reorient an organization around a cloud. Costs include everything from re-architecture to training courses offered by your cloud vendor. Cloud computing is an example of a disruptive technology. Disruptive technologies are expensive to implement.

 While these nontechnical challenges may be difficult to overcome, complacency is harder.

Your legacy deployment model, as inefficient and costly as it may be, is fully understood and likely to be trusted by executive management. Given the rapid growth of ecommerce, throwing money at a problem may just be easier and perceived as safer. The longer this move is postponed, the harder it's going to be in the future.

While there are benefits to adopting a full cloud-based solution, a hybrid approach is often the most pragmatic. There are just so many barriers to adopting a full cloud-based solution that it's often not practical yet. Hybrid works best when you have a direct connection from your cloud to a colo facility that's physically near your cloud. When you have just a millisecond or two connecting your cloud to your colo, it's as good as if they're colocated in the same data center. With a hybrid approach, you can deploy each hardware and software component where it makes the most sense. Table 12-1 shows the differences between public and private, with hybrid being somewhere in the middle.

*Table 12-1. Public versus private cloud characteristics*

| Public cloud | Private cloud |
| --- | --- |
| Full elasticity | No elasticity |
| Virtually unlimited capacity | Fixed capacity |
| Pay-as-you-grow metered pricing | Fixed pricing |
| Must develop or adapt apps to run | Any app will run without modification |
| Vendor sets up | You set up |
| Vendor manages | You manage |
| Limited ability to change underlying configuration | Complete ability to change underlying configuration |
| Limited ability to use custom hardware | Full ability to use custom hardware |

In reality, you'll probably deploy your database and other one-off bits of hardware and software in a colo, with as much as possible in a full cloud. A hybrid cloud can still give you many of the advantages of a full cloud, while negating some of the disadvantages.

# Path to the Cloud

When you decide to fully adopt the cloud for ecommerce, you'll find it's a mostly sequential process that takes time and competency to implement fully. Before you can get to the point where all of your software is running in a cloud, if you can ever get to that point, you have to start from the bottom of the pyramid in Figure 12-1 and work your way up to the top. This is where having a solid architecture and a high ability to execute matters.

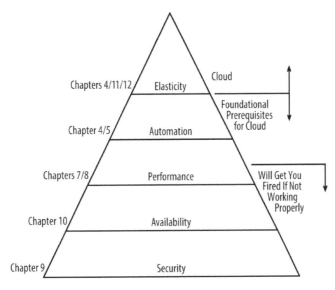

*Figure 12-1. Cloud competency pyramid*

Let's discuss each of these further:

*Security*

> Proper security must be established before any ecommerce may occur. That's just a prerequisite that neither vendors nor customers are willing to sacrifice. Proper security entails the use of security-related technology (firewalls of different kinds, distributed denial-of-service attack mitigation, reverse proxies) and the use of process-related best practices (proper change control, auditing, strong information protection policies). You can move on to availability only after security is properly established.

*Availability*

In today's omnichannel world, an outage increasingly has the effect of shutting down every single channel you have for generating revenue. It used to be that a website failure would be unpleasant, but it was isolated to that channel. Now, many point-of-sale systems, kiosks, and mobile applications use the same underlying platform. Outages today tend to be platform-wide and thus affect all channels.

*Performance*

Availability is important, but if your customers and store associates can't transact in a reasonable amount of time, it's just as useless as the platform being down. Performance is very important not only to successfully transact, but also to compete. Milliseconds of response time matter.

*Automation*

Once you've mastered security, availability, and performance, you can move on to automation. Automation, as we discussed in Chapter 4, is key to reducing configuration errors while improving efficiency. Automation is required for cloud computing because you need to rapidly build up servers after you've provisioned them.

*Elasticity*

Being able to elastically scale up and down is the true defining characteristic of the cloud. This is the end goal.

Elasticity, the primary focus of this book and the defining feature of cloud computing, can be broken up further, as shown in Figure 12-2.

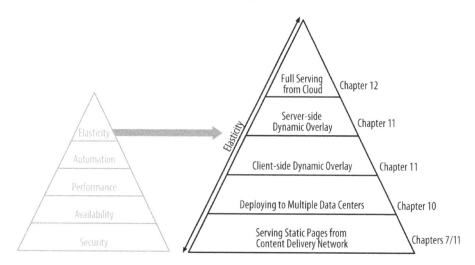

*Figure 12-2. The elasticity part of the cloud competency pyramid*

As in the previous hierarchy, you have to start at the bottom and work your way up:

*Serving static pages directly from a CDN*
When you use a CDN as a reverse proxy, you can serve entire static pages. As we discussed in Chapters 7 and 11, it's easy to offload the delivery of the majority of your page views and all of the HTTP requests you would normally receive for static content. By offloading a majority of your traffic, you've substantially reduced the scope of your platform while serving pages directly from the edge to individual customers.

*Deploying to multiple data centers*
Unless you jump straight to the top of the pyramid, you will be operating from two or more data centers concurrently for a period of time. Most systems are architected to be served out of a single data center. This was discussed in Chapter 10.

*Client-side dynamic overlay*
This refers to being able to retrieve a static page from a CDN or other intermediary and to overlay dynamic content on it on the client side. This is how most native mobile applications work today, and it's an easy way of dramatically increasing the number of page views that can be offloaded. The requests to retrieve content are typically some form of AJAX. This was discussed in Chapter 11.

*Server-side dynamic overlay*
Rather than deliver a static page to the client and then race back to the origin to overlay dynamic content, you can stitch together the dynamic and static page fragments in an intermediary, like a CDN or reverse proxy that you manage. With this approach, you can scale out your frontend delivery using a cloud while your less-used backend can remain on dedicated systems. It's a great option for many and the highest in the pyramid that most will reach. This was discussed in Chapter 11.

*Full serving from the cloud*
This is the most beneficial form of cloud computing, whereby your entire platform is hosted in a cloud. This is a fully elastic solution that offers the most benefits while also being the most challenging to implement. We'll discuss this shortly.

Again, it's important to gradually work your way up these pyramids as you gain competency. The more of these prerequisites you have in place, the easier it'll be to move your entire platform to the cloud.

# Architecture for Full Cloud

## Review of Key Principles

To begin, we must define what cloud computing actually is (Chapter 3), since the definition tends to vary from person to person. The three characteristics that best define the cloud are elasticity, on demand, and metered. Then there are service models (e.g., IaaS, PaaS, SaaS) and deployment models (public, hybrid, private). The characteristics of elasticity, on demand, and metered are best facilitated by public IaaS or PaaS, followed by hybrid IaaS or PaaS. By being able to specialize, cloud vendors almost always offer better availability, performance, security, and functionality at a lower cost than if you built a comparable solution. Always choose the service and deployment models highest up in the value chain for each function.

Next, once you've selected your flavor of cloud, you have to enable the elasticity, on demand, and metered parts of the cloud by implementing an auto-scaling solution (Chapter 4). An auto-scaling solution allows you to precisely match the amount of hardware you're using with the real-time traffic you're seeing. This allows you to pay for exactly the amount of hardware you need. The further down the value chain you move (toward IaaS), the more of this work you have to do yourself. That's why IaaS is generally less expensive than PaaS. Avoid provisioning ahead of anticipated load and instead provision in reaction to changing load. Purchase an auto-scaling solution if it meets your needs but be prepared to build one on your own.

Auto-scaling requires the ability to quickly and automatically install software on newly provisioned hardware (Chapter 5). If human intervention is required to add capacity, it's not cloud computing. You can install software by deploying a whole machine image, an archive (e.g., *.zip* or *.tar*), or by building from source. The approach doesn't matter, so long as it is fast and doesn't require human intervention.

Next, you have to select virtualization technology (Chapter 6). Cloud vendors often offer more than one, ranging from full hardware-level virtualization to paravirtualization to OS-level virtualization. Virtualization is a key enabler of the cloud but it is not the cloud itself. Depending on the flavor of virtualization you choose, you may be able to simply install an OS-level image rather than install all of the software from source. Choose lighter forms of virtualization where possible.

Once you have a solid foundation on which to deploy your platform, you then have to turn your attention outside of your cloud, between your end customers and your platform served in a cloud. CDNs (Chapter 7) are the silent enabler of ecommerce, providing reverse proxies, serving static content, hosting DNS, and optimizing performance, among many other functions. CDNs improve performance and reduce the amount of traffic hitting your platform by one or two orders of magnitude.

Next, we look inward to focus on building platforms natively for the cloud (Chapter 8). We must start by understanding what scalability is and isn't, followed by how to achieve it. The goals of building platforms natively for the cloud and achieving high scalability can be accomplished by adopting standard best practices—decoupling through the use of service-oriented architecture, asynchronous execution, reducing state, and storing it appropriately. Platforms that don't run well in a cloud generally don't run well outside of a cloud and vice versa. Since application architecture stems from the people you hire, you must hire a few top-quality architects as opposed to a large group. With hiring, it's quality over quantity.

Before discussing various approaches for a hybrid and using the full cloud, the topic of security (Chapter 9) must be addressed. While the cloud offers less-direct ownership, it provides more control, which is the key to remaining secure. The first step to security is defining an information security management system (ISMS) and then adhering to it. An ISMS defines the policies and procedures required for security along with provisions for self or third-party audits. Having an ISMS and following it is the single surest way to be secure, more than any specific technology or deployment architecture. Next to adopting and using an ISMS, the best technical recommendation is to minimize your attack profile by turning off unnecessary services, liberally using firewalls, and by using an identity and access management system to reduce the number of systems and functions your employees have access to.

Next, you must determine if you will deploy your platform across multiple data centers (Chapter 10). Availability has largely been the driving force of ecommerce architecture. Deploying the same application out of two or more geographically distant data centers helps to ensure even higher availability. The central problem with operating from multiple data centers is that you can have multiple customers logging in using the same account (e.g., username/password combination) from different data centers. If two customers update the same data at the same time from two different locations, one customer's action is going to succeed and the other is going to fail, possibly corrupting data along the way. You cannot resolve bidirectional replication conflicts. Instead, you must entirely eliminate the possibility of them occurring by ensuring that all updates terminate at the same database.

Short of adopting a full cloud-based architecture, you can adopt a hybrid cloud (Chapter 11) and get many of the benefits of a full cloud. To fully use a hybrid approach, you have to break apart your frontend from your backend. This splitting is a natural outcome of adopting an omnichannel-based architecture. Another approach is to use a colo facility that is physically near your cloud data center and has a direct connection to your cloud. Inserting HTML into a cached page does provide benefits, but more-comprehensive benefits come from pulling raw, structured data in the form of XML or JSON and then building a page in a cloud based on that data.

We covered a lot of ground in these chapters. If you haven't read them, please go back and review before proceeding.

## Architecture for Omnichannel

As we've previously discussed, omnichannel has been the dominant force driving platform architecture over the past few years. Adopting an omnichannel-based architecture allows your customers to transact with your backend across multiple frontends and have a consistent customer experience. The improved customer experience increases revenue.

An omnichannel architecture is not technically required for cloud computing, but it makes it a lot easier to adopt because of that natural split between your frontend and backend. But if everything is in a cloud, you could technically leave your frontend and backend merged, as many are today. You will eventually have to adopt a true omnichannel-based architecture because of pressure from your customers, but at least your deployment model won't be forcing you to make that change.

When you deploy both your frontend and your backend to a cloud, you should deploy them in pairs to the same data center, but with Global Server Load Balancing employed in the event of a failover, as shown in Figure 12-3.

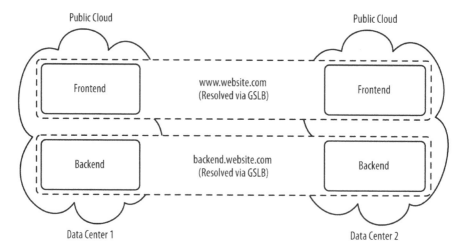

*Figure 12-3. Frontends and backends both in the cloud*

Most often, your frontend should be communicating with a backend that's local.

## Larger Trends Influencing eCommerce Architecture

Outside of ecommerce, the architecture principles behind all software architecture and development has radically changed over the past decade. The technology of the early Web and its guiding architecture principles no longer work in today's world.

Table 12-2 shows the differences between the old and new approaches to software development and deployment.

*Table 12-2. New versus old approaches to software development and deployment*

| Old | New |
| --- | --- |
| Sticky in-memory session | Shared memory cache session |
| Monolithic application | Service based |
| Monolithic software development | Teams organized around services |
| One data center | Multiple data centers |
| Statically scale for peaks | Full elasticity |
| Stateful | Stateless |
| ACID | BASE |
| Rigid schema | Flexible |
| CAPEX | OPEX |
| Manually deployed | Fully automated |

Your existing platform, people, and processes can be reoriented to take advantage of these new principles, but it takes time and a lot of effort. People become entrenched in the ways of the past and are often compensated for maintaining the status quo. Designate or hire and then empower a change agent to oversee the transformation. The shift to the cloud is about far more than technology. Only after you've built a capable organization, changed your processes, and updated your technology should you attempt cloud computing. Adopting the cloud without making those lower-level changes is unlikely to work.

# How to Select a Cloud Vendor

A large-scale ecommerce platform requires dozens, if not hundreds, of vendors, from a qualified security assessor for PCI audits to a database vendor. While all vendors must be carefully selected, no vendor is more important than your cloud vendor that will be providing you with Infrastructure-as-a-Service or Platform-as-a-Service. You're trusting your entire business and your job to this vendor.

What you're looking for in a primary cloud vendor is as follows:

*Breadth and depth of offerings*
What does it come with versus what will you have to build on top? For example, is their auto-scaling solution (Chapter 4) good enough to use, or will you have to build one?

*Maturity of offerings*
Is what the vendor offers stable? Does it actually work?

*Connectivity options*
What VPN connectivity options are offered? Does the vendor run lines to colos?

*Service-level agreements*
What does the vendor offer in terms of uptime guarantees? Will you always be able to provision hardware?

*Ability to colocate custom hardware*
Can you put your custom hardware-based VPNs, authentication devices, and other appliances in a cloud's data center?

Different vendors excel in different aspects, but you have to pick one vendor. It's possible to go with a multivendor solution, but that introduces an enormous amount of complexity without providing much benefit, given how rarely clouds suffer outages. Outages across a single vendor's fault domains is even more rare. Since outages are typically caused by your own misconfiguration, you double the number of misconfigurations you can make by deploying across two clouds.

Technology analysts such as Gartner and Forrester regularly produce reports on cloud computing and can help you select a vendor.

While the move to adopt the cloud may be partially fueled by price, price by itself shouldn't be a deciding factor. The elasticity provided by any vendor will save you more than enough money for you to care about the small differences in prices among cloud vendors.

Clouds appear to be entirely self-service with preset prices and credit cards as the only form of payment. But if you're going to make a substantial investment in a vendor, everything is up for negotiation. You can negotiate for better prices, price holds, additional levels of support, consulting support, and anything else of value. You're investing in a vendor, and that vendor is investing in you. As with any major vendor, you'll want to establish good relationships throughout your organization. Those back channels can mean the difference between your platform staying up or going down. Relationships matter.

# Summary

Both cloud and omnichannel retailing are fundamentally changing ecommerce for the better. The application and deployment architectures that have helped to make ecommerce mainstream over the past 20 years have outlived their usefulness. To succeed over the next 20 years and beyond, substantial changes are required. Adopting cloud and omnichannel principles is a multiyear journey that changes the way you do business.

The combination of cloud computing and ecommerce *just makes so much sense*, and the contents of this book should give you enough confidence to proceed. Good luck!

# Index

## A

A records, 200
    long TTL, 201
    short TTL, 202
    two A records for active/active data center
        assignment, 203
ability to execute, 193
access control, 175
accounting model
    advantages of cloud computing, 60
    for cloud deployment models, 67
ACID, 193
ACID-compliant databases, 42
active/active application tiers and active/passive
    database tiers, 209
active/active application tiers, mostly active/
    passive database tiers, 210
active/active deployment architecture, 212
    assigning customers to data centers, 203
active/passive deployment architecture, 207
    assigning customers to data centers, 201
agency dilemma, problem with cloud comput-
    ing, 73
Amazon Machine Image (AMI), 97
Amazon Web Services, 62
Amazon.com, 10
    on list of top ten largest U.S. retailers, 20
    physical warehouses, 8
Apache server, scalability, 147
APIs
    auto-scaling solutions, 92
    omnichannel architecture, 156, 222
Apple Computers, omnichannel retailing case
    study, 28

appliance-based hardware load balancers, 36
application delivery controllers, 34
application servers, 32, 35, 88
    health checking, 206
    managing state, 156
    modern, capabilities of, 36
    roles in current ecommerce platforms, 41
    taking over web server responsibilities, 38
architects, hiring, 160
architecture
    larger trends affecting ecommerce architec-
        ture, 249
    omnichannel, 248
archives
    building servers from, 99
    use of, advantages and disadvantages, 99
asynchronous processing, 150
    HTTP requests returning dynamic content,
        230
attacks, 134
    getting personally identifiable information
        (PII), 178
    reducing attack vectors in the cloud, 180
attribute-based personalization, 14
audit logging, 177
authentication, 175
    multifactor, for human users, 176
authoritative DNS servers, 200
authorization, 175
auto-scaling in the cloud, 81-94, 240, 246
    building auto-scaling solutions, 92
        interfacing with auto-scaling APIs, 92
        versus buying solutions, 94
    defining dependencies between tiers, 89

defining each tier that needs to be scaled, 88

defining ratios between tiers, 89

defining rules for scaling each tier, 89

how auto-scaling solutions work, 87

monitoring servers and aggregating data across each tier, 89

what can't be provisioned, 84

what needs to be provisioned, 82

when to provision, 85

automation, 244

availability, 46, 244

ensuring by operating out of multiple data centers, 189

in BASE consistency model, 194

in CAP Theorem, 195

public clouds, 73

superior, offered by cloud vendors, 240

## B

backend, 68

combined with frontend, 217

decoupled from frontend, 153, 217

fully decoupled from frontend, 233

needs of, 218

served from traditional data center, 217

stateless frontend, stateful backend, 213

Barnes & Noble, 22

BASE, 194

bastion host, 180

behavior-based personalization, 15

BIND DNS server, 33

blacklisting, CDNs, 134

blocking, 153

bookselling industry, changes in, 22

bootstrap script, 99

Borders, 22

bots

requesting too many pages too quickly, 134

web traffic from, 130

bursting (hybrid cloud), 66, 68

business

business reasons to use full cloud deployment, 239

collaboration with when building ecommerce platform, 161

control over ecommerce, 17

impact of omnichannel retailing, 25

## C

C10K problem, 148

C10M problem, 148

cache grid servers, 88

cache staleness, 196

caching

CDNs caching entire pages, 129

entire pages, with frontend in cloud and backend in traditional data center, 226

for increased scalability, 157

of DNS records, 200

overlaying HTML on cached pages, 228

page framents, 158

write-back cache to reduce database load, 151

CAP Theorem, 195

capital expenditures (CAPEX), 56, 60

CDNs (Content Delivery Networks), 36, 121-138

acceleration of HTML-based web pages, 121

additional offerings, 135

DNS, 136

frontend optimization, 135

throttling, 138

caching content, 157

cloud and, 124

defined, 123

edge side dynamic content overlay, 230

expansion of offerings, 123

offering global server load balancing, 205

outsourcing to, 62

serving as proxies, handling HTTP requests and responses, 228

serving as reverse proxies, advantages for active/active approach, 205

serving dynamic content, 128

caching entire pages, 129

pre-fetching static content, 132

security, 133

serving static content, 125, 245

loading a page with and without CDN, 127

taking over web server responsibilities, 38

CGI (Common Gateway Interface), 35

channels, retail, 23, 39

channel creation timeline, 24

mobile and other nonweb channels, consuming XML and JSON, 233 multichannel architecture with integration layer, 40, 220

single omnichannel platform, 221

Chef (configuration management tool), 101

client side dynamic content overlay, 229, 245

clients, maintaining state, 156

cloud competency pyramid, 243

cloud computing, 55, 80

  and active/passive deployment architecture, 208

  architecting for, 143-162

    scalability, 146-149

    scaling, rules for, 149-162

    uniqueness of ecommerce, 143

  auto-scaling (see auto-scaling in the cloud)

  case study, Amazon Web Services, 62

  CDNs (Content Delivery Networks) and, 124

  challenges with public clouds, 73

    availability, 73

    cost, 78

    over-subscription, 77

    performance, 75

  complementary cloud vendor offerings, 72

  deployment models, 66

    hybrid cloud, 68

    private cloud, 68

    public cloud, 67

  elasticity, 57

  evaluation criteria, 56

  exclusively using public cloud, 239-251

  generally accepted definition, 55

  hardware used in clouds, 69

  hybrid cloud, 217-237

  making operating from multiple data centers possible, 190

  metered, 59

  on demand, 58

  security, 164

    (see also security)

    study, enterprise security for the cloud, 165

  security principles for, 179

    protecting data at rest, 185

    protecting data in motion, 183

    reducing attack vectors, 180

  service models, 61

    Infrastructure-as-a-Service (IaaS), 65

    Platform-as-a-Service (PaaS), 64

    Software as a Service (SaaS), 63

  virtualization, 109-118

CloudFlare CDN, 134

code injection attacks, 134

command-line tools, interfacing with auto-scaling APIs, 92

commodity hardware, 70

compensation of employees for ecommerce sales, 25

complexity and innovation in ecommerce, 11

configuration, never replicating, 199

conflicts, data replication, detection and resolution, 195

consistency models, 193

  CAP Theorem, 195

  DNS as eventually consistent system, 200

  summary of ACID and BASE, 194

containers (see application servers)

Content Delivery Networks (see CDNs)

controls

  ISO 27001, 169

  policies on information access, retention, and destruction, 174

convenience of online shopping, 7

Corinthians soccer team, 15

costs

  challenges with public clouds, 78

  hardware/software costs, CAPEX versus OPEX, 60

  of traditions shopping versus online shopping, 7

  savings using full cloud, 240

credit card information, 167

credit card processing service, 169

cross-sells, 14

cross-site request forgery, 178

cross-site scripting, 134, 178

customer-friendly policies in ecommerce, 9

customizations of products, 12

# D

data centers

  assigning customers to, using DNS, 137

  deploying across multiple, 189

    (see also deploying across multiple data centers)

    initializing each data center, 198

    prerequisites for, 190

    selecting a data center, 197

uniqueness of ecommerce, 190
direct connections offered by cloud vendors, 225
health checking using GSLB, 206
hosted, 45
intra data center load balancing, 34
multiple, use in ecommerce, 33
data source identifiers, 211
data tier, 32
data-driven ecommerce applications, 18
databases
    as bottlenecks in the cloud, 151
    database firewall, 179
    database-backed inventory update, 153
    deploying your own relational database, 198
    distributed, consistency models, 193
    document based, 43
    everything but database in the cloud, 235
    fully denormalized, 43
    fully normalized, 42
    hosting options, 186
    multiple data centers with active databases, 210
    protecting data in, 185
    role in modern ecommerce architecture, 41
    writing to, using ORM model, 196
defense in depth, 172
    ecommerce security, 178
    protections in place for various layers, 172
Dell Computers, case study (price mishap), 50
denormalized data, 43
dependencies
    defining between tiers, 89
    resources having, provisioning order for, 85
deploying across multiple data centers, 189-215, 247
    approaches, 207
        active/active application tiers, active/passive database tiers, 209
        active/active application tiers, mostly active/passive database tiers, 210
        active/passive, 207
        full active/active, 212
        stateless frontends, stateful backends, 213
        summary of, 214
    architecture principles, 192
        initializing each data center, 198
        never replicating configuration, 199
        principles governing distributed computing, 193
        removing singletons, 198
        selecting a data center, 197
    assigning customers to data centers
        active/passive architecture, 201
        assigning to single data center, 201
        DNS, 200, 206
        global server load balancing, 203
    prerequisites for, 190
    uniqueness of ecommerce, 190
deployment across multiple data centers, 245
deployment architecture, legacy, 31-51
    application servers, 41
    databases, 41
    DNS, 33
    ecommerce applications, 39
    hosting, 44
    intra data center load balancing, 34
    limitations of current architecture, 46
        outages due to rapid scaling, 49
        scaling for peaks, 47
        static provisioning, 46
    three-tier architecture, 32
    web servers, 35
deployment models, cloud, 56, 66, 239
    hybrid cloud, 68
    private cloud, 68
    public cloud, 67
deployment units, 95
    monitoring health of, 102
developers
    hiring, 160
    working in small teams, 161
disintermediation, 6
distributed computing, principles governing, 193
    avoiding conflicts, 195
distributed denial of service attacks (DDoS), 133
DNS, 33
    disadvantages of self hosting, 136
    Global Server Load Balancing versus, 204
    in active/passive data center assignment, 202
    primer, 200
    services offered by CDNs, 136
    shortcomings, 201
    use of multiple A records, 203

using to assign customers to single data center, 201
document stores, 43
drop boxes, 9
drop shipping, 7

# E

eBay, 10
ecommerce
  deploying entire platform to public cloud, 239-251
  global rise of, 3-29
    better functionality, 11
    business control of ecommerce, 17
    changing face of retail, 19-28
    improvements in underlying technology, 18
    increasing maturity of offerings, 10
    increasing use of technology, 4
    inherent adantages of ecommerce, 5
    omnichannel retailing, Apple case study, 28
    personalized shopping, 14
    rich interfaces across multiple devices, 17
    social media and ecommerce, 16
  how enterprise ecommerce is deployed today, 31-51
  security principles for, 177
  traditional applications, written and deployed as a single package, 219
  unique characteristics of, 143, 190
    revenue generation, 143
    security, 144
    statefulness, 144
    unpredictable traffic spikes, 144
    visibility, 144
  using hybrid cloud, 217-237
ecommerce traffic funnel, 130, 145
ecommerce vendors with physical stores, 8
edge computing, 121
edge side dynamic content overlay, 230
Edge Side Includes (ESI), 231
edge-based proxying, 205
elasticity, 57, 244, 246
encapsulating TCP packets, 184
encryption
  hardware offload of encryption and decryption, 183
  protecting data at rest, 185
  protecting data in motion, 183
enterprise resource planning (ERP) platforms, 28
ESI (Edge Side Includes), 231
Ethernet networks, segmenting, 175
eventually consistent systems, 200

# F

Facebook, 16
fault domains, 197
FedRAMP (Federal Risk and Authorization Management Program), 134, 164, 171
firewalls, 175
  adding to hypervisor security, 182
  database firewall, 179
  operating system (iptables/nftables), 181
  provided by CDNs, 134
  restricting traffic by port and type, 180
flexibility, lack of, with PaaS, 65
FreeBSD Jails, 113
frontend, 68
  combined with backend, 217
  decoupled from backend, 153, 217
  fully decoupled from backend, 233
  HTML-based, marginalization of, 236
  needs of, 219
  optimization by CDNs, 135
  served from cloud, 217
  stateless frontend, stateful backend, 213
full serving from the cloud, 245
full virtualization, 115
  performance and, 117
functionality, better, in ecommerce, 11

# G

Global Server Load Balancing (GSLB), 63
  health checking, 206
  offerings by CDNs, 137
  primer, 203
  versus DNS, 34, 204
glue code, 160
graphical user interfaces (GUIs), interfacing with auto-scaling APIs, 92
grocery sales, combining physical stores with ecommerce, 9
growth of ecommerce, drivers of, 3
GSLB (see Global Server Load balancing)

## H

hardware
  scaling for peaks, 47
  used in clouds, 69
  utilized versus unutilized in scaling for
    peaks, 49
hardware security modules (HSMs), 186
hardware/software costs, CAPEX versus OPEX,
  60
health checking
  of data centers, 204
  of deployment units
    comprehensive, 105
    superficial, 103
  using Global Server Load Balancing, 206
hiring the right people, 160
horizontal scalability, 147, 148
hosting for ecommerce, 44
hot objects, 153
HSMs (hardware security modules), 186
HTML
  client side dynamic content overlay, 229
  data stored in, 43
  edge side dynamic content overlay by
    CDNs, 230
  marginalization of HTML-based frontends,
    236
  mobile-friendly, 17
  optimization by CDNs, 135
  server side dynamic content overlay, 232
  static, in early websites, 31
  use in web channel, marginalization by
    mobile and other channels, 233
HTTP GET requests, 225
HTTP requests, 125
  maintaining state across, 155
  number needed to pull up large ecommerce
    websites, 125
  statefulness, 144
HTTP responses, 227
HTTPS, 183
  using to post data from frontend to back-
    end, 225
hybrid clouds, 68, 217-237, 242, 247
  approaches
    caching entire pages, 226
    everything but the database in the cloud,
      235

fully decoupled frontends and backends,
    233
  overlaying HTML on cached pages, 228
  overlaying HTML on server side, 232
  summary of, 236
  using CDNs to insert HTML, 230
  as by-product of architecture for omnichan-
    nel, 219
  connecting to the cloud, 224
    direct connections to data centers, 225
    using public Internet, 224
hypervisor, 110
  bypassing to improve performance, 118
  in full virtualization, 110
  in operating system virtualization, 113
  in paravirtualization, 112
  security, 182

## I

IaaS (Infrastructure-as-a-Service), 45, 61, 164
  auto-scaling solutions, 87-94
  complementary cloud vendor offerings, 72,
    72
  content origination and delivery, 124
  installing software on newly-provisioned
    hardware, 95-108
  provisioning hardware from, 82-87
  vendor offerings, 65
IAM (identity and access management) systems, 176
identification (of users), 175
identity and access management (IAM) systems, 176
increasing use of technology, 4
information classification system, 173
  developing policies for each level, 174
information security management systems
  (ISMS), 166-172, 185, 247
  FedRAMP, 171
  ISO 27001, 169
  PCI DSS, 167
Infrastructure-as-a-Service (see IaaS)
initial provisioning versus auto-scaling, 81
innovations in ecommerce, 10
Internet
  access through mobile devices, 5
  increase in use of, 4
  using to connect separated backend and
    frontend, 224

inventory, updating, eliminating locking, 153
IP addresses
    as personally identifiable information (PII),
      167
    forcing clients to re-resolve, 212
    resolving via DNS, 33
    restricting traffic by, 181
IPsec, 184
IPsec-based VPN, 225
ISMS (see information security management
    systems)
ISO 27001, 134, 169
    central tenets for security framework, 166
    controls, 169
ISO 27002, 169
ISO snapshot format, 97
isolation, 109, 174
    fault domains, 197
IT
    collaboration with line of business, 161
    economics of, changes from cloud comput-
      ing, 59
    transfer of control over ecommerce to busi-
      ness, 17

## J

Java Virtual Machine (JVM), vertical scalabil-
    ity, 70
JavaScript-based franework, Node.js, 151
JDK 7, installing using Chef, 101
JSON, 233

## K

kernels, in paravirtualization, 112
key/value stores, 43

## L

latency
    calls from separated frontends to backends,
      224
    causes of, 138
    pulling up websites, 125
layering, security (see defense in depth)
least privileged access, 176
leveling, 49
lifecycle management, 107
Linux Containers (LXC), 113
Linux kernels, 112

Linux KVM, 111
load balancers, 228
    appliance-like hardware load balancers, 36
    application delivery controllers, 34
    health checking, 103
    modern, capabilities of, 36
    taking over web server responsibilities, 38
    throttling offered by, 138
    web servers as, 35
load balancing, 34
    (see also Global Server Load Balancing)
    DNS, using for, 33, 201
    intra data center, 34
load tests, 49
locking, reducing, 153
    lockless data structures, 154
logging, 177
login cookies, persistent, 130
logins, concurrent, for same user account, 191

## M

maturity of ecommerce offerings, 10
memory finder tools, 13
messaging servers, 88
metered (cloud computing), 59, 246
Microsoft Hyper-V, 111
mobile ecommerce offerings, 17
monitoring
    of data center health, 206
    of deployment unit health, 102
multifactor authentication, 176
multimaster architectute (see deploying across
    multiple data centers)

## N

Netshoes.com.br, 11
    personalization of shopping, 15
networks
    cloud security measures, 180
    segmentation and isolation, 175
Node.js, 151
nontechnical challenges to adopting full cloud,
    241
normalized data, 42
NoSQL solutions, 43

## O

object relational mapping (ORM) systems, 196

omnichannel retailing, 22, 39
  architecture for, 248
  business impact of, 25
  case study, Apple Computers, 28
  hybrid cloud as by-product of architecture
    for, 219
  technical impact of, 26
on demand (cloud computing), 58, 246
Open Systems Interconnection (OSI) model,
  175
Open Virtualization Format (OVF), 97
OpenStack, 92
operating systems
  firewall, 181
  in paravirtualization, 112
  installing on fully virtualized servers, 110
  operating system virtualization, 113, 115
operational expenditures (OPEX), 56, 60
optimizations offered by CDNs, 135
origin (data centers), 123
ORM (object relational mapping) systems, 196
outages, 46
  caused by rapid scaling, 49
  cloud-wide, 74, 197
  costs of, 144
  from security-related incidents, 177
  preventing by deploying across multiple
    data centers, 189
outsource, when to, 62, 159
over-subscription to public clouds, 77

**P**

PaaS (Platform-as-a-Service), 45, 61, 164
  limitations of, 65
  operting system virtualization, 115
  provisioning and responsibilities for, 83
  vendor offerings, 64
  when to use, 65
page fragments, caching, 158
paravirtualization, 112, 115
  performance and, 117
partition tolerance), 195
partitioning physical servers into virtual
  servers, 109
PCI DSS (Payment Card Industry Data Security
  Standard), 134, 164, 167
  limiting scope of cardholder data environ-
    ment, 169
  objectives and controls, 168

peak demand
  challenges for public clouds, 77
  scaling for peaks, 47
people, hiring, 160
perfectly scalable, 146
performance, 244
  biggest hindrance, calls to remote systems,
    117
  cause of problems in ecommerce, 118
  extensive use of SSL and TLS, 183
  full virtualization and, 111
  improving for virtualized software, 116
  paravirtualization and, 112
  public clouds, 75
  with everything but database in the cloud,
    235
personalization in ecommerce, 14, 130
personally identifiable information (PII)
  consequences of disclosure, 178
  defined, 167
photography, enhanced, of ecommerce products, 12
physical and ecommerce presence, combining,
  8
ping, power, and pipe, 44
Pinterest, 16
plan/do/check/act cycle, ISMS, 166
Platform-as-a-Service (see PaaS)
point-of-sale systems, 190
portability, 110
price discrimination, 16
pricing
  personalization used to price discriminate,
    16
  price advantage of ecommerce, 5
primary keys prefixed with unique identifier,
  211
private clouds, 68
  public cloud characteristics versus, 242
proactive provisioning, 85
product assortment, ecommerce vendors, 7
promiscuous mode, 182
provisioning, 81
  (see also auto-scaling)
  proactive, 85
  reactive, 87
  static, 46
proxying by appliance-based GSLB solutions,
  206

public clouds, 67
  challenges with, 73
    availability, 73
    cost, 78
    over-subscription, 77
    performance, 75
  deploying entire ecommerce platform to, 239-251
    architectue for full cloud, 246
    business reasons, 239
    path to cloud, 243
    reasons not to adopt full cloud, 241
    selecting a cloud vendor, 249
    technical reasons, 240
public utilities, analogy to cloud, 55
pure play ecommerce vendors, 6

**Q**

qualified security assessor (QSA), 168

**R**

ramp-up times, 49
ratios between tiers, defining, 89
RAW snapshot format, 97
reactive provisioning, 87
records (DNS), 200
recovery point objective (RPO), 193
  in active/passive deployment, 207
recovery time objective (RTO), 192
  in active/passive deployment, 207
Reddit, 77
relational databases, 42
  building out before deployment, 198
  NoSQL solutions versus, 43
  object relational mapping (ORM), 196
resources, 58
RESTful web services, 92
retail
  changing face of, 19
  omnichannel retailing, 22
  point-of-sale systems, 190
  traditional, closer tie-in with physical world, 8
returns
  customer-friendly policies in ecommerce, 10
  return rates in ecommerce, 9
revenue generation by ecommerce, 143
reverse proxy, CDN as, 129

  advantages over DNS for active/active approach, 205
  speeding up delivery of static content for all pages, 132
rich interfaces across multiple devices, 17
RPO (recovery point objective), 193, 207
RTO (recovery time objective), 192, 207

**S**

SaaS (Software-as-a-Service), 45, 61
  complementary cloud vendor offerings, 72
  DNS, 200
  provisioning, 83
  use within ecommerce platforms, 163
  vendor offerings, 63
safety factor, 84
scalability, 247
  defined, 146
  human factors, 150
  linear versus non-linear scaling, 149
  rules for scaling, 149
    caching, 157
    collaboration with line of business, 161
    converting synchronous to asynchronous, 150
    hiring the right people, 160
    reducing locking, 153
    removing state from individual servers, 155
    simplifying your architecture, 154
    using the right technology, 159
  scaling out, 148
  scaling up, 147
    C10K problem, 148
  versus throughput, 147
scale-down rule, defining, 90
scale-up rule, defining, 90
scaling, 246
  (see also auto-scaling in the cloud)
  elasticity in, 244
  outages due to rapid scaling, 49
  reasons to use full cloud, 240
  services offered by PaaS vendors, 64
scaling for peaks, 47
search, ecommerce, enhancements in, 12
security, 163-187, 243
  adopting an information security management system (ISMS), 166-172
    FedRAMP, 171

ISO 27001, 169
PCI DSS, 167
best practices, 172-177
  audit logging, 177
  defense in depth, 172
  identification, authentication, and
    authorization, 175
  information classification, 173
  isolation, 174
challenges in ecommerce and the cloud, 144
clouds and, 164
concerns with DNS self hosting, 136
connections between frontend in cloud and
  backend in traditional data center, 224
general principles, 165
principles for cloud, 179
  protecting data at rest, 185
  protecting data in motion, 183
  reducing attack vectors, 180
principles for ecommerce, 177
provided by CDNs, 133
superior, offered by cloud vendors, 240
threats from within and without, 165
server side dynamic content overlay, 232, 245
server-side includes, 232
servers
  C10K problem, 148
  dedicated instead of shared in the cloud, 182
  lifecycle, 107
  minimum and maximum server counts, 91
  removing state from individual servers, 155
  types of, 96
service level agreements (SLAs), 162
service models, cloud, 56, 61, 239
  case study, Amazon Web Services, 62
  complementary cloud vendor offerings, 72
  facilitation of cloud characteristics, 246
  IaaS (Infrastructure-as-a-Service), 65
  PaaS (Platform-as-a-Service), 64
  SaaS (Software-as-a-Service), 63
  versus value/cost margins, 72
services
  ancillary services offered by cloud vendors,
    72
  offered by ecommerce hosts, 45
session stickiness, 146, 162
shell infrastructure, 190
shell scripting, 102
shipping

drop shipping, 7
  problems with, 9
Shoe Fit Tool, Netshoes.com.br, 11
showrooming, 8
simplification to increase scalability, 154
single root I/O virtualization (SR-IOV), 241
singletons, 198
  avoiding, 199
  problems with, 199
SLAs (service level agreements), 162
snapshots
  building from, 97
  lifecycle management and, 108
  use of, advantages and disadvantages, 98
SOAP web services, 92
social media, effects on ecommerce, 16
software
  development and deployment, new versus
    old approaches, 249
  installing on newly-provisioned hardware,
    95-108
    building from archives, 99
    building from snapshots, 97
    building from source, 100
    deployment units, 95
    lifecycle management, 107
    monitoring health of deployment unit,
      102
  vertical scalability on a given hardware, 70
  web server, as bottlenect to vertical scalabil-
    ity, 148
Software-as-a-Service (see SaaS)
Solaris Containers/Zones, 113
source, building from, 100
SQL injection attacks, 134, 178
SR-IOV (single root I/O virtualization), 241
SSL (Secure Sockets Layer), 183, 224, 225
  not using when unnecessary, 155
  support by web browsers, 31
  termination, 184
  when to use, 183
state
  removing from individual servers, 155
  rules for minimizing harmful effects of, 156
  statefulness of ecommerce HTTP requests,
    144
  stateless frontends, stateful backends, 213
static provisioning, 46
static websites, 31

---

strong consistency (ACID), 193
synchronous processing, converting to asynchronous, 150

## T

tablets, Internet access via, 5
taxes, ecommerce vendors and, 6
TCP pings, testing response to, 103
technology
    impact of omnichannel retailing, 26
    improvements in underlying technology, 18
    increasing use of, 4
    technical reasons for not adopting full cloud, 241
    technical reasons for using full cloud, 240
    using the right technology, 159
threads, 151
    concurrency, 153
    eschewing in favor of event loop architecture, 149
throttling, 138
throughput, 146
    massive increases with modern web servers, 149
    scalability versus, 147
TLS (Transport Layer Security), 183, 224, 225
    not using when unnecessary, 155
    termination, 184
    when to use, 183
tokenization, 185
traffic
    estimating, 85
    from bots and humans, 130
    unpredictable spikes in ecommerce, 144
transaction capabilities, adding to static HTML, 31
Transport Layer Security (see TLS))
Twitter, 16

## U

unified omnichannel-based architecture, 27
unsticking a customer from a data center, 212
US
    compliance with FedRAMP, 167
    ecommerce retail sales, 20
    latency in pulling up websites, 125
    top 10 retailers in 1990 versus 2012, 19
usage metrics for metering/charge-back, 59

user interfaces, rich interfaces across multiple devices, 17

## V

vertical scalability, 147
    C10K problem, 148
    of software on a given hardware, 70
vertically integrated solutions, 72
virtual LANs (VLANs), 175
virtualization in the cloud, 109, 118, 246
    definition of virtualization, 110
    full virtualization, 110
    improving performance of virtualized software, 116
    operating system virtualization, 113
    paravirtualization, 112
    single root I/O virtualization (SR-IOV), 241
    summary of approaches, 115
visibility of ecommerce platforms, 144
VPNs (virtual private networks), 225
vulnerabilities
    leading to disclosure of PII, 178
    traditional environments and clouds, 165

## W

weak consistency (BASE), 194
web browsers
    ecommerce and, 17
    maintaining state, 156
web servers, 32
    C10K problem, 148
    deployment architecture without, 38
    ecommerce deployment architecture with, 37
    functions of, 36
    in early days of ecommerce, 35
    newer architectures, 149
    Node.js, 151
    replacement by load balancers, CDNs, and application servers, 36
web tier, 32
websites, static, 31
workload shifting, 110
write-back cache, 151

## X

Xen Hardware Virtual Machine, 111
XML, 233

# About the Author

**Kelly Goetsch** is responsible for Oracle's microservices initiatives. Previously, he was a product manager for Oracle Java Cloud Service, Oracle Java SE Cloud Service, and Oracle Exalogic Elastic Cloud. Kelly came to Oracle through the ATG acquisition, where he spent more than six years as a senior architect with ATG's Professional Services organization. He spent his last three years at ATG with Walmart Global E-Commerce, serving as chief ATG consultant. Kelly published eCommerce in the Cloud (O'Reilly Media, 2014) and numerous white papers on topics including distributed computing, large-scale e-commerce deployment architectures, performance tuning, and multimaster. He holds a MS in MIS and a BS in entrepreneurship from the University of Illinois at Chicago and has been granted three patents.

# Colophon

The animal on the cover of *eCommerce in the Cloud* is a Martial Eagle (*Polemaetus bellicosus*). This large eagle is found in sub-Saharan Africa in open and semi-open habitats. As the largest eagle in Africa, the Martial Eagle is notable for its size: 31–38 in (78–96 cm) in length, 6.6–13.7 lb (3–6.2 kg) in weight, and a wingspan of up to 6–8 ft (188–260 cm). The Martial Eagle is also the fifth heaviest eagle in the world, on average.

Adult eagles have a dark grey-brown plumage on its head and upper chest. On its underparts, the feathers are white with blackish-brown spotting. Female eagles are larger and more spotted than males, and more immature eagles are paler with less spotted underparts. In its seventh year, martial eagles reach adult plumage.

Their eyesight is 3–3.6 times human acuity, and they can spot potential prey from a great distance. The Martial Eagle is considered one of the world's most powerful avian predators. It is at the top of the avian food chain in its environment—an apex predator—and, when healthy, has no natural predators. Their diet depends greatly on opportunity and availability, but can consist of up to 45% birds such as game birds and Egyptian geese. They also feed on lizards, snakes, and other mammalian prey. Martial Eagles hunt while in flight, circling and stooping sharply to catch its prey.

Populations are naturally scarce because of a need for large territories and low reproduction rates, the Martial Eagle has experienced a major decline in numbers recently due to being directly killed by humans. Despite the small percentage of the eagle's diet actually represented by domesticated animals, the Martial Eagle is considered a threat to livestock, which is the main cause for persecution via shooting and poisoning by humans. In 2009, they were listed as Near Threatened; in 2013, they were uplisted to Vulnerable, and another uplisting is expected. Preservation depends on farmer education and an increase of protected nesting and hunting areas.

# Have it your way.

# Get even more for your money.

**Join the O'Reilly Community, and register the O'Reilly books you own. It's free, and you'll get:**

- $4.99 ebook upgrade offer
- 40% upgrade offer on O'Reilly print books
- Membership discounts on books and events
- Free lifetime updates to ebooks and videos
- Multiple ebook formats, DRM FREE
- Participation in the O'Reilly community
- Newsletters
- Account management
- 100% Satisfaction Guarantee

### Signing up is easy:

1. Go to: oreilly.com/go/register
2. Create an O'Reilly login.
3. Provide your address.
4. Register your books.

Note: English-language books only

**To order books online:**
oreilly.com/store

**For questions about products or an order:**
orders@oreilly.com

**To sign up to get topic-specific email announcements and/or news about upcoming books, conferences, special offers, and new technologies:**
elists@oreilly.com

**For technical questions about book content:**
booktech@oreilly.com

**To submit new book proposals to our editors:**
proposals@oreilly.com

**O'Reilly books are available in multiple DRM-free ebook formats. For more information:**
oreilly.com/ebooks